ELIZABETH CRAIG
was born in 1883. She has long been regarded as
the doyenne of British cookery writers, and
contributed a cookery column to *Woman's
Journal* on its birthday issue in 1926.

She now lives near Slough.

The Scottish Cookery Book

Elizabeth Craig

CORGI BOOKS

A DIVISION OF TRANSWORLD PUBLISHERS LTD

THE SCOTTISH COOKERY BOOK

A CORGI BOOK 0552 98087 0

First published by Andre Deutsch Ltd

PRINTING HISTORY

Andre Deutsch edition published 1956
Corgi edition published 1980

This book is set in Times 10/12 pt.

Corgi Books are published by Transworld Publishers Ltd.,
Century House, 61–63 Uxbridge Road, Ealing, London, W5 5SA

Made and printed in Great Britain by
Richard Clay (The Chaucer Press), Ltd., Bungay, Suffolk.

CONTENTS

FACTS AND FIGURES

GUIDE TO METRIC COOKING

Use these equivalents to make metric recipes that will fit your cake tins and bowls.

Present Measurement	Approx. Metric Equivalent	Present Measurement	Approx. Metric Equivalent
1 oz.	25 g.	9 oz.	250 g
2 oz.	50 g.	10 oz.	275 g.
3 oz.	75 g.	11 oz.	300 g.
4 oz.	100–125 g.	12 oz.	350 g.
5 oz.	150 g.	13 oz.	375 g.
6 oz.	175 g.	14 oz.	400 g.
7 oz.	200 g.	15 oz.	425 g.
8 oz.	225 g.	16 oz.	450 g.

LIQUID MEASURES

Use a 5-ml. spoon in place of a teaspoon and a 15-ml. spoon in place of a tablespoon. Handy equivalents: a 5-ml. pharmaceutical spoon or a set of American measuring spoons.

Present Measurement	Approx. Metric Equivalent
1 fl. oz.	25 ml.
2 fl. oz.	50 ml.
5 fl. oz.	150 ml.
10 fl. oz.	300 ml.
15 fl. oz.	400 ml.
20 fl. oz.	600 ml.
35 fl. oz.	1 litre

QUICK HANDY MEASURES		QUICK COMPARISON	
Approximate equivalent in level 15-ml. spoonfuls		*lb.*	*kg.*
Almonds, ground	25 g. = 3½	1	0·45
Breadcrumbs, fresh	25 g. = 7	2	0·9
Breadcrumbs, dried	25 g. = 3	3	1·36
Butter, lard, etc.	25 g. = 2	4	1·81
Cheddar, grated	25 g. = 3	5	2·26
Chocolate, grated	25 g. = 4	6	2·72
Coffee, instant	25 g. = 6½	7	3·17
Cornflour	25 g. = 2¾	8	3·62
Curry powder	25 g. = 4	9	4·08
Custard powder	25 g. = 2¾	10	4·53
Flour, unsifted	25 g. = 3	20	9·07
Suet, shredded	25 g. = 3	50	22·67
Sugar, caster/gran.	25 g. = 2		
Sugar, demerara	25 g. = 2		
Sugar, icing	25 g. = 3		
Syrup or honey	25 g. = 1		

AUTHOR'S NOTE

This is not a text book on Scottish fare but a selection of recipes with a Scottish background and a few traditional recipes that have survived the test of time. I hope they will appeal equally to the experienced and inexperienced cook, to all those who enjoy Scottish fare and to those who find as much pleasure in cooking as I do.

As soon as I was allowed to use a knife, I began to learn the rudiments of cookery. When mincemeat or plum puddings had to be prepared, or vegetables chopped for any broth, my mother propped me up beside the kitchen table in an old manse on the Braes of Angus, and I did my share. My mother had married without any knowledge of cookery and was determined that her daughters would be better prepared for housekeeping. It was she also who taught me as I grew older how to cook fish, meat and vegetables, but it was my father who showed me how to make candies, jams, jellies, liqueurs and wines.

When I was about twelve, I started to collect cookery recipes, transcribing some into exercise books and pasting others up. Some of these I am passing on to you with recipes from relatives in Aberdeenshire where my forebears on the maternal side tilled the land and bred Highland ponies, and from relatives in the Border country where my forefathers fed their flocks.

You will also recognize many from Angus and Edinburgh where I went to school, and from Dundee where I took a brides' class in cooking the better to edit the household pages in the *People's Friend*, and the *People's Journal*. Some of the recipes are for dishes met with wherever the Scots pitch their tents. Others are culled from an ancient book once treasured by my maternal great-grandmother in Edinburgh. I have had to modernize a few; for example, the haggis from which I banished the lights.

Scottish fare has always been wholesome fare, but it is sad to think that the Scottish kitchen like the English has lost so much of its individuality with the fret of years. This does not mean that the fare has deteriorated. On the other hand, the quality of most of it is higher than ever. Where can you find finer beef, mutton, fish or game, and when it comes to bread and teabread its equal is not to be found in these Islands. Unfortunately, though most of our food produce is of high quality, our cooking is not always of the same standard. In bygone days, our mothers had to cook all the food over peat fires and bake on the hearth in the peat embers; then coal ranges came in with no oven temperatures and no simmering plates to help them, which simplify the cooking of today. Yet I remember the cakes and pastry that we cooked in those ranges with nostalgia. . . .

We still have a national kitchen which in the days of the Auld Alliance learned much from the French cuisine. Let us try, with all the modern aids to housewifery that science has devised, to maintain it in its integrity. It is not enough to be praised for our Black Bun, Edinburgh Rock, Petticoat Tails and Shortbread.

Now I would like to thank one or two friends, including Dr Cramond and Bruce Russell, for coming to my assistance when I was preparing this book. Without their help it would not have been possible to include some of the traditional recipes.

As we used to say in Angus when wishing folks well: 'Lang may their lums reek.'

ELIZABETH CRAIG

They say in Fife
That next to nae wife
The best thing is a gude wife.

I would change this saying to 'a gude housewife'. When I lived in my ain country we spoke of the husband as 'the gudeman'. When my father had been away visiting his flock in the glens, my mother used to urge us girls on to prepare for his return by singing in her lovely voice:

There's nae luck aboot the hoose,
There's nae luck ava,
There's little pleasure in the hoose
When oor gudeman's awa'.

Rise up an' mak' a clean fireside,
Put on the muckle pot,
Gie little Kate her cotton goon
An' Jock his Sunday coat;
An' mak' their shoon as black as sloes,
Their hose as white as snaw;
It's a' to please my ain gudeman:
He likes to see them braw.

For there's nae luck aboot the hoose,
There's nae luck ava,
There's little pleasure in the hoose
When oor gudeman's awa'.

INTRODUCTION

MEASURING

All measurements given in this book are level unless otherwise stated.

TO MEASURE DRY INGREDIENTS IN A CUP

If a cup of any dry or liquid ingredient is suggested in recipes, this refers to an average-sized teacup, if my standard measuring cup manufactured in aluminium is not available. $1\frac{1}{4}$ cups of any liquid equals $\frac{1}{2}$ pint. If measuring a dry ingredient in it, fill up to the cup level and shake level. If using an average-sized teacup, level off with a palette knife.

TO MEASURE DRY INGREDIENTS BY SPOON

Take a slightly heaped spoonful of ingredient, and slide a palette knife across the top, taking care not to press ingredient. The result will be a level spoonful of ingredient. To measure $\frac{1}{2}$ a spoonful, (if you haven't a measuring spoon for this purpose), divide ingredient through the middle, lengthwise if spoon is oval shaped, crosswise if round, and carefully scoop out one half. To obtain $\frac{1}{4}$ spoonful, measure $\frac{1}{2}$ spoonful, then divide remaining half in two crosswise, and carefully scoop out half.
NOTE: Sift flours and icing sugar before measuring.

Fill spoon only up to the rim, not to overflowing. To save waste, particularly where essences are concerned, it is safer to use measuring spoons than parts of a spoon.

TABLE OF EQUIVALENTS

Ingredient	Approximate equivalent to 1 measuring cup	Approximate equivalent to 1 tablespoon
Almonds, ground	¼ lb.	⅓ oz.
Arrowroot	5 ozs.	¼ oz.
Barley, pearl	½ lb.	1 oz.
Breadcrumbs, dried	6 oz.	½ oz.
stale	2 oz.	¼ oz.
Cheese, grated	4 oz.	¼ oz.
Cocoa	¼ lb.	¼ oz.
Coconut, desiccated	¼ lb.	¼ oz.
Cornflour	5 oz.	¼ oz.
Dried fruit (except stone fruit)	6 oz.	
Fats	½ lb.	½ oz.
Flour	¼ lb.	¼ oz.
Gelatine, powdered		½ oz.
Minced meat	½ lb.	½ oz.
Nuts, chopped	¼ lb.	¼ oz.
Oatmeal, medium grain	6 oz.	⅓ oz.
Rice	½ lb.	¾ oz.
Sago and semolina	6 oz.	½ oz.
Sugar, brown (closely packed)	7 oz.	About ½ oz.
caster	½ lb.	½ oz.
Sugar, granulated	7½ oz.	About ½ oz.
icing	5 oz.	Fully ¼ oz.
Tapioca	6 oz.	½ oz.

1 lb. bacon	yields	15–20 slices
1 lb. chocolate	,,	about 3 cups grated
1 square chocolate	,,	1 oz.
1 medium-sized lemon	,,	2–3 tablespoons juice and 1 rounded teaspoon grated lemon rind
1 medium-sized orange	,,	$\frac{1}{2}$ cup juice and $\frac{3}{4}$ tablespoon rind
8 lumps of sugar	,,	1 oz.

APPROXIMATE OVEN TEMPERATURES

	Degrees F.
Very slow	250° F.
Slow	300° F.
Moderately slow ⎫ Fairly slow ⎬	325° F.
Moderate	350° F.
Moderately hot ⎰ ⎱	375° F. 400° F.
Fairly hot	425° F.
Hot	450° F.
Very hot ⎰ ⎱	475° F. 500° F.

FRYING TABLE
(Deep Fat)

Food	Fat temperature	Oil temperature	Bread test
Uncooked mixtures (doughnuts and fritters)	360–375° F.	375–385° F.	1 minute
Cooked mixtures (croquettes, fish cakes, etc.)	375–385° F.	385° F.	40 seconds
Fish	375° F.	375° F.	1 minute

Food	Fat temperature	Oil temperature	Bread test
Onions	360–375° F.	375° F.	1 minute
Potatoes (crisps, chips, straws, etc.)	390° F.	395° F.	20 seconds

I prefer to fry potatoes by the 'two step' method: (1) 375° F. till soft and starting to brown. Drain on absorbent paper. (2) Fry at 390° F. till brown and crisp.

BREAD TEST

Use this test when you have no thermometer to test temperature. Drop an inch square of bread into hot fat or oil. If it browns at specified time, fat or oil is at right temperature for frying. If it browns in less time, cool fat or oil and test again. If it takes longer, heat a little and test again.

THE
SCOTTISH COOKERY
BOOK

SOUPS

Mony cooks ne'er made gude kail

Scots are very proud of their reputation for good soup and most Scottish housewives take the making of soup very seriously. In spite of the modern tendency to follow the quickest way to the table, many Scottish women believe, as I do, that though some good soups can be made without stock, there are many soups that would not be worth supping if it were not for the stock that is their basis.

Some of our soups are traditional, such as Bawd Bree, Cullen Skink, Kail and Powsowdie. These you seldom enjoy except at a St Andrew's or Burns Night Dinner. Most of our soups take the edge off the appetite, but others of a French origin, dating from the days of the Auld Alliance, are of a more delicate consistency. Unlike the former, they are only a prelude to courses to follow, not a course in themselves. I would like you to get to know both.

BROWN STOCK

2 *lb. shin of beef*	1 *sliced parsnip or turnip*
4 *pints cold water*	1 *celery stick*
1 *small carrot*	½ *teaspoon salt*
1 *small onion*	1 *teaspoon peppercorns*

Remove all fat and skin from meat, then wipe meat and cut up into dice. (If bone is included scrape carefully, remove the marrow and rinse bone in boiling water.) Melt enough marrow from the bone, or clarified butter if not using bones, to cover bottom of soup pan. Add meat. Fry slowly till the fat is absorbed, then add water. Cover and stand for 30 minutes, then remove lid and add a pinch of salt. Bring slowly to boiling point, then carefully skim off any scum. Add prepared vegetables, salt and peppercorns. Simmer, uncovered, for 3 hours, then strain through a hair sieve into a basin. When cold, remove any fat before using stock.

WHITE STOCK I

2 *lb. knuckle of veal*	*a few parsley stalks*
2 *quarts cold water*	3 *white peppercorns*
1 *scalded onion*	1 *teaspoon salt*

Wipe the meat with a damp cloth. Remove all fat and any greasy skin from the knuckle. Cut up meat into small pieces, putting them into the cold water as you cut.

Add the bones. Bring very slowly to the boil and skim well.

Add onion and parsley stalks, peppercorns and salt. Simmer very gently for 5 or 6 hours. Strain through a fine sieve.

WHITE STOCK II

Substitute 1 lb. raw chicken bones for the veal and add a celery stick and blade of mace, as well as the onion, parsley and peppercorns. Increase water by a pint. Follow method given for No. 1.

GARNISHES FOR SOUPS

Garnish cream soups with minced parsley or fried croûtons. (If wanted for a party, top each bowl with a heaped teaspoon of switched cream, then sprinkle lightly with minced chervil, chives, paprika or parsley.)

FRIED CROÛTONS

Cut bread into slices ⅓ inch thick. Remove crusts. Cube. Fry in deep fat, 375°–390° F., for about 40 seconds until crisp and golden brown. Drain on absorbent paper. If preferred, slice $\frac{1}{4}$ inch thick and stamp into rounds the size of sixpence. Fry in a little butter or margarine till golden brown. Drain on absorbent paper.

ARTICHOKE PURÉE

1 *lb. Jerusalem artichokes*	*salt and pepper to taste*
1 *oz. butter*	$\frac{1}{2}$ *oz. cornflour*
1 *medium-sized onion*	$\frac{1}{2}$ *gill milk*
1 *pint white stock*	*cream to taste*

Scrub and wash artichokes. Peel them very thinly, throwing each as peeled into a basin of acidulated water to preserve their colour. Melt butter. Add artichokes. Slice in onion. Fry very slowly, stirring frequently, till the butter is absorbed, but take care that the vegetables do not change colour. Add stock and salt and pepper to taste. Simmer gently until the artichokes are tender, in about an hour. Rub through a hair sieve. Mix the cornflour to a cream with the milk and stir into soup. Simmer gently for about 5 minutes, stirring constantly. Remove from heat. Stand for 2 or 3 minutes, then add cream slowly, from $\frac{1}{2}$ gill to $1\frac{1}{2}$ gills, according to whether a purée or a creamy soup is wanted. Garnish with minced parsley. Serves 4 or 5.

BAWD BREE HARE SOUP

1 *fresh brown hare*	*salt to taste*
2 *lb. shin of beef*	1 *teaspoon sugar*
4 *quarts water*	6 *whole cloves*
2 *medium-sized onions*	1 *blade mace*
2 *medium-sized carrots*	1 *teaspoon mustard*
1 *small turnip*	$1\frac{1}{2}$ *oz. butter*
1 *small parsnip*	2 *oz. flour*
3 *celery sticks with foliage*	1 *or 2 glasses of port wine*
strip of lemon rind	*squeeze of lemon juice*
2 *sprigs parsley*	1 *teaspoon red currant jelly*
1 *teaspoon black peppercorns*	*small forcemeat balls*
2 *bay leaves*	

When skinning and cleaning the hare, be careful to retain all the blood. Rinse well, then break the diaphragm, and hold the hare over the vessel containing the blood when removing the lungs. Joint hare and remove very small steaks from the back, rump and shoulders. Cut shin into small pieces. Place in a saucepan with the water and remainder of hare. Bring to boil. Skim if necessary. Slice in prepared onion, carrot, turnip, parsnip and celery. Add lemon rind, parsley, peppercorns, bay leaves, salt to taste, sugar cloves, mace and mustard. Bring to boil. Skim if necessary. Simmer very gently for 3 hours, then strain. Beat the steaks from the hare with a meat bat or rolling pin. Melt the butter in a soup pan. Dredge the steaks with flour, and fry slowly in the butter till slightly browned on both sides, then remove to a plate. Add remainder of flour. When frothy, stir in the strained stock and fried hare. Simmer very gently for 1½ hours. Skim. Strain the blood. Gradually stir in a little of the hot soup. Continue until all the soup is added, then return to pan. Stir till almost boiling, but do not allow to boil, or the soup will curdle. When I make this soup, I generally leave it for about 10 minutes over boiling water and stir it occasionally. Meanwhile, I pound the parboiled liver of the hare with the pieces of cooked hare boiled for stock and rub this through a hair sieve. Gradually stir a little of the soup into the purée, then when creamy in texture, stir this into the soup in pan. Gradually add the port wine, lemon juice, red currant jelly, and salt and cayenne pepper to taste. In some parts of Scotland forcemeat balls are added as I have suggested, but the hare steaks can take their place as a garnish. Serves 15.

TO VARY: Reduce flour to 1 oz. and use it only for dredging the steaks. Mince 2 slices of fat bacon and fry slowly till crisp, then remove from pan. Add butter to bacon fat. When melted, brown steaks, then add strained stock and 4 oz. medium oatmeal.

FORCEMEAT BALLS: Mix the reserved finely chopped cooked hare liver with ¼ lb. sausage meat or breadcrumbs. Season with salt and pepper. Add 1 teaspoon grated onion, 1 tablespoon melted butter and hare stock to moisten. Make into balls the size of a marble. Either flour or 'egg and crumb', and fry in deep fat till they rise to the top and are evenly cooked.

TO MAKE BAWD BREE FROM COOKED HARE: Chop, pound and sieve the meat left over from a cooked hare. Dredge with flour, 1 tablespoon to a pound of the purée. Gradually stir in hot, rich brown, onion-flavoured stock until you have a thin cream. Stir till boiling. Simmer gently for 5 minutes, stirring constantly, then season with cayenne pepper and flavour to taste with boiling port wine, allowing at least a tablespoon to each cup of soup. Garnish with forcemeat balls.

CABBAGE AND PEA SOUP

¾ lb. streaky bacon
3 pints boiling water or stock
2 small cabbages
1 scraped carrot
1 medium-sized peeled turnip

2 peeled onions
1 small head celery
¾ pint dried peas
salt and pepper to taste

Place bacon in a saucepan. Add boiling water or stock. Trim and remove leaves from cabbages, then chop cabbage. Place in pan. Chop and add carrot, turnip, onion and celery, and peas soaked overnight in cold water to cover, then drained. Cover and simmer till peas are tender in 2–3 hours. Skim off all fat and remove bacon. Season to taste with salt and pepper. Thin if necessary with stock. Serves 6.

CARROT SOUP

2 large carrots
1 medium-sized onion
½ oz. butter or dripping
2 oz. rough scraps fat bacon
  or ham

1 quart stock
1 lump of sugar
salt and pepper to taste
1 dessertspoon minced parsley

Grate the carrots. Slice onion. Melt butter or dripping and bacon or ham scraps together in a saucepan. Add carrot and onion. Stir over moderate heat till all the fat is absorbed by the vegetables, then add stock. (If first stock is used, allow only 1 pint, and add 1 pint of water.) Bring to boil. Skim well just before boiling and after boiling. Simmer very gently for $1\frac{1}{4}$ hours. Rub through a hair sieve. Pour into a saucepan. Add sugar, salt and pepper to taste and parsley. Serve when it comes to boiling point. Serves 4.

COCK-A-LEEKIE

Lang may ye live, an' lang enjoy
Ilk blessin' life can gie,
Health, wealth, content, and pleasure,
An' cock-a-leekie.

This is a traditional soup which frequently figures as the first course at a Burns Supper or St Andrew's Night Dinner. It is usually made with an old cock, but an old fowl can be substituted.

1 *old cock or fowl*	2 *tablespoons rice*
2 *quarts cold water*	1 *tablespoon chopped parsley*
1 *large teaspoon salt*	*salt and pepper to taste*
6 *shredded leeks*	

Draw and truss the cock or fowl in the usual way, then place in a large saucepan with the cold water. Wash giblets and add with salt. Bring to boil. Skim thoroughly. Simmer very gently for 2 hours, skimming as necessary. Rinse and add leeks and rice. Simmer gently till the cock or fowl is tender. Remove bird and giblets, and any grease from the soup. Add parsley and salt and pepper to taste. Serve the bird as a separate course, coated with caper sauce. Serves 4 or 5.

COW HEEL SOUP

1 *cow's heel*	1 *tablespoon sago*
3 *pints water*	1 *dessertspoon chopped parsley*
salt as required	*squeeze of lemon juice*
1 *sliced onion*	*pepper to taste*
1 *sliced carrot*	*pinch of grated nutmeg*
1 *sliced celery stick*	

Clean heel. Place in a saucepan. Cover with cold water. Bring to boil, then drain off water. Divide heel in four. Place in saucepan. Add cold water as given and a pinch of salt. Bring to boil. Skim. Add onion, carrot and celery. Bring again to boil. Simmer gently for 3–3½ hours. Strain stock into another saucepan. Remove some of the meat from the bones. Chop and add to soup. Bring again to boil. Stir in sago. Simmer gently for 25 minutes, then add parsley, lemon juice, pepper and nutmeg. Serves 6.

CREAM OF ALMONDS

¼ lb. almonds
½ pint of milk
2 tablespoons sieved breadcrumbs
1 oz. butter

1 oz. flour
1 quart chicken stock
salt and cayenne pepper to taste
pinch of ground mace
½ pint cream

Chop the almonds. Place in a mortar. Pound with a teaspoon of water, then add to the milk. Cover and simmer very gently until soft. Add crumbs. Simmer for 3 minutes, then rub all through a hair sieve. Melt the butter. Add the flour and almond purée, then gradually stir in the stock, salt, cayenne pepper to taste and mace. Boil for about 5 minutes, stirring constantly. Remove pan from heat. When slightly cooled, gradually stir in the cream. Stir till nearly boiling. Serve with Melba toast. Serves 6 to 8.

CREAM OF BARLEY

2 quarts chicken stock
¼ lb. pearl barley
2 tablespoons chopped onion
1 blade mace
1 inch cinnamon stick

1 oz. butter
salt and pepper to taste
2 egg yolks
½ pint cream or rich milk

Pour stock into a saucepan. Rinse and add the barley with onion, mace and cinnamon. Bring to boil. Skim if necessary. Simmer very gently for 2½–3 hours, till barley is soft, then rub through a sieve. Return to pan. Add butter, and salt and pepper to taste. Beat the egg yolks. Gradually beat in the cream. Stir a little of the soup into the mixture, then pour this into the soup in pan, stirring constantly. When blended and piping hot—but it must not boil—pour into heated tureen. If too thick for your taste (Scots favour thick soups), thin the purée with hot chicken stock before adding the egg yolk and cream. Serves 6.

CREAM OF CARROT

2 oz. butter
2 tablespoons grated carrot
1 finely chopped large onion
½ teaspoon salt
2 large carrots, cut into balls
1 bay leaf

1 pint white stock
1 oz. flour
½ pint milk
salt and pepper to taste
2 teaspoons minced parsley

Melt butter in a saucepan. Add grated carrot and onion. Fry slowly for 5 minutes, stirring occasionally. Do not allow to brown. Add salt, carrot balls, bay leaf, and stock. Bring to boil. Skim if necessary. Simmer very gently for 45 minutes. Remove bay leaf. Cream flour gradually with milk, then stir in remainder of milk. Stir into soup. Boil for 4 minutes stirring constantly, then season to taste and add parsley. Boil for 1 minute. Serve, garnished with switched cream, if liked. Serves 3.

CREAM OF CELERY

2 heads of celery
1 sliced medium-sized onion
3 pints white stock

2½ oz. flour
½ pint cream
salt and pepper to taste

Trim and wash celery thoroughly. Cut in shreds. Place in a saucepan. Add onion and stock. Bring to boil. Skim if necessary. Simmer very gently for about 40 minutes. Mix the flour smoothly to a cream with milk. Stir into soup. Stir till boiling, then simmer for 5 minutes, stirring constantly. Rub through a sieve. Pour purée into a saucepan. Gradually stir in the cream. Stir till almost boiling. Season with salt and pepper. Serve with fried croûtons. Serves 6.

STRATHMORE CREAM OF GREEN PEAS

2 *pints shelled green peas*
1 *quart boiling strained white*
  stock
1 *sprig mint*

salt and pepper to taste
1 *teaspoon sugar*
3 *egg yolks*
½ *pint cream*

Rinse the peas. Place in a saucepan. Add stock and mint. Bring to boil. Boil until tender. Rub through a wire sieve into a clean saucepan. Add salt and pepper and sugar. Stir occasionally until boiling, then remove pan from stove. Beat egg yolk. Stir in a little of the soup, then stir this into remainder of soup in pan. Stir in cream. Stir over moderate heat till piping hot, but do not allow to boil. Serves 6.

FAMILY GREEN PEA SOUP

Place ¾ pint green peas in a saucepan. Add 1 quart boiling white stock, 1 chopped medium sized onion, 1 shredded lettuce, salt and pepper to taste, 1 teaspoon sugar and a sprig of mint. Simmer very gently for 40 minutes. Rub through a wire sieve. Melt 1 oz. butter. Stir in 1 oz. flour. When frothy, gradually stir in the purée. Stir till boiling. Simmer gently for 3 minutes. Garnish with ¼ pint boiled green peas.

MY MOTHER'S CREAM OF SORREL

When I was a child we used to suck the leaves of wild sorrel, or sourock, when I was gathering the sorrel for soup making. Nowadays I grow sorrel, which Mary, Queen of Scots is said to have introduced to Scotland, from seed bought in Paris.

27

½ lb. sorrel leaves
2½ oz. butter
3½ pints chicken or veal stock
½ lb. chopped potato
1 teaspoon salt
pepper to taste
¼ pint cream
whipped cream to taste

Carefully pick over sorrel. Wash and rinse in a colander under cold water tap. Melt butter in a saucepan. Add sorrel. Stir over moderate heat until the sorrel wilts, then gradually stir in stock. Bring to boil. Add potato and salt. Cover and simmer very slowly for 1 hour, then rub through a sieve. Rinse saucepan. Add the soup. Season with pepper. Slowly stir in cream. Reheat, stirring constantly, but do not allow to boil. Serve in heated soup cups. Garnish with whipped cream. Serves 6–8.

CREAM OF SPLIT PEAS OR LENTILS

1½ cups split peas or lentils
3 pints ham bone liquor
2 tablespoons chopped onion
½ cup chopped celery
1 pint milk
1 tablespoon flour
1 teaspoon finely chopped mint
salt and pepper to taste

Rinse and drain peas or lentils. Soak overnight in cold water to cover. Pour ham bone liquor into a saucepan. Drain peas or lentils and add. Stir in onion and celery. Cover. Simmer very gently for 2 hours, then rub through a wire sieve into a basin. Rinse saucepan. Add purée and milk, reserving 2 tablespoons of milk. Mix the flour to a paste with the reserved milk. Stir into soup with mint. When boiling, simmer for a minute or two, stirring constantly, then re-season if necessary. Serve with fried croûtons. Serves 6.

CULLEN SKINK

1 Finnan haddock
1 chopped peeled onion
1 pint milk
mashed potato as required
1 tablespoon butter
salt and pepper to taste

Skin a medium-sized haddock. Place in a shallow saucepan. Add just enough boiling water to cover. Bring slowly to boil. Add onion. When the haddock turns creamy, remove it from pan and carefully take flesh from the bones. Flake fish. Add the bones to the water in pan. Cover and simmer very gently for 1 hour. Strain stock. Return to saucepan. Bring to boil. Bring milk to boil in separate pan and add to stock with the fish. Simmer gently for about 5 minutes, then stir in enough hot mashed potatoes to make a creamy soup. Add butter, bit by bit, and salt and pepper to taste. If liked, stir in a tablespoon or two of cream, and a heaped teaspoon of minced parsley. Serves 4.

FEATHER FOWLIE

This is a version of a soup frequently served at national banquets.

1 *fresh roasting fowl*
salted water as required
1 *slice lean ham*
1 *sliced medium-sized onion*
1 *sliced celery stick*
2 *or 3 slices of carrot*
2 *sprigs parsley*

1 *sprig thyme*
1 *blade mace*
1½ *gills white stock*
3 *slightly beaten egg yolks*
2 *tablespoons hot cream*
1 *dessertspoon minced blanched parsley*

Remove skin from fowl. Rinse the inside thoroughly with salted water, then joint bird. Place in a basin. Cover with cold salted water. Soak for 30 minutes. Rinse thoroughly again, then place the joints in a deep saucepan with the ham, onion, celery, carrot, parsley, thyme and mace. Add 3 pints of cold water. Cover and bring to boil. Skim if necessary. Simmer very gently for 1½ hours. Strain into a basin. Leave until cold, then remove all grease. Pour into a clean saucepan. Add white stock. Bring very slowly to boil. Simmer very gently, uncovered, for 20 minutes. Draw pan to side of stove. Strain the egg yolks and stir gradually into the cream. Stir into soup. Add parsley and minced poached chicken breast to taste. Stir for a moment or two over the stove. Serve in a hot soup tureen or in hot soup cups. Serves 6.

To use up boiled chicken, serve cold with ham and salad at a later meal, or curry it.

FIFE BROTH

2 *or* 3 *ribs of pork*
2 *oz. pin-head barley*
salt and black pepper to taste
6 *potatoes*

Wash the ribs, which should be used when the meat has been taken off for baking. Place in a saucepan. Add 2 quarts of cold water. Rinse and add the barley. Bring to boil. Skim if necessary. Simmer very gently for at least 3 hours. Season with salt and pepper to taste. After cooking for 2½ hours, slice and add potatoes, and finish cooking. Re-season as necessary. Remove ribs before serving. Serves 5 or 6.

FINNAN HADDOCK SOUP

2 *slices of onion*
½ *cup sliced carrot*
½ *cup sliced celery*
water as required
1–1½ *lb. Finnan haddock*
2 *pints thin white sauce*
salt and pepper to taste
pinch of ground mace
hot milk as required
¼ *cup thick cream*

Place onion, carrot, celery and water to cover in a saucepan. Bring to boil. Simmer for 20 minutes. Add fish. Cover and bring to the boil. Skim. Cover and simmer till fish and vegetables are tender, then remove skin and bone from fish. Strain off liquor into a basin. Rub fish and vegetables through a fine sieve. When making the white sauce use 1½ pints hot milk and ½ pint of the hot strained fish liquor. Season to taste with salt, pepper and mace. Stir into purée. Reheat, stirring constantly. Draw pan to side of stove. Thin to taste with hot milk. Serve in soup cups with whipped cream floating on each portion. Serves 6.

MY MOTHER'S FISH SOUP

6 *fresh haddock heads*
1 *small fresh haddock*
1 *small sliced carrot*
1 *slice of turnip*
2 *oz. butter*
2 *oz. flour*
½ *pint milk*
1 *tablespoon chopped parsley*

1 or 2 sliced celery sticks	salt and pepper to taste
1 handful of parsley	1 egg yolk
½ teaspoon salt	1 tablespoon thick cream

Clean and rinse the heads, and the haddock. Place in a saucepan. Cover with cold water. Bring to boil. Skim carefully. Add carrot, turnip, celery sticks, parsley and salt. Bring again to boil. Cover and simmer very gently until the vegetables are tender, then strain. Melt the butter in a saucepan. Add flour. Stir till frothy, then gradually stir in 2 pints hot fish stock. When boiling, simmer stirring constantly for 2 or 3 minutes, then add the milk, parsley and salt and pepper to taste. If liked, add 1–2 teaspoons of mushroom ketchup. Mix the egg yolk with the cream till blended. Gradually stir into soup. Stir over low heat until soup is thickened and re-season if necessary. Serves 6.

FRIAR'S CHICKEN SOUP

Sir Walter Scott claimed this soup was a favourite of James VI. In his day, the chicken was removed from the soup, carved and served in the soup. There are various versions of this. Here is one popular in Victorian days.

2lb. knuckle of veal	1 jointed skinned roasting fowl
1 medium-sized onion	salt and pepper to taste
½ head celery	3 egg yolks
1 blade of mace	¼ pint milk
12 peppercorns	¼ pint cream
3 cloves	1 tablespoon minced parsley
2 quarts cold water	

Wipe veal with a damp cloth and place in a saucepan. Prepare and add onion and celery, then mace, peppercorns, cloves and water. Bring to boil. Skim carefully. Cover and simmer very gently for 1½ hours. Strain stock into another saucepan. Add joints of fowl. Bring to boil. Skim if necessary. Simmer gently for 45 minutes. Remove all white meat. Simmer soup gently for 30 minutes. Add salt and pepper to taste. Strain into another saucepan. Beat the egg yolks. Stir in the milk and cream. Gradually add to soup. Stir till thickened, but do not allow to boil, then add diced white meat and parsley. Serve at once. Serves 8.

CLEAR GAME SOUP

remains of cold game
1 large onion
1 medium-sized carrot
1 bay leaf
1 sprig thyme
1 sprig parsley
1 blade mace
2 cloves

6 black peppercorns
2 white peppercorns
1 lump sugar
2½ quarts beef or veal stock
2 egg shells and egg whites
2 oz. lean raw ham
sherry as required
salt to taste

Take the remains of any cold roast black cock, grouse or pheasant. Place in a saucepan. Slice in the onion and carrot. Add the herbs, spices, sugar and stock. Bring to boil. Skim. Simmer very gently for 3 or 4 hours with lid tilted, skimming occasionally, then strain. Leave until cold. Carefully remove any fat. Wash egg shells. Remove their inner skins. Turn stock into a clean saucepan. Add egg shells and slightly beaten egg whites. Stir well. Add ham and from 1 to 2 glasses of sherry according to taste. Whisk well until blended. Bring to boil. Simmer very gently for 4 minutes, then strain through a jelly bag, dipped in scalding hot water and wrung dry. Season with salt. Reheat. Garnish with custard dice and minced chervil or parsley, or with Game Quenelles. Serves 8.

HIGHLAND CLEAR GAME SOUP

Put any carcase of grouse, partridges or scraps of venison, raw or cooked, in a saucepan. Add 1 sliced onion and carrot, 1 blade mace, 1 bay leaf, 3 cloves, 2 sprigs parsley and salt and pepper to taste. Cover with beef stock. Bring to boil. Skim carefully. Simmer gently for 2 hours, then strain. Bring again to boil, then add 1 oz. coarsely chopped raw lean beef. Bring again to boil. Strain through a jelly bag. It may be necessary to add another ounce of beef and bring soup again to the boil, and strain before it is perfectly clear. Flavour to taste with Marsala or sherry. Reheat. Serve in hot cups with fairy toast.

HOTCH-POTCH

1½ lb. neck of mutton
½ teaspoon salt
2 quarts water
2 chopped onions
2 diced carrots
1 slice of turnip

½ lettuce
½ pint green peas
1 medium cauliflower
1 teaspoon sugar
pepper to taste

Place the mutton, with bones, salt and water in a saucepan. Bring slowly to the boil, then skim. Simmer 1 hour. Add onion, carrot and turnip. Cover and cook gently for 30 minutes, then chop and add lettuce, and peas. Divide cauliflower into small sprigs. Trim off stalks and add. Cover and simmer for 30 minutes till all the vegetables and the meat are tender, then remove bones and meat. Add sugar, pepper and more salt as required. Serves 6. If mutton is to be served as a separate course, following the soup, keep it hot, then serve it coated with caper sauce, with mashed potatoes and mashed turnip or swede. This soup is generally made when the young vegetables come into season, but can be prepared for winter meals, substituting quick-frozen peas, 10 minutes before dishing up, for the fresh peas. In some parts of Scotland, shredded cabbage is substituted for cauliflower. If you happen to have mutton stock, you can substitute it for the mutton and water. In that case, use only 3 pints of stock and add the vegetables as soon as the stock comes to the boil as described.

HOUGH SOUP

BROWN SOUP

1 lb. shin of beef
1 oz. butter or dripping
1 large sliced carrot
2 slices turnip

1 sliced onion
2 pints water
1 oz. sago
triangles of toast

Wash and cut the meat into small pieces. Melt fat in a saucepan. Add meat and vegetables. Fry, turning frequently, till brown. Add water. Bring to boil. Skim, then simmer gently for about 3½ hours. Skim again. Strain into a clean saucepan. Add sago. Bring again to boil, then simmer gently until the sago is cooked. Season with salt and pepper to taste. (Sometimes my mother thickened this soup with flour creamed with cold water in place of thickening with sago.) Serve with triangles of crisp toast. Serves 3.

KAIL BROSE

In early days this was a staple food in Scotland. It was usually made with water for breakfast, sometimes with stock for supper.

KAIL BROSE WITH WATER: Allowing 2 tablespoons of oatmeal per person, add salt and pepper to taste and a walnut of dripping per portion. Pour boiling water in which kail has been cooked over the oatmeal, stirring rapidly as you pour until thinned to taste and forming knots. Serve at breakfast with soor dook.

KAIL BROTH WITH BROSE: Boil a cleaned cow heel or ox head in 6 pints salted water until the fat rises to the top. Shred 2 lb. of kail. Add to stock. Simmer gently until tender in about 15 minutes. Meanwhile, toast a teacup of medium oatmeal lightly in a moderate oven, then place it in a basin. Add a pinch of salt. Stir in a ladleful, or more, of the fatty top of the broth until the oatmeal forms knots. Remove cow heel or cow head from broth. Add the oatmeal brose. Stir well.

SUTHERLAND BROSE: Mix toasted oatmeal with cabbage bree until it thickens in the form of knots. Serve with soor dook.

THURSO BROSE (Brochain): Season toasted oatmeal with salt, then stir in enough boiling water, flavoured with onion and cheese when liked, to make a porridge so thick that the spoon can stand in it. Sup with cream or milk from a dish at side of plate, without onion and cheese if for breakfast.

STRONE KAIL BROTH

½ teacup barley   1 quart stock
1 small piece of turnip   1 teacup chopped kale
1 medium-sized carrot   salt and pepper to taste
2 leeks

Rinse and drain the barley. Peel and dice turnip. Scrape and chop carrot. Trim and slice leeks. Pour the stock, made from beef, ham or mutton, into a saucepan. Add the barley and vegetables, minus the kail. Bring to boil. Skim if necessary. Simmer for 2½ hours. Add the kail. Simmer for ½ hour, then add salt and pepper to taste. Serves 4.

KILMENY KAIL

1 jointed rabbit   1 lb. green kail
¼ lb. diced pickled pork   seasoning to taste

Place rabbit in a basin. Cover with warm water. Stand for a minute or two, then drain off water. Place in a saucepan with the pork and cold water to cover. Rince and shred the kail and add. Simmer very gently for 3 hours. Season with pepper to taste, and salt only if required. Serve with oatcakes. Serves 6.

SCOTCH KAIL

3 lb. mutton   1 teaspoon salt
3 quarts cold water   1 oz. pearl barley
3 medium-sized onions   1 stalk curly kail
3 medium-sized leeks   salt and pepper to taste

Wipe the meat with a damp cloth. Place in a large saucepan. Add water. Halve and slice onions and leeks and add with the salt. Bring to boil. Simmer gently for about 1 hour. Place barley in another saucepan. Cover with cold water. Bring to boil. Strain and add to soup. Simmer gently for 1 hour. Remove the heads from the stalk of kail. Rinse thoroughly in a colander under cold water tap, then drain and shred finely. Add to soup. Simmer gently for 1 hour. Remove meat. Cut up enough into small pieces to fill 1 cup. Place in soup tureen. Season kail with salt and pepper to taste. Pour over meat. Reserve mutton for another meal. Serves 6 or 7.

MY MOTHER'S KIDNEY SOUP

1 *medium-sized carrot*	1 *bouquet garni*
½ *small turnip*	1 *quart second stock*
1 *large chopped onion*	1 *ox kidney*
1 *celery stick*	½ *oz. butter*
1 *teaspoon black peppercorns*	*flour as required*
1 *blade of mace*	*salt and pepper*

Slice the vegetables into a saucepan. Add peppercorns, mace, bouquet garni (1 sprig each parsley, thyme and marjoram and 1 bay leaf) and stock. Bring to boil. Skim if necessary. Simmer gently for 1 hour. Skin, split, core, wash and dry kidney, then cut in slices. Melt the butter. Add kidney and fry slowly till well browned. Add 1 quart water. Cover and simmer very gently for 1 hour, then strain off stock. Chop the kidney finely. Add to kidney stock. Strain in vegetable stock. Simmer very gently for 1 hour. Thicken to taste with flour creamed with water. Season with salt and pepper. If preferred, the soup can be made with 6 sheep's kidneys, or with half calves' liver and half ox kidney. Both makes a more delicate soup than ox kidney alone. Serves 6.

LENTIL AND TOMATO SOUP

¼ *lb. lentils*	6 *peppercorns*
½ *pint tinned tomatoes*	3 *pints second stock*
1 *medium-sized onion*	*salt to taste*
1 *small parsnip*	1 *oz. flour*
1 *sliced turnip*	1 *cup milk*
2 *whole cloves*	*butter as required*

Rinse and drain lentils. Place in a saucepan with the tomatoes.

Prepare and slice onion, parsnip and turnip. Add to lentil mixture. Stir in cloves, peppercorns and stock. Stir frequently till boiling, then skim. Add salt to taste. Simmer until lentils are tender, then rub through a wire sieve. Place purée in a clean saucepan. Cream the flour with a little of the milk. Heat remainder of milk to boiling point. Quickly stir in creamed flour. Stir till boiling. Reheat purée, stirring constantly, till boiling, then remove pan from stove and stir in the white sauce and a walnut of butter. Season again if necessary. (If wanted richer, increase butter to 1 oz. Melt it, Stir in the flour without creaming and then the milk.) Serve with fried croûtons. Serves 6.

WHITE LENTIL SOUP

This was a soup that was often served on Good Friday when I was a child. It was followed by boiled salt cod and egg and parsely sauce, served with fluffy mashed potatoes.

½ *lb. Egyptian lentils*	6 *black peppercorns*
2 *celery sticks*	1 *oz. flour*
1 *medium-sized carrot*	½ *pint milk*
1 *medium-sized onion*	¼ *pint cream*
1 *oz. butter*	2 *sprigs parsley*
3 *pints cold water*	*salt and pepper to taste*
1 *blade mace*	*fried croûtons*

Rinse the lentils well under cold water tap, then drain. Slice celery, carrot and onion. Melt butter in a saucepan. Add the lentils and vegetables. Fry slowly, stirring frequently until all the butter is absorbed, then add the water, mace and peppercorns. Bring to boil. Skim. Cover, and simmer gently until the lentils are tender in about 2 hours. Cream the flour gradually with the milk. Stir till boiling, then add a little of the soup. When blended, stir into the remainder of soup, and heat until boiling, stirring constantly. Gradually stir in cream, parsley, and salt and pepper to taste. Serve with fried croûtons. Serves 6.

TO VARY: Substitute white stock for all the water, or half the water.

In cold weather, sprinkle the lentils before frying with a table-spoon of curry powder and add a teaspoon of curry paste before liquid. Sometimes I garnish lentil soup with minced fresh mint, and serve it with dice toast instead of fried croûtons.

LORRAINE SOUP

This is a modern, very economical version of the Potage à la Reine, once so fashionable in Edinburgh, and claimed to be called after Mary of Lorraine, wife of James V, who did so much for the Scottish kitchen.

½ lb. cold, cooked chicken or
  rabbit
½ lb. cold, cooked veal
2 oz. blanched almonds
2 hard-boiled egg yolks
crumbs of a dinner roll

3½ pints white bone stock
salt and pepper to taste
squeeze of lemon juice
pinch of ground mace
hot cream to taste
minced parsley

Pound the chicken or rabbit and the veal, weighed without skin or bone, in a mortar with the almonds and egg yolks. Remove crusts from roll. Bring to boil in milk to cover and pound into the meat mixture when cold. Gradually stir in the stock. Season with salt, pepper, lemon juice and mace. Stir till piping hot. Just before serving, stir in hot cream to taste. Garnish with minced parsley. Serves 8.

MUSHROOM SOUP

6 oz. mushrooms
2¾ pints chicken stock

salt, paprika and pepper to taste
cream

Wash, peel and stem mushrooms. Place the peelings and stems, after chopping, in a saucepan with the stock. Simmer gently for 1 hour. Season with salt and pepper, then strain. Return to saucepan. Slice mushrooms and add. Cook very gently for 5 or 6 minutes until tender. Serve in soup cups. Garnish with whipped cream, flavoured with paprika. Serves 5.

NETTLE BROTH

Some Scottish soups are very distinctive, such as soups containing kail, oatmeal and nettles. In the Highlands, young nettles used to be made into broth with chicken stock thickened with barley, but when I learned to cook, kail broth, which had always been more popular in the Lowlands than in the Highlands, had taken the place of nettle broth.

3 *pints chicken stock*   ½ *pint finely chopped nettles*
½ *cup pearl barley*   *salt and pepper to taste*

Remove any fat from stock. Turn stock into a saucepan. Rinse and drain the barley and add to stock. Bring slowly to boil. Meanwhile, wash young nettle tops thoroughly in salted water, then drain and chop very finely. Add to stock. Simmer very gently until the barley is tender. Season with salt and pepper to taste. Serves 4 or 5.

ONION SOUP

Use beef stock or half beef and half game stock for this soup.

4 *large onions*   1 *lump sugar*
2 *oz. butter*   1 *saltspoon mustard*
2 *pints brown stock*   *pepper to taste*
½ *teaspoon salt*   ½ *oz. flour*

Scrub and trim the onions. Remove the skins. Place the onions in a saucepan. Cover with cold water. Bring to boil. Strain off water. Melt butter in a saucepan. Slice and add onions. Fry very slowly, turning frequently, until a rich brown, then add stock, salt, sugar, mustard, pepper and onion skins. Bring to boil. Remove skins. Simmer very gently for about 2 hours. Rub through a hair sieve. Pour into a clean saucepan. Stir in flour, creamed with stock. When boiling, simmer for 5 minutes. Serve with fairy toast or with a round of toast in each portion, sprinkled thickly with grated cheese. (Sometimes I chop the onions and do not sieve the soup.) Serves 4.

OYSTER SOUP

24 *small oysters*
1 *quart chicken or fish stock*
2 *oz. butter*
2 *oz. flour*
salt and pepper to taste

¼ *pint milk*
1 *blade mace*
½ *teaspoon anchovy essence*
¼ *pint cream*
1 *teaspoon lemon juice*

Beard and scald the oysters in the stock, then remove from stock and halve. Melt butter in a saucepan. Stir in flour. When frothy, gradually stir in the stock. Stir till boiling. Season with salt and pepper to taste. Add milk, mace and anchovy essence. Bring very slowly to the boil. Stand for 10 minutes, then remove mace. Bring again to the boil. Slowly stir in cream, then lemon juice. Add oysters. Stir gently till piping hot, but do not allow to boil. Serves 6.

PARTAN BREE

CRAB SOUP

1 *large boiled crab*
3 *oz. rice*
1 *pint milk*
1 *pint chicken or veal stock*

salt and white pepper to taste
dash of anchovy essence
¼–½ *pint cream*

Remove all the meat from a boiled crab, but lay aside that taken from the larger claws. Rinse the rice. Place in a saucepan. Add the milk. Boil till soft but not into a pulp. Rub it with the crab meat through a sieve. Place purée in a clean saucepan. Gradually stir in stock. Stir till boiling, then season with salt and white pepper to taste and a dash of anchovy essence. Add the pieces of meat from the claws and stir till reheated, but do not allow to boil. Add cream to taste, stirring it in gradually. When piping hot, serve in heated soup cups. Serves 4 to 6.

PENTLAND SOUP

2 oz. butter
2 dessertspoons flour
2 pints hot milk
1 peeled clove of garlic
2 separated eggs

salt and pepper to taste
3 tablespoons grated nippy
 cheese
1 dessertspoon chopped parsley
fried croûtons

Melt butter. Stir in flour. When frothy, gradually stir in milk.
Add garlic. Bring slowly to boil. Remove from stove. Leave until
cold. Remove garlic. Stir a tablespoon or two of the milk into the
yolks, then stir yolks into milk in pan. Return pan to stove. Stir
till piping hot. Season with salt and pepper. Add cheese. Stir
only until melted, then add stiffly beaten egg whites and parsley.
Serve at once in heated soup cups with fried croûtons. Serves 4 or
5.

LARGO POTATO SOUP

1 lb neck mutton
3 quarts cold water
2 lb. potatoes

1 medium sized carrot
3 onions
salt and pepper to taste

Wipe mutton with a damp cloth. Place in a saucepan. Add the
water. Bring to boil. Skim carefully. Peel, slice and add potatoes.
Grate carrot and mince onions and add to soup. Season with salt
and pepper. Simmer gently for about 2 hours, then remove
mutton. Re-season if necessary. Add minced parsley to taste.
Beat with an egg beater till frothy. Serves 8.

POWSOWDIE

SHEEP'S HEAD BROTH

This is a national Scottish broth that has survived the test of
ages. In olden days it was the custom, when a sheep's head was
available, to make it into a Sunday dinner. You started with
Powsowdie, now more familiar as Sheep's Head Broth, and followed with either the head dressed with brain sauce or baked.

In Scottish manses, it is said, Powsowdie was always served on Saturday and the head was served cold at Sunday dinner.

1 *sheep's head*	*salt and pepper to taste*
4 *quarts cold water*	1 *grated carrot*
2 oz. *barley*	1 *dessertspoon chopped*
1 *pint mixed vegetables*	*parsley*
2 oz. *chopped onion*	

Order a large fat head and get the butcher to singe it and split it. Ask for the trotters as well, and have them singed and split. Our grandmothers had to clean the head and trotters themselves, but nowadays it is usual, unless you live on a farm, to buy both head and trotters ready for cooking. Wash head and trotters thoroughly. Remove the brain from head and soak it in cold water sharpened with vinegar, to whiten it. It is used to make into sauce to serve with the head. Place head and trotters in a saucepan. Cover with cold water. Bring to boil. Skim well, then rinse. Place both in a large saucepan. Add the cold water. Rinse the barley in a strainer under the cold water tap and add. Bring to boil. Skim well. Add the mixed vegetables, equal quantity of diced carrot, turnip and sliced leeks and the onion. Season with salt and pepper. Simmer very gently for 3 or 4 hours according to age of animal and size of head. Remove the trotters when they are tender. Half an hour before broth is ready, add the grated carrot. When ready, remove head and add the parsley, and bring to boil again. Serve in a hot tureen.

TO VARY: Add 2 tablespoons of fine oatmeal 30 minutes before serving. If liked, add the chopped meat from the head at the same time.

TO MAKE A RICHER BROTH: Add 2 or 3 lbs. of scrag of mutton with the barley and 2 cups of soaked, dried peas. Do not add the other vegetables until the head has simmered for about 1½ hours.

PRINCE ALFRED SOUP

3 *large peeled onions*
4 *large peeled potatoes*
1 *quart well-flavoured stock*
1 *egg or 2 egg yolks*

1½ *pints milk*
salt and pepper to taste
fried croûtons

Place the onions and potatoes in a large saucepan. Add the stock. Bring to boil. Skim if necessary. Cover and simmer gently for 1 hour, then rub through a sieve. Beat up egg or egg yolks. Mix with the milk. Stir into soup. Place over moderate heat. Stir until piping hot. Do not allow to boil. Remove from stove. Season with salt and pepper. Serve with fried croûtons. Serves 6.

RABBIT SOUP

1 *rabbit*
2 *quarts white stock*
¼ *lb. bacon*
1 *onion*
1 *clove*
1 *sliced carrot*
1 *celery stick*
1 *sprig parsley*

1 *sprig thyme*
½ *bay leaf*
1 *blade mace*
1 *oz. butter or margarine*
1 *oz. flour*
½ *pint milk*
salt and pepper to taste
fried croûtons

Wipe rabbit with a damp cloth and joint. Place in a basin. Cover with boiling water. Stand for 1 minute, then drain off water. Place joints in a saucepan. Add stock. Bring to boil. Skim. Add bacon, onion stuck with clove, carrot, celery and herbs. Bring to boil. Simmer very gently for 1½ hours, or till rabbit is tender. Remove best joints of rabbit and herbs. Melt butter or margarine. Add flour. Stir till frothy, then stir in milk. When smooth and boiling, stir gradually into soup. Cover and simmer for 20 minutes. Season with salt and pepper to taste and a pinch of nutmeg if liked. Strain into a clean saucepan. Remove meat from bones. Place with the bacon in a mortar and pound with a pestle to a paste. Rub through a sieve. Add purée to soup. Stir till boiling. Gradually stir in 1½ gills cream if liked. Serve with fried croûtons. Serves 8.

RED POTTAGE

8 oz. haricot beans
2 celery sticks
1 medium-sized onion
1 small, boiled beetroot

4 medium-sized tomatoes
1 oz. butter
3 pints stock
salt and pepper to taste

Rinse and drain beans. Soak overnight in cold water to cover. Drain well. Slice vegetables. Melt butter in saucepan. Add beans and vegetables. Fry gently for 5 minutes, stirring occasionally. Add stock and salt and pepper to taste. Bring to boil. Skim if necessary. Simmer gently for about $3\frac{1}{2}$ hours, then remove beetroot slices. Rub remainder through a sieve. Reheat. Serve garnished with chopped mint. Serves 6.

EDINBURGH RICE SOUP

3 oz. rice
1 cup white stock
3 pints milk

$\frac{1}{2}$ teaspoon salt
pinch of sugar

Pour boiling water over the rice, placed in a strainer, then rinse under the cold water tap and drain well. Place in a saucepan. Add stock and milk. Simmer very gently for 1 hour, then add salt and sugar. Serves 6.

DUNDEE SCOTCH BROTH

In my young days the meat used for making this broth was kept hot in the oven and served as the main course with caper sauce. In the West Highlands, I have been served with broth of this kind accompanied by a dish of boiled potatoes which was passed round the table.

2 quarts of cold water
1 lb. neck of mutton, flank
   of beef or tip end of ribs
salt to taste

1 medium-sized onion
$\frac{1}{2}$ cabbage or Savoy
1 celery stick
1 sprig parsley

44

2 tablespoons pearl barley
2 medium-sized carrots
¼ swede
2 leeks

about 1 cup dried peas, soaked
12 hours
1 dessertspoon minced parsley

Pour water into a large saucepan. Prepare meat. If using neck wash it. Wipe flank of beef or tip end of ribs with a damp cloth. Place in saucepan. Bring very slowly to the boil. Skim just before boiling. Add 1 teaspoon of salt. Skim again. Add barley and prepared vegetables. Bring slowly to boil. Simmer very gently for about 2 hours. Season to taste. Add parsley 2 minutes before serving. Serves 6–8.

SKIRT SOUP

1½ lb. beef skirt
1 large scraped carrot
1 medium-sized peeled turnip
5 pints cold water

1 heaped tablespoon minced
  onion
salt and pepper to taste
sippets of toast

Remove all skin and fat from the skirt, then wipe skirt carefully. Cut into small dice. Place in saucepan. Add roughly chopped carrot and turnip and water. Bring to boil. Skim carefully. Add onion and salt to taste. Simmer very gently for 2 hours, then season with pepper. Serve with sippets of toast. Serves 8.

SPRING SOUP

2 dozen rhubarb sticks
1 sliced onion
1 sliced carrot
½ oz. lean ham
½ oz. butter

1 quart rich stock
1 or 1½ oz. breadcrumbs
salt and pepper to taste
fried croûtons

Wash, peel and trim the rhubarb, then place in boiling water. Boil for 3 or 4 minutes, then drain. Slice into a saucepan. Add onion, carrot, ham and butter. Cover and simmer very gently till the vegetables are tender. Add stock. Bring to boil, then sieve.

Return to pan. Add breadcrumbs. Cover and simmer very gently for about 75 minutes. Skim off all fat. Season with salt and pepper. Serve with fried croûtons. Serves 6.

MISS BRECHIN'S TOMATO BISQUE

1 *level teaspoon bicarbonate of soda*
1 *quart tinned tomatoes*
1½ *pints milk*
1 *oz. cornflour*
1½ *oz. butter*
salt and pepper to taste
fried croûtons

Stir the bicarbonate of soda into the tomatoes. Stand for ½ hour. Rub through a sieve. Bring milk to boiling point. Cream cornflour with additional cold milk. Gradually stir in the hot milk, then return to saucepan and stir till boiling. Simmer for 5 minutes. Remove pan from stove. Heat tomato purée. Gradually stir into the hot white sauce. Stir to boiling point, then whisk well. Add the butter, bit by bit. Season with salt and pepper. Serve with fried croûtons. Serves 6.

TOMATO AND MILK SOUP

2 *lb tomatoes*
1 *oz. butter*
1 *small carrot*
1 *medium-sized onion*
1½ *pints white stock*
1 *oz. cornflour*
½ *pint milk*
salt and pepper to taste

Wash tomatoes. Melt butter in a saucepan. Slice in carrot and onion. Fry very slowly till onion is clear, stirring occasionally. Slice in tomatoes. Add 2 sprigs of parsley and 1 whole clove. Cover. Simmer very gently for 15 minutes. Add stock. Bring to boil. Simmer gently till the carrot is tender, then sieve. Reheat. Cream cornflour with the milk. Pour into a saucepan. Stir till boiling. Simmer gently for 5 minutes, then gradually stir into soup. Season with salt and pepper to taste. Serve at once. Serves 6.

ANGUS VEGETABLE SOUP

1 *medium-sized carrot*
1 *medium-sized turnip*
1 *medium-sized onion*
1 *leek*
1½ *oz. butter*
1½ *pints white stock or water*
pinch of sugar

½ *teaspoon celery salt or 2*
  celery leaves
1 *blade mace*
1 *bay leaf*
1 *clove*
rich milk as required
salt and pepper to taste

Cut the carrot and turnip into strips like wax vestas, and the onion and leek into rings. Melt butter in a deep saucepan. Add the vegetables. Fry slowly until all the butter is absorbed. Add stock or water, brought to the boil, sugar, celery salt or leaves, mace, bay leaf and clove. Bring to boil. Skim if necessary. Simmer very gently for about 2½ hours. Rub through a sieve, after removing mace and clove. Pour back into saucepan. Gradually stir in milk. Season with salt and pepper. Stir till almost boiling. Serve garnished with minced parsley. Serves 4.

IONA WHELK SOUP

1½ *lb. whelks in shells*
1 *quart water or stock*
1 *oz. medium oatmeal*

1 *small minced onion*
½ *oz. butter*
salt and pepper

Boil whelks till they are ready for picking out of shell. Remove from shells and set aside. Pour water or stock into a saucepan. Stir in oatmeal. When boiling, add onion, butter and seasoning to taste. Simmer slowly for 45 minutes. Add whelks. Boil up and serve. Serves 6.

MOTHER'S WINTER BROTH

3 *pints chicken or turkey stock*
½ *cup diced carrot*
½ *cup diced turnip*
½ *cup sliced celery*
½ *cup sliced leek*

½ *cup shredded cabbage*
¼ *cup of diced parsnip*
¼ *cup of chopped onion*
2 *tablespoons rice*
salt and pepper to taste

Pour the stock into a saucepan. Add the vegetables. Bring to boil. Skim if necessary. Cover and simmer for fifteen minutes, then add rice rinsed under the cold water tap and drained. Simmer gently until the vegetables and rice are tender in about $\frac{1}{2}$ hour. Season with salt and pepper. Serves 6.

FISH

Scotland has been famous for her fisheries ever since the eleventh century, when her rivers and lochs and the seas around her shores teemed with fish. It was written of the Firth of Forth:

> *In her the skate and codlin' sail,*
> *The eel, fu' souple, wags his tail,*
> *Wi' herrin', fluke, an' mackerel,*
> *An' whitin's dainty;*
> *Their spindle shanks the lobsters trail*
> *Wi' partans plenty.*

In her great rivers salmon, which I consider the finest salmon in Europe, was so plentiful at one time that it ranked with the humble herring of today. My father often told me that when he was a boy in Roxburghshire the ploughmen when engaged always stipulated that they should not be served salmon more than once a week.

Every time I go back to Scotland I marvel at the quality of the fish which, unlike so many things, seems to remain as good as it used to be. In my youth, we had to depend on the fisher lasses from Arbroath and Montrose for our supply of fresh fish. Dressed in their picturesque blue and white kilted costumes, they came to our back door with creels on their backs packed with flukies, haddies, herring and mackerel smelling still of the sea. They were followed in later years by fish cadgers in pony traps.

Sometimes I long to hear again the cry of 'Wha'll buy ma caller herrin'. They're bonny fish and halesome farin'.' which used to echo through the Scottish streets, and the cry of 'Wastlin' herrin' ' announcing that the succulent Loch Fyne herring were for sale.

Herring is one of the most delicious fish that swims in Scottish waters. Perfectly grilled, it is the gourmet's delight.

In medieval days, fish in Scotland was usually seethed (boiled). Later it was also made into soup. Nowadays, in the north, it is as popular fried as it is in the south. The last time I lunched off fried fillets of plaice at the Peacock Inn at Newhaven, the fillets were so good that I asked to be shown how they were cooked:

'Dip the fillets in seasoned flour. Shake lightly, then draw each in turn through cold water and dip in sieved rusk crumbs. Fry in deep, hot fat till pale golden brown. Drain and garnish with lemon. Serve with fried chips.'

ANCHOVY AND CELERY BUTTER

4 *whole anchovies*　　　　　2 *oz. unsalted butter*
4 *celery sticks*　　　　　　*cayenne pepper to taste*

Wash and bone anchovies preserved in brine. Drain and pound to a paste in a mortar. Boil celery in fresh water. Drain and rub through a sieve. Beat into butter, then gradually beat into anchovy paste. Season with cayenne pepper. Beat till blended. Make into pats. Use for garnishing fish.

CABBIE CLAW

MODERN VERSION

1 *medium-sized haddock,*　　3 *sprigs parsley*
　about 3 lb. in weight　　1 *tablespoon grated horseradish*
boiling water as required　*egg sauce*

Clean, skin, and dry a freshly caught haddock. Leave the head on, but remove the eyes. Rub it inside and out with salt, and leave for 12 hours. Hang it up in the shade in the open air for at least 24 hours. On a windy day, you can hang it in a draughty passage. This is to impart a slight 'highness' to the fish. (In earlier days, I am told, it was left hanging sometimes for 2 or 3 days before it was cooked.) Place in a saucepan of boiling water to cover. Add the parsley and horseradish. Simmer very gently till cooked.

Remove fish to a platter. Lift all the flesh from the bone, dividing it up into small pieces. Arrange on a flat, hot dish. Cover with egg sauce, made with half milk and half fish stock. Dredge lightly with cayenne pepper or paprika, and spoon mashed potatoes round. Serves 5 or 6.

COD OR HADDOCK CAKES

1 cup flaked boiled cod or
   haddock
1 tablespoon grated onion
1 cup mashed potato
salt and pepper to taste

pinch of crushed thyme
about ¼ cup thick white sauce
2 teaspoons minced parsley
½ teaspoon made mustard
lemon

Mix the fish in a basin with the onion, potato, salt and pepper to taste, thyme, sauce, parsley and mustard. Stir till blended. Cool on a plate. Divide into 6 equal portions. Shape with floured hands into flat cakes. Melt enough butter or margarine to cover the bottom of a large frying pan. Fry cakes slowly till golden brown below, then turn and brown on other side. Drain on absorbent paper. Arrange on a hot dish. Garnish with sprigs of parsley. Serve with lemon, parsley or Sauce Tartare. Serves 6.

GLASGOW COD

1 lb. skinned cod
salt and pepper to taste
1 oz. butter
½ pint hot milk
1 small cup medium oatmeal

¼ cup shredded suet
½ teaspoon minced parsley
½ teaspoon minced chives
1 teaspoon minced onion
salt and pepper

Wipe the cod with a damp cloth. Place in a buttered fireproof dish. Season with salt and pepper. Dab with the butter. Pour the milk round. Mix the oatmeal to a very firm paste with the suet, parsley, chives, onion, salt and pepper to taste and milk as required. Shape into small balls like marbles. Place round the cod. Bake in a moderate oven, 350° F., for about ½ hour. Serve with creamed or mashed potatoes. Serves 4.

CRAPPIT HEIDS

HEBRIDEAN

4 *haddock heads of equal*
  size
4 *haddock livers*

medium oatmeal as required
salt and pepper to taste
milk to bind

Clean the heads thoroughly. Rinse the livers and chop. Measure.
Mix with equal quantity of oatmeal. Season with salt and pepper.
Moisten with the milk. Stuff heads loosely to give room for the
oatmeal to swell. Place in a saucepan. Cover with fish stock.
Simmer very gently for 30 minutes. This dish, which is also
popular in Shetland, is sometimes served alone, but the heads are
more generally cooked with the fish from which they are taken and
served with the fish.

CROPADEU (1781)

Make a paste of oatmeal and water. Shape it like a dumpling.
Tuck a haddock's liver into the middle of the paste. Season it
well with salt and pepper, then draw the paste round it. Place in
a floured pudding cloth. Boil for ½ hour. Nowadays Cropadeu is
sometimes cooked in a covered greased basin for 1 hour. During
cooking, the liver dissolves and flavours the oatmeal.

STEWED EELS

1 *eel*
1 *tablespoon clarified butter*
6 *small, peeled onions*
½ *oz. flour*

¼ *pint brown stock*
2 *tablespoons claret*
salt and pepper to taste
parsley and croûtons

Remove head, then wash fish thoroughly in cold, salted water.
Soak in cold, salted water to cover for 15 minutes. Skin and clean,
then rinse again. Cut in slices, 1½ inches thick. Dry thoroughly.
Melt butter. Add onions. Fry slowly till turning brown, then add
flour. When frothy, gradually stir in the stock and claret. Stir till
boiling. Season with salt and pepper. Add eel. Cover and simmer

gently until cooked in about 30 minutes. Dish up fish. Arrange onions round. Skim, then strain the sauce over the fish. Garnish with minced parsley and ½ pint of fried croûtons.

BOILED EELS WITH PARSLEY BUTTER

Prepare and slice eels as for stewed eels. Place in a saucepan. Cover with boiling salted water. Add a dash of vinegar or the juice of ½ lemon. Cover and simmer gently until tender in about 30 minutes. Drain thoroughly. Dish up. Coat with Parsley Butter. Serve with boiled potatoes.

DUNDEE VERSION OF RUSSIAN FISH PIE

¾ *lb. pastry*
1 *lb. fillet of fish*
1 *hard-boiled egg*
grated rind ½ lemon

1 *heaped teaspoon minced*
  parsley
4 *tablespoons white sauce*
salt and pepper to taste

Roll out puff, rough puff or flaky pastry into a square about ¼ inch thick. Trim edges neatly. Turn upside down on a lightly floured board. Weigh fish, free from skin and bone, using haddock, halibut or sole. Shell the egg. Cut fish and egg into small pieces. Mix with the parsley, lemon rind, sauce and salt and pepper to taste. (If liked, stir in a minced truffle.) Place in the centre of the pastry square. Brush the edges with beaten egg. Fold the corners of the pastry to the centre, leaving open spaces in between, or close the edges firmly instead of leaving open spaces in between. Brush with beaten egg. Decorate with pastry leaves, brushed also with egg. Place on a wet baking sheet. Bake in a hot oven, 450° F., for about ½ hour. Serves 4 or 5.

FISH AND POTATO PUDDING

2 *tablespoons golden*
  breadcrumbs
¾ *lb. mashed potatoes*
3 *tablespoons grated cheese*

1 *beaten egg*
salt and pepper to taste
½ *lb. flaked boiled fish*
3–4 *tablespoons parsley sauce*

Line a well-greased pudding basin with the crumbs. Mix the potatoes with the cheese, egg, and salt and pepper to taste and line the basin with three-quarters of this mixture. Mix the fish with the sauce. Season with salt and pepper. Pack into basin. Cover with remainder of potato mixture. Dab with bits of butter. Bake in a moderate oven, 350° F., till golden brown in 30 to 45 minutes. Turn out on to a hot dish. Serve with mushroom or parsley sauce. Serves 3.

FISH TOASTS

½ pint flaked cold fish
½ oz. butter
2 or 3 tablespoons milk

1 beaten egg
salt and pepper to taste
hot buttered toast

Place fish in a saucepan with butter and milk. Stir till blended and fairly hot, then stir in egg and salt and pepper to taste. When thick, but not boiling, spread thickly on 2 slices of hot buttered toast. Garnish with chopped parsley. Serves 2.

BAKED STUFFED FLUKIES
FLOUNDERS

3 flounders
3 minced shallots
1 teaspoon minced parsley
½ teaspoon beef extract

1 oz. butter
3 teaspoons lemon juice
½ pint white wine
seasoned breadcrumbs

Choose flounders weighing about 1 lb. each. Skin both sides, then make a cut from head to tail down the centre of the thick sides of the fish. Mix shallots, parsley, beef extract, butter and lemon juice to a paste. Raise the fillets from the bone in the centre with a sharp knife, then push a little of the paste into each pocket. Place the fish in a lightly-buttered shallow fireproof dish. Pour the wine over. Sprinkle with seasoned breadcrumbs to taste. Dab with butter. Bake in a moderate oven, 350° F., for about 30 minutes. Serves 3.

54

FRIED FLUKIES

FLOUNDERS

Clean the fish 2 hours before cooking and rub them lightly on both sides with salt to firm them. When required, wipe them dry. Dip in seasoned flour, then in beaten egg and sieved breadcrumbs. Fry in hot, shallow fat till golden brown below, then turn and fry on other side. Drain on absorbent paper. Garnish with fried parsley sprigs and quarters of lemon. When eggs are scarce in winter, dip in seasoned flour, shake well and fry without egging and crumbing. Allow 1 per person.

POACHED FRESH HADDOCK

*A January haddock an' a February hen
Are nae to be marrowed in the ither months ten.*
Old Morayshire Proverb

4 *fillets of haddock*   4 *tablespoons clarified butter*
salted water as required   *parsley sprigs*

Wipe fillets, each large enough for 1 person, with a damp cloth. Place in a shallow saucepan, half full of salted water at boiling point. Simmer gently for about 20 minutes, then drain thoroughly. Dish up. Garnish with parsley sprigs. Serve with clarified butter and boiled potatoes. Serves 2.

RIZZARED HADDIES

Clean fresh haddocks thoroughly. Rub with a little salt. Leave for 12 hours, then dry them carefully and hang them up to dry in the open air for several hours, shading them from the direct rays of the sun. Dip in flour and toast before a clear fire, turning frequently to prevent scorching. When the colour of toast, in about 25 minutes, serve for breakfast in a folded napkin, with melted butter. This is an old method of cooking medium-sized haddocks, when toasters were manufactured to hook onto the fire bars. Today the Scottish cook generally grills them after preparing as described.

SCOTCH HADDOCK PUDDING

10 oz. flaked cooked haddock
2 cups mashed potatoes
salt and pepper to taste
1 tablespoon lemon juice
1 teaspoon minced onion

dash of celery salt
pinch of crushed herbs
1½ tablespoons minced parsley
1½ oz. butter or margarine
3 separated eggs

Stir fish into potato. Season to taste with salt and pepper. Stir in lemon juice, onion, celery salt, herbs and parsley. (If wanted highly seasoned, add a dash of tobasco.) Melt butter and stir into mixture. Beat egg yolks. Stir into mixture. Beat egg whites to a stiff froth and fold in. Place in a large shallow buttered fireproof dish. Bake in a moderate oven, 350° F., for about ½ hour, until puffy and golden brown. Serve with a green salad. Serves 6.

FISH MAYONNAISE
(Chef Kenneth Milne's recipe)

Poach as many fillets of haddock as required in salted water with 2 or 3 sprigs of parsley, a squeeze of lemon juice, and chopped onion to taste. When ready, cool and drain. Arrange in a circle on a flat dish, leaving a space in the middle. Coat fish with tomato mayonnaise. Fill the middle with potato or Russian salad. Garnish round the edge alternately with slices of hard-boiled egg and peeled tomato.

CASSEROLE OF HALIBUT

2 peeled onions
2 large carrots
1 cup sliced celery
3 oz. butter

2 lb. halibut steaks (6)
salt and pepper to taste
1 tablespoon lemon juice
1 tablespoon minced parsley

Mince onions. Scrape and mince carrots. Place onion, carrot and celery in a saucepan. Cover with boiling salted water. Cover. Simmer very gently for 20 minutes. Meanwhile, melt butter in another pan. Add halibut. Fry slowly till slightly browned below, then turn and brown on the other side. Lift carefully into a shallow casserole. Sprinkle with the butter from the pan and salt and pepper to taste, then with the lemon juice. Add the boiled, drained vegetables and a cup of the vegetable stock. Cover closely. Bake in a moderate oven, 350° F., for ½ hour. Dish up. Arrange vegetables round. Pour liquor into a saucepan. Thicken to taste with cornflour creamed with vegetable water. Bring to boil. Stir in parsley. Pour over fish. Serves 6.

FARMHOUSE HALIBUT

1 *tablespoon butter*　　　　　½ *pint cream*
2 *lb. middle-cut halibut*　　　1 *tablespoon flour*
salt and pepper to taste

Melt butter and pour into a casserole. Carefully remove skin from halibut. Place halibut in casserole. Season with salt and pepper. Pour cream over fish. Bake in a slow oven, 325° F., for about 25 minutes. Dish up. Stir flour, creamed with a little milk, into the cream in casserole. When blended, transfer to an enamel lined saucepan. Stir constantly till boiling. Season with salt and pepper if necessary. Pour over the fish. Garnish with parsley. Serves 4 to 6.

BAKED STUFFED HERRINGS

Ye may ca' them caller herring,
Women ca' them lives o' men.

Herring are no good till they smell the new-mown hay.

4 *herrings*　　　　　　　　　1 *teaspoon minced parsley*
1 *small peeled onion*　　　　*salt and pepper to taste*
½ *teacup stale breadcrumbs*　2 *chopped mushrooms*
1 *large soft roe*　　　　　　1 *teaspoon butter*
½ *teaspoon crushed herbs*　　*fried chips*

Remove heads. Clean and wash fish. Split open and remove backbones. To make the stuffing, mince onion finely. Add crumbs, roe, herbs, parsley and salt and pepper to taste. Stir in mushrooms and butter. Season inside of each herring with salt and pepper. Divide stuffing in 4 equal portions. Spread a portion over each herring, then roll up carefully and tie securely with coarse cotton. Place side by side in a greased piedish. Dab with butter. Cover with greased paper. Bake for 35 minutes at 375° F., then remove paper and allow to brown. (If preferred, you can simply fold the sides of herring together again instead of rolling them up.) Remove cotton. Serve with fried chips, mustard sauce and any green salad. Serves 4.

TO VARY: Mix 2 oz. minced, peeled mushrooms with 1 tablespoon breadcrumbs, 1 tablespoon minced parsley, salt and pepper to taste, the strained juice of ½ lemon, ½ teaspoon creamed butter and either 1 large, washed soft roe, or 2 hard roes. Stuff herrings. Bake side by side in a buttered pie dish, with a lid on top at 350° F. for 2 minutes, then uncover, and bake until brown in about 5 minutes. Serves 4.

In some seaside resorts enough water is placed in the baking dish to cover the base before adding the rolls.

HERRINGS IN BUTE FASHION

6 *fresh herring*
salt and granulated sugar
cold water as required
strained juice of 1 *lemon*

6 *boiled potatoes*
2 *chopped hard-boiled eggs*
pinch of crushed herbs
mayonnaise or salad cream

Clean herring, then remove heads, tails and fins. Cut them down the middle and carefully remove their backbones. Place side by side on a flat dish. Sprinkle liberally with salt and granulated sugar. Leave for 4 hours, then dry thoroughly. Roll them up, starting at the heads. Place side by side in a deep fireproof dish. Cover with water. Sprinkle with the lemon juice. Cover. Bake in a moderate oven, 350° F., for about ¾ to 1 hour. Dish up. Chill. Dice potatoes. Lightly stir in eggs, herbs, and salad cream or mayonnaise to moisten. Pack into centres of rolls. Garnish to taste with sprigs of parsley or watercress, diced pimiento and slices of hard-boiled egg. Serves 6.

HERRING AND TATTIES

On the north-east coast boiled salt herring with jacket potatoes are very popular, especially with the fisher folk. In Helmsdale the herring are taken out of a firkin as required and soaked in fresh water overnight. Next day they are placed in a saucepan of boiling water to cover and boiled for 20 minutes. They are then served with jacket potatoes and a glass of milk. Both herring and potatoes are eaten with the fingers. Now here is how I have had them in the Pentlands:

THE PENTLAND WAY: Allow 2 or 3 salt herring to 2 lb. potatoes. Peel or scrub potatoes. Place them in a saucepan (in olden days a three-legged pot was used). Add enough cold water to half fill pan. Place the fish over the potatoes. Cover pan. Simmer gently until the herring is cooked, then remove herring and keep hot while finishing the cooking of the potatoes. Drain when ready, and cover with a cloth. Place lid on top. Leave for a minute or two until the tatties are dry and mealy, then serve with butter and the herring.

GRILLED HERRING

fresh herring with soft roes   *melted butter as required*
seasoning to taste

Remove heads from herring. Clean, then scrape. Wash insides thoroughly. Wash, drain, and brush roes with butter, then place inside. Season insides with salt and pepper, and brush with melted fat. Make 3 gashes equal distance apart across each side, cutting from head end. (I more often gash them across the backbone.) Brush well on both sides with the butter. Grill slowly for about 20 minutes, basting each time you turn fish. I generally turn them thrice. They must be cooked slowly. Serve for breakfast with toast. If wanted for any other meal serve garnished with lemon, chip potatoes and mustard sauce. Allow 1 herring per person.

PICKLED HERRING

6 *medium-sized herring*
salt and pepper to taste
1 *Spanish onion*
2 *whole cloves*

6 *peppercorns*
½ *bay leaf*
1½ *gills white vinegar*
1½ *gills water*

Clean herring. Cut in halves lengthwise and clean the inside. Season with salt and pepper to taste. (If liked, dip in flour, then shake.) Roll up each fillet neatly with the skin on the outside. Brush a shallow fireproof dish with melted butter. Arrange rolls alternately with the roes in dish. Peel and slice onion. Sprinkle fish with onion, cloves and peppercorns. Add bay leaf. Mix vinegar and water. Pour over fish. If not enough liquid to cover fish, add more vinegar and water in the same proportions. Cover dish. Bake in a slow oven, 300° F., for fully 1 hour, then uncover and bake for about 20 minutes. Remove from oven. Leave until cold. Serve with potato salad. Serves 3 or 6.

KEDGEREE

½ *lb. flaked, cooked fish*
¼ *lb. cooked rice*
2 *oz. butter*
1 *or* 2 *hard-boiled eggs*

salt and pepper to taste
cayenne pepper to taste
pinch of grated nutmeg

Use either cooked smoked or fresh haddock. Remove all skin and bones from the fish and chop or flake fish roughly. Mix with the rice. Place in a saucepan. Add the butter, and egg white if liked, finely chopped. Stir till piping hot. Season with salt and pepper, cayenne pepper and nutmeg. Dish up in the shape of a pyramid on a hot flat dish. Garnish with minced parsley and sieved egg yolk. If preferred, cut the egg white in strips and arrange round the kedgeree instead of mixing it with the fish. You can extend the kedgeree by increasing the cooked rice to ½ lb.

TO VARY: 1. Stir a teaspoon of curry powder into the butter, then add the fish and rice. 2. Substitute flaked tinned salmon for the fresh or smoked fish.

BAKED LING

*Ling would be the beef of the sea
If it had always salt enough, butter
enough and boiling enough.*
Old Gaelic Proverb

4 *lb. sliced ling*   3 *oz. fresh butter*
2 *dessertspoons salt*   1 *tablespoon flour*
white pepper to taste $\frac{1}{2}$ *pint hot milk*
1 *saltspoon ground mace*

Dip ling in flour seasoned with salt, pepper and ground mace.
Shake lightly. Place in 2 layers in a greased pie dish. Dab with
the butter. Cream flour with a little of the milk, then stir in remainder of milk. Pour over fish. Bake in a slow oven, 325° F., for
about 50 minutes. Dish up. Garnish with sippets of toast. Serves
6.

TO FRY LING

Cut 2 lb. ling into slices about $\frac{3}{4}$ inch thick. Dip in seasoned flour.
Egg and crumb. Fry in smoking hot fat until golden brown below,
then turn and brown on the other side. Dish up. Garnish with
lemon and parsley. Serves 3 or 4.

BAKED STUFFED MACKEREL

2 *medium-sized mackerel*   1 *teaspoon minced shallot*
4 *tablespoons breadcrumbs*   *salt and pepper to taste*
1 *teaspoon minced parsley or*   *melted butter as required*
  chives

Clean and fillet mackerel. Lay 2 fillets side by side in a greased
fireproof dish, insides uppermost. Mix crumbs with parsley or
chives, shallot and salt and pepper to taste. Moisten to a paste with
melted butter. Spread over fillets. Cover each with another fillet,
inside downwards. Press together. Cover with greased paper. Bake
in a moderate oven, 350° F., for 20–30 minutes. Serve with fennel
or mushroom sauce. Serves 2.

TO GRILL MACKEREL

Clean 3 mackerel. Split and fillet if large, but do not skin. Soak fish in a marinade for 1 hour, turning occasionally. Drain. Grill until slightly browned below, then turn and grill on the other side. Dish up. Place a pat of maître d'hôtel butter on each fish or fillet. Garnish with lemon butterflies and parsley sprigs. Serves 3.

SOUSED MACKEREL

3 *medium-sized mackerel*
$\frac{1}{2}$ *pint vinegar*
$\frac{1}{2}$ *pint water*
1 *bay leaf*
6 *peppercorns*
2 *allspice berries*
salt and cayenne pepper to taste
sprigs of fennel or parsley

Clean and boil mackerel gently to avoid breaking, then cool and drain carefully. Remove the fillets from the bones. Pour vinegar and water into a saucepan. Add bay leaf, peppercorns, allspice berries and salt and cayenne pepper to taste. Simmer gently for 5 minutes, then strain into a jug. Leave until cold. Pour over fish. Leave for 5 to 6 hours. Remove fillets to a serving dish. Garnish with fennel or parsley. Serves 3.

TO BOIL SALMON (1851)

> '*Tibby*' *was for cuttin't in twa cuts, but I like a saumon to be served up in its integrity.*
> CHRISTOPHER NORTH

There are many excellent ways of dressing this favourite fish, but perhaps none equal to plain boiling when well performed. Scale and clean the fish without unnecessary washing or handling, and without cutting it too much open. Have a roomy and well-scoured fish-kettle and if the salmon be large and thick, when you have placed it in the strainer and in the kettle, fill up, and amply cover it with cold spring water so that it may heat gradually. Throw in a handful of salt. When the water comes to a boil, skim carefully, then let the fish boil slowly, allowing twelve minutes to the pound. The minute the boiling is completed, lift the fish strainer and rest it across the pan until the fish is thoroughly drained. Throw a folded soft cloth or flannel over it. Never leave fish, after it is cooked, in hot water or it will become soft. Dish on a hot fish platter covered with a napkin. Besides the essences to be used with salmon at discretion, which are now found on every sideboard of any pretension, Anchovy, Lobster and Shrimp Sauce are served with salmon, also plain melted butter. Where the fish is got fresh, and served in what is esteemed by some the greatest perfection, crisp, curdy and creamy, it is the practice to send in a sauce-tureen of the plain liquor in which it was boiled. Fennel (which can be grown like parsley) and butter are still heard of for salmon but are nearly obsolete. Garnish with a fringe of curled green parsley and slices of lemon. The carver must help a slice of the thick part with a smaller one of the thin, which is the fattest, and the best-liked by those in the secret. Sliced cucumber is often served with salmon and indeed with all boiled fish.

TO BOIL SALMON TO SERVE COLD

Wash a middle cut of salmon thoroughly under the cold water tap. Pour into a shallow saucepan, fitted with a rack, enough cold water to cover the salmon. Add salt until you find the brine strong enough to float an egg. Remove egg. Lower salmon on to rack. Add 3 or 4 black peppercorns, 1 thin slice of lemon, 1 or 2 sprigs of parsley, a sprig of fennel when available, $\frac{1}{2}$ bay leaf and a glass of white wine if liked. Cover pan closely. Bring slowly to the boil. Simmer for 1 minute, then remove pan, without uncovering, from stove. Leave until quite cold. Remove salmon on the rack from stock. Drain thoroughly. Garnish with sprigs of fennel or parsley and slices of cucumber. Serve with mayonnaise or Sauce Tartare.

SALMON CAVEAC

2 salmon cutlets, ½ inch thick   1 small blade mace
1 quart vinegar   ¼ oz. black peppercorns
2 peeled shallots   salt to taste
2 cloves   olive oil as required

Place cutlets in an earthenware dish. Bring vinegar to the boil
with all the ingredients except the oil, then strain and cool. Pour
over cutlets. Sprinkle as much olive oil over the vinegar as will
float on top of it. Stand for ½ hour. Drain cutlets. Grill for about
¼ hour, turning once or twice, until evenly cooked through. Serves
2.

SALMON CUTLETS

½ lb. cold, boiled salmon   salt and pepper to taste
½ oz. butter   squeeze of lemon juice
1 oz. flour   1 beaten egg
¼ pint milk or fish stock   4 tablespoons breadcrumbs
1 dessertspoon cream   lemon and parsley

Flake the salmon. When not available, substitute drained, tinned
salmon. Melt butter in a small saucepan. Stir in flour. When
frothy, stir in milk. Bring to boil, stirring constantly, and simmer
for 2 minutes, then stir in cream, salt and pepper to taste, lemon
juice and salmon. Turn onto a plate. When cool enough to
handle, shape into cutlets. Egg and crumb. Slip a tiny piece of
macaroni in each. Fry in deep hot fat till golden brown. Drain on
absorbent paper. Garnish with lemon and parsley sprigs. Serve
with tomato or Sauce Tartare. Serves 3.

CRAWFISH OR LOBSTER CUTLETS: Follow recipe for salmon, but
substitute ½ lb. chopped crawfish or lobster, and add a little
crawfish or lobster spawn. Reduce milk to ½ gill and increase
cream to ½ gill. Flavour with a drop or two of anchovy essence.
Serves 3.

STEAMED SALMON CUTLETS

2 *salmon cutlets, 6 oz. each*   *squeeze of lemon juice*
salt and pepper to taste   *olive oil*

Wipe cutlets. Season with salt and pepper to taste on both sides.
Sprinkle with lemon juice. Brush with olive oil. Wrap in greaseproof paper. Place on a rack over boiling water. Steam for 15–20
minutes, depending on thickness of cut. Serve with Sauce Tartare,
cucumber and boiled new potatoes. Serves 3.

SALMON SCALLOPS

2 *tablespoons melted butter*   4 *tablespoons stale breadcrumbs*
½ *pint thick white sauce*   ½ *lb. sieved boiled potatoes*
2 *cups flaked cooked salmon*   *hot milk and butter as required*
salt and pepper to taste   4 *sprigs parsley*

Brush 4 scallop shells with melted butter. Place a tablespoon of
the sauce in the bottom of each. Divide the fish between the shells.
Season to taste with salt and pepper. Cover equally with the remainder of sauce, then with the crumbs. Sprinkle lightly with
remaining melted butter. Mash potatoes. Beat with hot milk and
butter to taste and season. Pipe round scallops. Bake in a fairly hot
oven, 425° F., until brown on top. Garnish each scallop with a
sprig of parsley. Serves 4.

BAKED SALMON STEAKS

2 *thick salmon steaks*   *salt and pepper to taste*
2 *oz. butter*   ¾ *pint tomato sauce (p. 111)*
1 *tablespoon minced parsley*

Wipe the steaks with a damp cloth. Grease a baking tin, large
enough to take the steaks side by side, with a little of the butter.
Lay steaks in tin. Dab with the remainder of the butter. Sprinkle
with the parsley and salt and pepper to taste. Cover with greased
paper. Bake in a moderate oven, 350° F., for about 25 minutes.
Dish up. Pour the tomato sauce round. Serves 4.

GRILLED SALMON STEAKS

1 tablespoon olive oil
1 teaspoon salt
pepper and paprika to taste

3 thick salmon steaks
anchovy butter as required
lemon and parsley

Mix the oil with the seasoning on a large plate. Wipe steaks with a damp cloth and place in the marinade. Soak, turning occasionally, for 45 minutes. Grill for 6 minutes on each side. Spread each steak with anchovy butter. Dish up. Garnish with lemon and parsley sprigs. Serves 3.

ESKHILL SALMON TROUT

1 salmon trout, 3 lb. in
   weight
2 peeled shallots
1 stick celery
2 sprigs parsley
½ green pepper

½ cup stale breadcrumbs
2 eggs
salt and pepper to taste
dash of paprika
½ cup white wine
½ cup water

Carefully remove the skin without breaking from the trout after it is cleaned, then bone trout. Put the flesh with the shallots, celery, parsley and pepper through a meat grinder with a fine knife. Stir in crumbs. Beat eggs. Add with salt, pepper and a little paprika. Stir in wine and water. Mix well. Pack into the skin of the fish Close skin carefully. Smear a large fireproof dish thickly with butter. Add fish. Sprinkle with lightly-dried sieved breadcrumbs. Bake in a moderately hot oven, 400° F., for ¾–1 hour. Serve from dish with creamed potatoes or boiled new potatoes, and Lemon Sauce. Serves 4 or 5.

Note: The original recipe had no green pepper. I think it an improvement.

DRIED SILLOCKS

Dried Sillocks used to be very popular with school children in Orkney and Shetland. They were eaten uncooked with their midday 'piece' of bannock or oatcake, as a relish. They are the fry of the saith, a member of the cod family, better known in England as 'coal-fish'. Clean and wash fish well in salted water. Tie up in bunches and hang in the fresh air until they are quite hard.

A MONTROSE WAY WITH SKATE

3 *lb. skate*	2 *sprigs parsley*
1 *teaspoon salt*	$\frac{1}{2}$ *gill vinegar*
1 *sliced carrot*	1 *quart water*
1 *sliced onion*	2 *tablespoons capers*
1 *bay leaf*	1 *teaspoon minced parsley*
1 *clove*	1 *oz. butter*

Prepare the skate and cut off fins. Divide fish into 6 equal-sized pieces. Wash and dry thoroughly. Place the salt, carrot, onion, bay leaf, clove, parsley, vinegar and water in a saucepan. Bring to boil. Boil for 5 minutes. Add fish. Bring again to boil. Simmer gently for 15 minutes. Lift with a skimmer on to a hot dish lined with a cloth. Drain well. Remove skin. Transfer to a hot serving dish. Sprinkle with capers and parsley. Melt butter. Cook till pale brown and dribble over the fish. Serves 6.

BAKED STUFFED SOLE

1 *large sole*	1 *peeled Spanish onion*
1 *oz. butter*	1 *peeled large tomato*
1 *teaspoon minced parsley*	2 *tablespoons breadcrumbs*
essence of anchovy to taste	2 *tablespoons grated cheese*
cayenne pepper to taste	$\frac{1}{4}$ *pint tomato sauce* (*p.* 111)

Wash sole in cold, salted water, then dry and skin. Trim off fins and tail and cut off the beard. With a knife knead the butter to a paste with the parsley and an anchovy essence, or anchovy paste if preferred, to taste. Season with cayenne pepper. Mix well. Make an incision down the centre of the fish on one side only, and carefully lift the flesh on either side of the incision to form a pocket. Slip into the pockets three-quarters of the stuffing, spreading it with a knife. Smear the bottom of a greased, shallow fireproof dish with the remainder. Lay the sole in the dish, stuffed side upwards. Slice the onion and tomato very thinly, and place the slices, overlapping, alternately down the centre of the fish. Mix the crumbs with the cheese and sprinkle over the fish. Pour the tomato sauce round. Cover with a buttered paper. Bake in a moderate oven, 350° F., from 10 to 15 minutes. Place dish on a platter covered with a paper doyley. Serve with new potatoes. Serves 2.

SOLE IN THE DUART WAY

When I was about twelve years old, Sir Fitzroy Maclean of Duart, Chief of his clan, took Inshewan for the shooting. He came to Angus year after year, and our parish was the richer for his presence. Once when he was in possession, my mother gave birth to a son, so the waggonette was sent to take the five of us children, or it might have been six, to lunch and tea. That was the first time I tasted sole, so I asked for the recipe.

4 *large fillets of sole*	1 *dozen button mushrooms*
salt and pepper to taste	1 *egg yolk*
½ *oz. butter*	*salt and pepper to taste*
2 *or* 3 *tablespoons water*	2 *tablespoons thick cream*

Place the fillets side by side in a shallow well-buttered fireproof dish. Season with salt and pepper to taste. Fleck the butter over, then sprinkle with the water. Cover with buttered paper. Bake in a moderately hot oven, 375° F., until milky white in a few minutes. Meanwhile place the bones and trimmings of sole in a saucepan with 2 or 3 slices each of carrot and onion and a sprig of parsley. Cover with water and simmer for 5 minutes, then strain. Thicken the stock from the fish and the trimmings with creamed flour. Add a large pat of butter and the mushrooms, steamed in a little butter, and the egg yolk and cream. Stir over moderate heat for a moment or two until thickened to taste. Do not allow to boil. Arrange fillets on a flat hot dish. Coat with the sauce. Garnish with lemon and parsley. Serves 4.

SOLE WITH A DELICATE AIR

6 *fillets of sole*
milk *as required*
4 *white peppercorns*
1 *oz. butter*
1 *oz. flour*

salt and pepper to taste
½ *gill cream*
4 *or* 5 *drops lemon juice*
parsley

Place bones and skins of fish in a saucepan. Add milk to cover and peppercorns. Simmer very gently for 5 minutes. Remove from fire. Fold each fillet in two, or roll them up into turbans. Place in a shallow saucepan. Strain the milk over. Simmer gently for 6 minutes. Lift each up with a skimmer onto a hot serving dish. Measure milk. If reduced to below ½ pint, add enough additional milk to make up ½ pint. Melt butter. Stir in flour, then milk. When smooth and boiling, season with salt and pepper to taste and paprika if liked. Stir in cream, lemon juice and minced parsley to taste. Add fillets and reheat. Dish up. Serves 3.

BAKED STUFFED FILLETS OF SOLE

6 *fillets of sole*
squeeze of lemon juice
salt and pepper to taste
½ *oz. butter*
½ *oz. flour*

fish stock or milk as required
6 *oz. minced smoked haddock*
½ *gill sherry*
½ *pint Lemon Sauce (p.* 105)

Wipe fillets with a damp cloth. Sprinkle lightly with lemon juice. Season with salt and pepper to taste. Melt butter in a saucepan. Add flour. When frothy, stir in ½ gill of fish stock or milk or half and half. Stir till smooth and boiling. Add haddock, salt and pepper to taste, and a little cream if necessary. (If too thin, thicken with sieved breadcrumbs.) Spread fillets thinly with the stuffing. Beginning at the thick ends, roll fillets up. Place side by side in a shallow greased fireproof dish containing ½ gill hot fish stock mixed with the sherry. Cover with a greased paper. Bake in a moderate oven, 350° F., until creamy in about 10 minutes. Drain well. Make remainder of stuffing into tiny balls. Egg, crumb and fry till golden. Dish up fillets in a circle. Coat with the sauce. Pile balls in the centre. Garnish with sprigs of parsley. Serves 6.

FRIED SPRATS

Wash thoroughly and draw at the gills. Dry gently on a cloth. Dredge with flour. Fry a few at a time in hot fat about 390° F. Season with cayenne pepper. Sprinkle with lemon juice. (If preferred, fry in batter.) Garnish with lemon. Serve with thin brown bread and butter. Allow 6–8 per person.

TROUT

I have eaten trout in many parts of the world, lake trout in Canada, trout caught in Alpine and other Continental streams, but none so good to me as the small speckled trout my brother used to guddle from the White Burn in Angus, and the sea trout he brought home from the Esk. I attribute this to the fact that the trout were cleaned and cooked sometimes within ½ hour of being caught. Never more than one or two hours.

MOTHER'S WAY WITH BURN TROUT

4 *burn trout*	2 *oz. medium-sized oatmeal*
salt and pepper to taste	2 *oz. butter*

Split, clean, bone and rinse trout. Drain and dry thoroughly. Season with salt and pepper to taste on both sides. Smooth out with a broad-bladed knife. Place oatmeal on a sheet of greaseproof paper. Coat the trout on both sides with the oatmeal. Melt the butter and fry trout, first on the skin side, then turn and fry on the other side, till cooked through and the oatmeal is crisp. Serve for high tea with toast.

Note: Sometimes the trout were cooked without boning, when the flesh was slashed across slantwise on each side to prevent the skin curling.

SEA TROUT: THE MEMUS WAY

6 *large fillets of sea trout*   2 *tablespoons butter*
salt and pepper to taste   3 *tablespoons sieved*
juice of ½ *lemon*   *breadcrumbs*
1½ *teaspoons minced parsley*

Butter a shallow fireproof dish large enough to take the fillets side by side. Season fillets on both sides with salt and pepper to taste and paprika if liked, then place them in the dish. Sprinkle with lemon juice. Dab with butter. Cover with a buttered fireproof plate or lid. Bake in a moderate oven, 350° F., for 8–10 minutes according to size. When almost ready, uncover. Mix the crumbs with the parsley. Sprinkle evenly over the fillets. Baste with the liquor in the dish. Bake at 350° F., till golden brown. Serves 6.

WHITEBAIT

If not able to cook when delivered, store in a refrigerator if possible. Wash gently in salted water, handling as little as possible, then lay each on a spread-out cloth to dry. Shake gently on to another dry cloth, then dredge carefully all over with seasoned flour. Place a few of the fish at a time in a frying basket. Cook in hot fat, about 380° F., for about 1½ minutes, then turn them on to a sieve. When all are cooked, reheat fat to 400° F., and turn all the fish into frying basket. Lower into the fat and fry for a moment or two till crisp, then slightly brown them. Shake the basket of fish gently over the fat to drain well, then turn them gently on to absorbent paper. Season with cayenne pepper and salt. Serve with thin brown bread and butter and lemon.

WHITING IN A SCOTS WAY

Choose small, freshly caught fish. Dip in seasoned flour, then shake lightly. Fry very slowly in melted butter, turning when cooked below, but do not allow to brown. Cook for a minute or two on second side, then add minced parsley and chives or the green of spring onions and fish stock or milk and cream, in the proportion of 1 teaspoon each of parsley and chives or onion and 4 tablespoons stock or milk and 2 or 3 tablespoons of cream, mixed till blended, to 4 whiting. Baste the fish well with the liquor and finish cooking, adding seasoning if necessary. Serves 2.

FRESH FISH ROES

Hard roes are popular for breakfast in Scotland while soft roes are greatly favoured as an after-dinner savoury, as well as for high tea.

BOILED COD'S ROE

Wash roe thoroughly. Place in boiling, salted water to cover. Add a dash of vinegar or lemon juice. (If the roe is burst, tie it in a piece of butter muslin before boiling.) Simmer for 15–20 minutes if thin. If thick, allow about 30 minutes. Remove from pan. Leave until nearly cold, then remove muslin if used. When quite cold, skin carefully, then cut in slices about $\frac{1}{2}$ inch thick.

TO FRY: 1. Dip each slice in seasoned flour. Fry in a little hot fat till crisp and golden brown on both sides. 2. Dip in seasoned batter, flavoured minced parsley, and fry in deep hot fat till golden brown. Drain on absorbent paper. 3. Dip in seasoned flour then egg and crumb. Fry in deep hot fat as in 2.

TO SERVE: Garnish with sprigs of fresh or fried parsley and lemon. If shallow-fried in bacon fat, garnish each slice with a curl of crisply fried bacon.

ACCOMPANIMENT: Tartare or tomato sauce, and fried chips if liked.

TO SCALLOP COD'S ROE: Boil only for 10 minutes, then cut into dice. Measure. Mix with equal quantity of Béchamel Sauce, and half quantity of chopped fried mushrooms. Pack into buttered scallop shells. Cover with sieved breadcrumbs. Dab with butter. Bake in a fairly hot oven, 425° F., till golden brown in about 8 minutes.

COD'S ROE ELIZABETH: Cut boiled cod's roe in slices fully ½ inch thick. Dip in seasoned flour. Fry in a little hot onion butter (see below), very slowly, till golden brown, then turn and fry on the other side. Dish up. Add thin cream to the butter, allowing 1 tablespoon for each 2 slices of roe. Stir till piping hot, then spread over the roe. Garnish with minced parsley. Serve with crisp, hot toast and butter.

ONION BUTTER: Fry grated onion in the butter before adding the roe, allowing 1 dessertspoon of onion to each 2 or 3 slices of roe. Fry slowly till clear, then draw to one side of pan or remove from pan, and fry roe.

BREEKS

Christened by my brother Ernest, who, when asked as a school-boy what he would like for breakfast, invariably answered 'Breeks'.

These are haddock roes. Prepared in the following way, or fried, they make an excellent breakfast dish. Wash and soak in salted water for 1 hour, then boil for 2 or 3 minutes in salted water to cover, and drain thoroughly. Cover with milk. Add a good pat of butter and cook slowly till tender, then add salt and pepper to taste, minced parsley, and a little cream if liked. Serve with toast. To fry, dredge lightly with seasoned flour then fry in plenty of bacon dripping until crisp and golden.

HERRING ROES ON TOAST

Wash, drain and dry roes and treat them in one of the following ways:

1. Season with salt, dredge with flour and brush with melted butter. Place side by side on a greased or oiled grill rack. Grill first on one side, then on the other. Cut each roe in two. Serve on hot buttered toast. Season with cayenne pepper. Sprinkle with a few drops of lemon juice. Garnish with parsley.
2. Season with salt and pepper. Dip in olive oil. Grill quickly on both sides. Serve with Maître d'Hôtel Butter.

73

TO DEVIL SOFT ROES

Season with salt and pepper. Brush them with made mustard, mixed with Worcester sauce to taste. Grill for a moment or two on one side, then turn and grill on the other. Sprinkle with paprika. Place side by side on fingers of hot buttered toast. Garnish with lemon.

SOUSED FISH ROES

1 *lb. fish roes*	2 *sprigs parsley*
1 *sliced medium-sized carrot*	6 *black peppercorns*
2 *chopped celery stalks*	2 *cloves*
1 *sliced medium-sized onion*	1 *blade mace*
1 *bay leaf*	*vinegar or white wine and water*

Wash roes and place in a greased shallow fireproof dish. Sprinkle with the carrot, celery stalks, onion, bay leaf, parsley, peppercorns, cloves and mace. Cover with equal quantity of vinegar or white wine and water. Bake in a moderate oven, 350° F., till cooked through. Time depends on size of roes. Chill. Serve with potato salad on individual plates, arranging roes on top of small mounds of salad. Garnish with watercress. Serves 6.

SALT AND SMOKED FISH

It was not until the late twelfth century that speldings and other cured fish became generally popular in Scotland. Speldings are small, split, salted and rock-dried haddocks and whitings. At one time Aberdeen was the source of most of this type of fish. When I was young, one was able to choose small haddock, for example, in varying guises from the pale delicate fish known as Moray Firths to the nutty flavoured Finnan haddocks, and the close-smoked haddocks known as Smokies which hailed from Arbroath and Auchmithie.

Smoked haddocks are met with more on the East coast of Scotland than on the West. In Crail, in Fifeshire, famous for its crabs, haddocks smoked in the lum were very popular, and used to be known as 'Crail Capons'. In olden days, when a Fifer wished to ask you to a meal a common invitation was 'Come an' ha'e a a capon wi' us.'

SALT COD BALLS

1 *lb. salt codfish*	1¼ *oz. butter*
6 *medium-sized potatoes*	2 *eggs*

Put fish in a saucepan. Cover with cold water. Bring to boil. Drain off water, and add fresh water to cover. Cover pan. Bring again to boil. Simmer gently till tender. Flake fish finely with your fingers while hot. Have potatoes ready, mashed, seasoned with salt and pepper and creamed till fluffy with hot milk and butter. Measure potatoes. Allow fish and potatoes in the following proportions: to 3 cups of prepared potatoes allow 1½ cups flaked fish. Stir till blended. Add butter to taste. Beat eggs lightly and stir into mixture. Beat until light, then leave until cold and firm. Shape into small balls, handling mixture lightly. Roll balls in flour. Place in a basket. Fry in deep smoking hot fat until golden brown. Drain on absorbent paper. Dish up. Garnish with sprigs of parsley. Serves 6.

CREAMED SALT COD WITH
POTATO BORDER

2½ *gills shredded salt cod*	1 *hard-boiled egg*
2½ *gills medium-thick white*	1 *teaspoon chopped parsley*
sauce	1 *lb. mashed potatoes*

Cover cod with water in a saucepan. Heat slowly until boiling. Drain off water. Repeat this once or twice, depending how salt the fish is. Add white sauce. Stir in chopped egg white and parsley. Arrange in the centre of a hot dish. Ring with well-seasoned mashed potatoes, enriched with butter and milk to taste. Sprinkle fish lightly with the sieved egg yolk. Serves 4 or 5.

BOILED SALT FISH

2 *lb. salt cod or ling*   1 *pint Egg or Mustard Sauce*
cold water as required   (*p.* 113)

Cut fish into suitable portions for serving. Wash thoroughly. Soak in cold water to cover for 12 hours, changing the water occasionally. Scrape or pull off skin. Place in a pan of cold water to cover. Bring slowly to the boil. Skim well. Simmer gently until tender in about ¾ hour. Drain carefully. Dish up. Pile on a hot ashet. Serve with Egg, or Mustard Sauce, and fluffy mashed potatoes. Serves 4 to 6.

Note: This was a popular main course for dinner on Good Friday in the East coast of Scotland when I was a school girl. When served with Egg Sauce, 2 eggs were allowed to 1 pint of white sauce, and the yolk of one was sieved over the dressed fish.

CREAMED SALT FISH: Flake 1 lb. boiled salt fish. Stir into ½ pint Egg or White Sauce with salt, pepper and lemon juice to taste. Garnish with slices of hard-boiled egg or with sieved yolk of 1 or 2 hard-boiled eggs and the shredded white or whites. Serve with fluffy mashed potatoes. Serves 3.

SALT FISH PUDDING

Boil a piece of dried fish, then remove and skin. Take out the bones. Pound fish in a mortar with a pestle, then measure. Mash equal quantity of potatoes. Season with salt and pepper and moisten with hot milk and butter to taste. Beat well. Add fish. Beat till blended. Place in a buttered fireproof dish. Smooth the top with a knife. Dab with bits of butter. Reheat in a moderate oven and bake till lightly browned. Serve with egg, or egg and parsley sauce.

FINDON OR FINNAN HADDOCKS

There is a tendency to think of all smoked split haddocks as Finnan or Findon haddocks. These haddocks, called after a hamlet in Kincardineshire, are distinguished for their rich, golden colour and their nutty flavour. They used to be dried over sea weed smoke, and sprinkled with salt water during the process, claims Sir Walter Scott. Today, I am told, the most flavourful are dried over peat smoke, while the others, sold also as Finnan Haddies, are usually dried over smoking hardwood sawdust, or chips of birch or oak. I am talking of Scottish smoked haddies, not some of the dyed imitations sold in their name across the Border.

TO COOK FINNAN HADDOCKS

These haddocks are usually grilled, or steamed or poached.

TO GRILL: Brush with creamed or melted butter and grill lightly on both sides. Place on a hot ashet. Top each haddock with two lightly-poached eggs.

TO POACH: Trim and cut each haddock in two down the middle.

Place in a saucepan with boiling water to cover. Simmer very gently for 5 minutes.

TO DRESS: Drain off water. Melt $\frac{1}{2}$ tablespoon butter. Cream a teaspoon of cornflour with milk taken from $\frac{1}{2}$ pint. Stir in remainder of milk. Turn into a saucepan. Stir till boiling. Pour over the fish. Season. Simmer for 1 minute. Dish up fish. Pour the sauce over, adding a chopped hard-boiled egg and a teaspoon of minced parsley if liked.

TO STEAM: Trim haddocks and cut in two lengthwise, then across. Place in a saucepan with just enough water to cover bottom of pan. Add a rasher of bacon. Cover closely. Steam for about 5 minutes. Dish up fish. Coat with melted butter.

FINNAN HADDOCK LOAF

2 *cups flaked boiled Finnan*
  haddock
½ *cup stale breadcrumbs*
2 *oz. butter*
1 *dessertspoon minced parsley*

2 *beaten eggs*
salt and pepper to taste
1 *saltspoon crushed herbs*
1 *tablespoon minced fried*
  mushrooms

Mix all the ingredients together till blended. Pack into a greased
pudding basin, filling it to within fully an inch from the rim. Cover
tightly with greased paper. Steam for 1 hour. Or pack into a
greased loaf tin, cover with a greased fireproof plate and bake in
a moderately hot oven, 375° F., for about 50 minutes till firm in
centre and golden brown. Unmould. Serve hot with parsley sauce
or cold with mayonnaise. Serves 6.

FINNAN NESTS

1 *oz. butter*
1 *teaspoon flour*
3 *tablespoons grated cheese*
½ *teacup top milk*
salt and pepper to taste

1 *teaspoon Worcester sauce*
1¾ *cups flaked, boiled Finnan*
  haddock
hot milk and butter to taste
4 *cups mashed seasoned potato*

Melt the butter in the top of a double saucepan over hot water.
Stir in flour, then cheese. Stir until melted, then slowly stir in top
milk, salt and pepper to taste and Worcester sauce. Add Finnan
haddock. Stir constantly till piping hot. Add hot milk, butter and
seasoning to potatoes. Beat till fluffy. Divide equally between 4
hot plates. Shape into rounds. Make a hollow in centre of each.
Pour in creamed Finnan. Sprinkle filling lightly with paprika or
chopped parsley. Serves 4.

FINNAN SPUDS

3 *large baked potatoes*
salt and pepper to taste
½ *oz. butter*
¼ *pint cheese sauce*

3 *tablespoons boiled Finnan*
  haddock
grated cheese as required

Remove top of potatoes, then carefully scrape out the potato into a saucepan, taking care not to cut the skins. Arrange potato shells in a greased fireproof dish. Mash the potato. Season with salt and pepper to taste, and beat in the butter. Line the potato shells with this. Place a teaspoon of cheese sauce in each potato shell. Flake haddock. Divide it equally between the potatoes. Fill up with the remainder of sauce. Sprinkle with grated cheese. Brown under grill. serves 3

RED HERRINGS

Red herrings are smoked, salted herring, sometimes called 'buffed'. They are usually eaten at breakfast, high tea or supper.

Open fish and clean thoroughly under running water. Place in a shallow saucepan. Cover with boiling water. Soak for about 5 minutes, then drain well. Fry or grill like kippers.

TO GRILL KIPPERS

Wash and remove heads. Allow ½ oz. butter to each fish and melt it. Brush kippers on both sides with butter, and also the grill rack. Grill steadily until half cooked, in about 3 minutes, using moderate heat, then turn and grill on the other side. To grill kippers successfully, the rack should be hot before using and the 'grill' on full. Reduce the heat slightly before cooking. I always baste my kipper occasionally, once on each side, with the butter while cooking. Season with pepper. Serve with toast.

FRIED KIPPERS

Melt a large walnut of butter in a frying pan large enough to take 2 kippers side by side. Lower heat and place kippers in pan, skin side downwards. Fry for $3\frac{1}{2}$–$4\frac{1}{2}$ minutes, then turn and fry for the same length of time on the other side, adding more butter to the pan if necessary. Dish up. Pour remaining butter over.

SMOKIES

Smokies are fresh haddocks of a small size which have been cleaned, cured and smoked whole, as opposed to herrings and Finnan haddocks which are split, cured and smoked flat. The term close fish, meaning whole fish, is also applied to smokies

They need only reheating as they are cooked in the process of curing. Slit them up. Remove the backbones carefully. Spread with butter, rather lavishly. Season with black pepper and close again. Heat in a moderate oven until piping hot. Serve with toast and butter for breakfast or high tea.

CREAMED SMOKIES: Bring haddocks to a boil in cold water, then drain, skin and flake. Measure. Add equal quantity of cream sauce made by mixing $\frac{1}{2}$ cup white sauce with 1 cup thin cream. Heat in the top of a double boiler over hot water, then season with black pepper and salt to taste. Serve on a hot dish with creamed or mashed potatoes and green peas, in hot pastry cases, or on hot buttered toast or fried bread.

AN EDINBURGH WAY WITH SMOKIES: Head and tail fish. Place in a saucepan with enough water to prevent burning. Cover closely. Bring slowly to boil. Drain. Serve with parsley butter.

SMOKIES, THE MANSE WAY

4 *Arbroath haddocks*
cold water as required
2 *tablespoons flour*
1 *pint milk*

1 *dessertspoon butter*
salt and black pepper to taste
2 *chopped hard-boiled eggs*
1 *dessertspoon minced parsley*

Place the haddocks in a shallow saucepan. Cover with cold water. Bring to boil, then skin them. Cream flour with fish liquor. Heat milk with butter till fairly hot, then stir in creamed flour. Stir till smooth and boiling. Season with salt and black pepper. Place the smokies in a casserole, after boning if liked. Pour the sauce over. Sprinkle with the egg and parsley. Heat in oven.

SMOKED FISH PUDDING

$\frac{1}{2}$ *lb. boned, smoked fillet*
$\frac{1}{2}$ *lb. boiled cod or haddock*
$\frac{1}{4}$ *lb. shredded suet*
1 *teaspoon finely chopped*
  parsley

2 *oz. stale breadcrumbs*
salt and pepper to taste
1 *teaspoon grated onion*
2 *beaten eggs*
$\frac{1}{2}$ *pint milk and fish stock*

Flake the fillet into a basin. Add cod or haddock to fillet, then stir in suet. Mix and mash well together, then rub through a sieve into another basin. Add breadcrumbs, parsley, salt and pepper to taste, and onion. Mix well. Stir eggs into milk and stock, using half milk and half stock made from fish trimmings. Stir till blended. Add fish mixture and mix well. Three-quarter fill a greased pudding basin. Cover tightly with greased paper. Steam gently for about $1\frac{1}{2}$ hours. Serve with anchovy or parsley sauce. Serves 4 or 5.

SHELLFISH

The herring loves the merry moonlight
The mackerel loves the wind
But the oyster loves the dredging song
Because he comes of gentle kind.

This is a song the fishermen used to sing as they trailed their dredging nets for oysters in the Firth of Forth.

Shellfish in bygone days was a staple article of diet in Scotland. In the eighteenth century, oyster suppers were so popular and cheap that they were the fashion with the gay bloods of Edinburgh, who made 'high ploy' in the taverns renowned for oyster fare. In those days, 'Caller oo', the cry of the oyster vendors, was often heard in and out the closes and wynds of Cowgate, and its neighbourhood where many of the taverns were then situated. That cry alas! is heard no more.

CRAB CUTLETS

6 oz. flaked, cooked crab	$\frac{1}{4}$ pint milk
1 oz. butter	salt and pepper to taste
1 oz. flour	egg and breadcrumbs

Use most or all of the white meat of the crab. Melt butter in a small saucepan. Add flour. When frothy, stir in milk. Stir till boiling. Simmer gently for a minute or two, stirring constantly, then season with salt and pepper to taste and add the crab. When blended, spread on a plate and leave until cool. Shape into cutlets. Egg and crumb. Fry in deep hot fat till golden brown. Arrange on a hot dish lined with paper doyley. Garnish with sprigs of parsley and lemon butterflies. Serves 2.

DRESSED CRAB
(COLD)

Place a freshly-boiled, medium-sized crab on its back on a board. Holding shell firmly with one hand, and the body in the other hand, pull it apart. With a spoon, remove the stomach bag, just below the head, from the shell part, and throw it away. Carefully scrape out all the meat from the shell into a basin. Wash and dry shell, and knock off its edge as far as the dark line round the edge. Dry and polish with olive oil. Stir 1 tablespoon of freshly sieved breadcrumbs into the removed meat. Season with salt and pepper and flavour with lemon juice or vinegar and minced parsley to taste. Divide this mixture in two. Place a half of it into each side of the shell, leaving a space in the centre. Now remove all the greyish-white pieces from the body, as they are inedible. Crack the large claws with nut crackers and remove all the flesh from inside them, as well as from the body. (I use the handle of a small teaspoon or coffee spoon for doing this.) Season this flesh with salt and cayenne pepper, and flavour with lemon juice or vinegar. Pile into the middle of the shell. Garnish with the small claws and with sprigs of parsley.

TO VARY: Mix the meat with a French dressing flavoured with French mustard, or with mayonnaise. Return to shell. Garnish with sieved hard-boiled egg yolk, chopped hard-boiled egg white and parsley, capers and watercress.

DRESSED CRAB (HOT): Chop all the meat. Melt $\frac{1}{2}$ oz. butter in a saucepan. Add $\frac{1}{2}$ oz. flour. When frothy, stir in $\frac{1}{4}$ pint milk. Stir till boiling. Season with salt, pepper and cayenne pepper. Flavour with $\frac{1}{2}$ teaspoon anchovy essence and a few drops lemon juice. Stir in the crab meat. When blended, pack into prepared shell. Sprinkle with sieved breadcrumbs. Dab with butter. Cook under the grill until crumbs are crisp and golden brown.

PARTAN PIE

This is Meg Dods' recipe.

Remove the meat from the claws and body of a crab. Clean the shell thoroughly. Season the crab meat with salt, white pepper and grated nutmeg to taste. Add 1 or 2 pats of unsalted butter and a tablespoonful of breadcrumbs. Stir till blended. If liked, stir in half a wineglass of vinegar. Turn into a small saucepan. Add a mustard spoon of made mustard and stir over moderate heat till piping hot. Return meat to the shell. Brown with a salamander or under the grill. Serves 1.

Lobsters are generally served boiled and either turned into a lobster salad or lobster mayonnaise in Scotland. The meat from a hen lobster is preferred. Shell, and remove the coral. Rinse, dry and pound the coral, then rub it through a sieve. Cut tail into neat slices and half the claws lengthwise. Soak lobster in Vinegar Sauce for 3 hours, then drain thoroughly.

LOBSTER SALAD: Mix 1 lb. diced lobster meat with 1 teaspoon of capers, a little diced cucumber or beetroot and chopped gherkin, and mayonnaise to moisten. Garnish with slices of hard-boiled egg, mustard and cress, or watercress, and heart of lettuce leaves. If preferred, French dressing can be substituted for the mayonnaise. Serves 4.

LOBSTER MAYONNAISE: Prepare the lobster but do not soak in Vinegar Sauce. Coat lightly with thin mayonnaise, or French dressing. Pile in a salad bowl. Mix $\frac{3}{4}$ gill of mayonnaise with $\frac{3}{4}$ gill of aspic jelly. Leave until beginning to set, then pour over the lobster. (If liked, add $\frac{1}{4}$ pint of pricked prawns or shrimps to the lobster before coating.) Garnish with the coral, sliced stuffed olives, 1 tablespoon of capers, 2 tablespoons diced pickled beetroot, heart of lettuce leaves, and wedges of hard-boiled egg or tomato if liked. Serves 4.

ASPIC OF LOBSTER

$\frac{3}{4}$ *pint aspic jelly*   1 *freshly boiled lobster*
salad to taste   *watercress*

Melt half the aspic jelly. Pour into a wet flat dish. Leave until set. Cut into rounds about $1\frac{1}{2}$ inches across. Dish them up in a circle. Remove all the flesh from lobster. Cut up the flesh. Crack claws and remove flesh. Place lobster in centre of aspic rounds, using the claw meat for garnish. Garnish round the edge with sprigs of watercress and chopped aspic jelly. Serve with mayonnaise. Serves 4.

LOBSTER CUTLETS

¼ lb. boiled lobster
1 oz. butter
1 oz. flour
½ gill fish stock
½ gill milk

1 egg yolk
squeeze of lemon juice
cayenne pepper and salt to taste
a drop or two of carmine
fried parsley and lemon

Mince the lobster finely. Melt butter. Stir in flour. When frothy, stir in fish stock and milk. Stir till boiling, then add lobster, egg yolk, lemon juice, cayenne pepper and salt and carmine. Cook over slow heat till mixture firms slightly, but do not allow to boil. Turn onto a plate. When cold, shape into neat, small cutlets. Egg and crumb. If rather soft, repeat. Fry in deep hot fat till golden brown. Garnish with fried parsley and lemon. Serves 2.

QUEENSFERRY LOBSTER SALAD

1 boiled medium-sized
    lobster
2 crisp lettuces
1 bunch watercress

½ lb. firm tomatoes
2 hard-boiled eggs
½ cucumber
salt and pepper to taste

Cut the flesh of lobster in neat pieces. Mix to taste with mayonnaise. Pack into the tail shells. Make a circle on a flat dish with the heart of lettuce leaves and tuck a little watercress in between each leaf. Scald, peel, chill and slice tomatoes. Shell and slice eggs. Peel and slice cucumber. Shred remainder of lettuce and cress. Arrange the tomato slices, egg slices, cucumber slices, and the shredded lettuce mixed with the cress in alternate layers in the centre of the circle. Lean the stuffed lobster shells on the salad towards each other. Place the head in the centre. Garnish in between the shells with the claws, and one or two slices of egg and tomato. Serve with mayonnaise, or with mayonnaise mixed with a third of its quantity of whipped cream. Serves 2.

OYSTERS AS A FIRST COURSE

Open oysters carefully just before they are required, taking care not to spill the liquor in their deep shells. Remove their beards and place one oyster in each shell. Arrange carefully in a circle on a bed of cracked ice when possible. Offer cayenne pepper, tabasco, lemon juice and brown bread and butter with oysters. Allow 6 or 12 per person.

HOT OYSTERS: Dip bearded oysters in beaten egg, then in sieved breadcrumbs. Season with salt and cayenne pepper and grate nutmeg to taste. Butter the deep shells lavishly. Place one oyster in each shell, crowned with a small pat of butter. Bake in a moderately hot oven, 400° F., for about 5 minutes.

OYSTER PATTIES

12 *patty cases 2 inches across*
1 *dozen oysters*
1 *oz. butter*
1 *oz. flour*

¼ *pint milk*
½ *gill cream*
squeeze of lemon juice
salt and cayenne pepper to taste

Make patty cases of puff pastry. Beard the oysters. Pour the liquor into a small saucepan and add the oyster beards. Bring to a boil, then strain off liquor and throw away the beards. Halve oysters. Melt butter in a small saucepan. Add flour. When frothy, stir in milk and cream. Stir till boiling. Simmer for 2 or 3 minutes, still stirring, then add the liquor, oysters, lemon juice and salt and cayenne pepper, stirring constantly. When piping hot, fill the cases. Reheat for a moment or two in the oven if wanted hot, or serve cold.

OYSTER AND SOLE PIE

6 *oysters*
1 *small filleted sole*
squeeze of lemon juice
salt and cayenne pepper to taste

1 *egg*
1 *dessertspoon flour*
½ *gill milk*

Beard and drain oysters, reserving their liquor. Grease a shallow fireproof dish. Sprinkle sieved breadcrumbs thinly over the bottom. Lay the fillets of sole in the bottom. Add the oysters, lemon juice, salt and cayenne pepper to taste. Beat the egg till frothy. Strain in the oyster liquor. Add flour. Stir till smoothly blended, then stir in the milk. Pour this over the fish. Sprinkle fairly thickly with sieved breadcrumbs. Dab with butter. Bake in a moderate oven, 350° F., for 15 to 20 minutes. Serve with mashed potatoes and buttered green peas. Serves 2.

SCALLOPED OYSTERS

2 *dozen oysters*   2 *oz. butter*
½ *cup sieved breadcrumbs*   *salt and cayenne pepper to taste*

Open the oysters and place them with their liquor in a small saucepan. Bring to boiling point. Remove oysters to a plate and trim off their beards and any hard portions. Strain liquor into a basin. Smear 4 large scallop shells with butter. Sprinkle about a teaspoon of the crumbs into each. Divide the oysters equally between the shells. Sprinkle each with a dessertspoon of bread-crumbs. Fleck with 4 small dabs of butter. Season with salt and pepper. Divide the oyster liquor equally between each, sprinkling it over the top. Spread a smooth layer of crumbs over the oysters. Dab with butter. Place shells on a tin. Bake in a hot oven, 425° F., for about 10 minutes, until pale brown. Arrange in a hot dish on a folded napkin. Serves 4.

COCKLES

Wash the shells thoroughly in 3 or 4 changes of cold water to remove all sand. Place in salted water to cover. Leave for 30 minutes, then transfer to a shallow saucepan, containing just enough water to cover the bottom of pan. Tuck a wet towel over them. Shake the pan constantly over moderate heat to prevent them burning, until the shells open. Serve hot with vinegar and pepper and bread and butter or treat in one of the following ways:

FRIED: Shell boiled cockles. Dip in seasoned flour, then deep-fry. Drain. Serve with lemon and brown bread and butter.

PICKLED: Boil, then drain off the liquid through muslin and measure. Place in a small saucepan with equal quantity of vinegar, and mace and sherry in the proportion of 1 blade of mace and ½ gill of sherry to a pint of liquid. Bring to boil and leave until cold. Place cockles in screw top jars, then pour in the liquid and seal closely. Use as a garnish or in fish sauces.

COCKLE SAUCE: Strain the liquor from a pint of boiled cockles. Melt 2 oz. butter in a saucepan. Add the strained juice of 1 lemon, pepper to taste and the liquor. Heat almost to boiling point, but do not allow to boil. Serve with boiled cod, haddock, hake or saith.

MUSSELS

Brush shells thoroughly, then wash in several changes of cold water to remove all grit and sand.

TO BOIL: Boil as suggested for cockles, or place in a deep saucepan and sprinkle with a little salt. Cover with a wet towel, then with lid, and shake briskly over strong heat till the mussels are scalded and the shells open. Remove at once, for if cooked too long they turn tough. Strain liquor from shells into a basin. Examine mussels and remove any bit of weed lurking under the black tongue before dressing and serving.

AS AN HORS D'ŒUVRE: Prepare mussels as described. When cold, dip in thin mayonnaise or Sauce Tartare, and return each to its shell. Allow 4–6 per person.

TO FRY: Spear each mussel with a fork and dip in batter, made with half milk and half strained mussel liquor. Roll each in sieved breadcrumbs. Fry in deep hot fat or oil till golden brown.
    Mussels can also be cooked by any method suggested for oysters, or served after boiling, when cold, with lemon juice or vinegar and brown bread and butter.

PERIWINKLES

Wash these little sea-snails thoroughly in several changes of cold water to remove any grit or sand, then shake them well. Place in a saucepan of boiling salted water to cover. Boil rapidly for 20 minutes, then strain and cool. Serve with brown or white bread and butter.

WHELKS

When gathering whelks, discard all large specimens as they are inclined to be tough. Wash them in several changes of cold water as soon as they are gathered, then shell them. In Scotland, they are usually tossed in seasoned flour, then egged and crumbed and fried in deep hot fat or oil. Serve with a light sprinkling of vinegar and with brown bread and butter.

If there is any doubt about cockles, mussels, periwinkles and whelks being fresh, place a silver spoon in the water when they are being boiled and if they are stale or 'bad', the spoon will turn black, when on no account must they be eaten. (Whelks can also be boiled, but are tastier fried.) Eat cockles and periwinkles with a two pronged fork. Mussels are frequently used in Scotland as a garnish for cold fish dishes, and elaborate hot dishes.

MILK CHEESE FILLING (1910)

Cover 1 or 2 quarts of milk and leave for three days, or longer if the weather is cold, till it becomes thick. Cover a basin with butter muslin and pour the milk on to it. Break the curds up with a fork. Tie the ends of the muslin together, then suspend from a hook with the basin below to catch the whey. Leave for at least 12 hours. Untie the muslin. Shape cheese into a pat with butter hands. Place on a sieve to drain still more. Leave for 24 hours, then place in a basin. Beat in a little salt and mould in a basin.

FINNAN HADDOCK FILLING

1 *small finnan haddock*
2 *tablespoons milk*
1 *oz. butter*
2 *tablespoons cream*

$1\frac{1}{2}$ *teaspoons minced parsley*
salt, pepper and cayenne to taste
toast

Scald, skin and remove fillets from haddock, then halve and cook in the milk and butter in a covered dish very slowly till tender. Flake fillets. Stir in cream, parsley, pepper, salt and cayenne to taste. Stir in liquor from dish. Cool. Use as a filling between slices of bread toasted on the outside and thinly buttered inside.

POTTED HAM

1 *lb. lean boiled ham*	1 *saltspoon made mustard*
½ *lb. fat boiled ham*	1 *saltspoon cayenne pepper*
¼ *teaspoon ground allspice*	½ *teaspoon piquant sauce*
¼ *teaspoon ground mace*	2 *oz. butter*

Put the ham through a mincer into a mortar. Pound well with a pestle, gradually working in the seasonings. When thoroughly blended, rub through a sieve. Press into small sterilized pots. Add melted, clarified butter to a depth of ½ inch. Serve with crisp toast and butter. This ham keeps fresh for several days.

LAMB'S LIVER SPREAD

1 *tablespoon bacon fat*	½ *lb. lamb's liver*
1 *sliced small onion*	*butter or margarine as required*
1 *tablespoon chives or spring onion*	*salt and black pepper to taste*

Heat the fat in a strong frying pan. Add onion. Fry slowly till lightly browned, stirring frequently. Cut liver in thin slices. Dip in seasoned flour. Remove onion with a perforated spoon, so that all the fat drips back into pan. Place liver in pan with more bacon fat if required, and fry slowly till firm, but not browned. Remove and leave until cold. Put the onion and liver through a mincer with the chives or spring onion, and a sliver of garlic. Put again through mincer into a basin. Add the bacon drippings and enough creamed butter or margarine to make a spreadable consistency. Season with salt, and freshly ground black pepper. Mash well, then pack tightly into a jar. Store in a refrigerator, and leave for at least 1 day before using.

PARTRIDGE PASTE

1 *young partridge*	*thick cream as required*
salt and pepper to taste	

Wipe a cleaned partridge, trussed for roasting, with a damp cloth. Brush bird with melted butter. Roast on a trivet in a baking tin in a hot oven, 500° F., until brown. Pour 3 tablespoons of water into baking tin. Add a large walnut of butter. When butter is melted, baste the bird well. Lower oven temperature to 375° F. Return bird to oven. Roast for 15 or 20 minutes until tender, basting at half time. Remove to a dish. Leave until cold. Skin, bone and put the flesh through a mincer. Strain the liquor from the baking tin into a small saucepan. Bring to boil. Simmer until reduced to half a tablespoon, then cool. Stir into paste. Season with salt and pepper. Thin to taste with the cream. Use as a sandwich paste or filling for small éclairs or choux pastry buns for buffet parties.

PRAWN CREAM

Moisten finely minced cooked prawns with white sauce and thick cream in the proportions of 1 tablespoon white sauce to 2 oz. prawns and cream to make a spreadable mixture. Season with salt and pepper. Flavour with a few drops of vinegar and colour a pale pink.

SALMON AND SHRIMP PASTE

1 *lb. flaked steamed salmon*
$\frac{1}{4}$ *pint unshelled shrimps*
$2\frac{1}{2}$ *oz. butter*

salt and cayenne pepper to taste
ground mace to taste

Place salmon in a mortar. Shell shrimps. Chop finely. Add to salmon with the butter. Pound to a paste with a pestle. Season to taste with salt, cayenne pepper and mace. Rub through a fine sieve. Pack tightly in sterilized pots. Cover with clarified butter.

ANCHOVY AND EGG SANDWICHES

12 *anchovy fillets*
3 *hard-boiled egg yolks*
dash of curry powder
dash of cayenne pepper

2 *tablespoons grated Parmesan*
   cheese
butter or thick cream to taste

Pound and mash the anchovy fillets, drained from their oil, with the egg yolks. Beat in the curry powder, cayenne pepper, grated Parmesan cheese and enough creamed butter, or thick cream, to make a smooth paste. Use as a filling for 24-hour-old bread.

CRESS BUTTER SANDWICHES

Beat ¼ lb. salt butter till creamy. Add mustard and cress, carefully picked over and washed and dried, allowing 1½–2 tablespoons according to taste. Beat till blended. Season with pepper. Add a drop or two of green colouring. Use as a filling for 24-hour-old thinly sliced unbuttered bread. If liked, sprinkle the filling with picked prawns, allowing 6 to each covered slice, then cover with thinly buttered bread.

GEORGE SANDWICHES

Stamp out rounds of white or brown bread and butter. Spread with white mayonnaise, cream mixed with beaten egg white and flavoured lemon juice. Cover with shredded chicken, ham or tongue. Sprinkle lightly with minced olives, then cover with buttered bread rounds to fit.

LAURETTA SANDWICHES

3 *oz spiced beef*	*salt and black pepper to taste*
1 *cream cheese*	*2 teaspoons made mustard*

Mince the beef, then pound it to a paste. Pound cheese with salt, pepper and mustard till of the consistency of butter. Spread 24-hour-old bread, thinly sliced, half with the cream cheese and half with the beef. Pair slices. Trim off crusts. Cut in triangles.

POTTED SALMON SANDWICHES

1 *lb. cold, boiled salmon*	*cayenne pepper to taste*
2 *oz. butter*	*black pepper to taste*
½ *teaspoon ground cloves*	*salt if necessary*
2 *teaspoons anchovy sauce*	½ *a cucumber*
1 *teaspoon lemon juice*	*sprigs of watercress*

Pound the salmon in a mortar with the butter, cloves, anchovy sauce, lemon juice, cayenne pepper, black pepper, and salt if necessary. Take a pan loaf 24 hours old, and spread, after removing the end slice, with butter or mustard butter, then with the salmon paste. Cut off slice, and top with thinly sliced cucumber cut in strips. Now butter the bread again and remove slice. Place on top of cucumber. Press down firmly. Cut into small rounds with a sharp cutter. Repeat. One loaf takes 6 oz. of butter. Garnish with watercress.

MUSTARD BUTTER: Beat 2 oz. butter till creamy, then beat in 1 teaspoon made mustard, a squeeze of lemon juice, and cayenne pepper and salt to taste. Use for buttering sandwich bread and bridge rolls for fish or meat fillings.

SHRIMP SANDWICHES

2 *sieved hard-boiled eggs*	2 *teaspoons stiffly-whipped*
1½ *oz. fresh butter*	*cream*
1 *oz. salmon and shrimp paste*	1 *tablespoon peeled shrimps*

Beat the egg gradually into the butter, then beat in the paste. Stir in cream and shrimps. Season carefully with salt and cayenne pepper. Use as a spread for thinly cut unbuttered brown bread, 24 hours old. Sandwich 3 slices together. Remove crusts. Cut in fingers.

TOMATO SALAD SANDWICHES

¼ pint tomato pulp   colouring if necessary
¼ oz. powdered gelatine   pepper and salt to taste
¼ pint whipped cream   shredded celery as required

Use ripe tomatoes for making the pulp. Slice and rub them through a hair sieve. Add gelatine. Stir till dissolved, then fold in the cream and a drop or two of red colouring if necessary and salt and pepper to taste. Chill. Spread on thin bread and butter. Sprinkle filling lightly with celery. Cover with thin bread and butter. Remove crusts. Cut into triangles.

EGGS AU GRATIN

6 *hard-boiled eggs*
1 *tablespoon melted butter*
1 *teaspoon minced parsley*
1 *teaspoon grated onion*
½ *teaspoon minced chives*

5½ *tablespoons stale*
 breadcrumbs
salt and pepper to taste
1 *pint Béchamel sauce*
¾ *cup grated cheese*

Shell and halve eggs crosswise while hot. Remove yolks to a basin. Stir in butter, parsley, onion and chives. Moisten 1½ tablespoons of the crumbs with milk. Season with salt and pepper to taste. Stand for 3 minutes. Stir into yolk mixture. When blended, pile into egg whites. Place side by side in a shallow buttered fireproof dish. Cover with the sauce. Mix remainder of crumbs with the cheese. Sprinkle over the top. Dot with flecks of butter. Bake in a moderate oven, 350° F., till golden brown in about 15 minutes.

TO VARY: Place 3 or 4 picked shrimps or a prawn in the bottom of each egg white before adding filling, or place a layer of the sauce in bottom of dish, then add stuffed eggs and fill spaces in between with boiled green peas. Cover with the sauce. Finish off as described. Serves 6.

EGG SALAD

4 *hard-boiled eggs*
2 *tablespoons chopped boiled*
 fowl
salt and pepper to taste

a few drops of vinegar
radish roses
lettuce leaves as required

Shell eggs. Halve crosswise. Remove yolks to a basin. Mash with fowl meat, salt and pepper to taste, and vinegar. Divide in 8 equal portions. Shape into balls. With a sharp knife, cut a thin slice from bottom of white shells to make them stand evenly. Cut round the tops into points. Slip a yolk ball into each. Arrange on a bed of crisp lettuce leaves. Wreath with radish roses. Serves 4.

DEVILLED EGGS

6 *hard-boiled eggs*　　　　　　1 *teaspoon Worcester sauce*
½ *tablespoon vinegar*　　　　　*salt and pepper to taste*
½ *teaspoon mustard*　　　　　　1 *tablespoon mayonnaise*

Cut the eggs in half. Remove the yolks and press them through a sieve. Add the seasonings and mayonnaise and beat until smooth and fluffy. Refill egg whites and garnish with chopped chives and parsley. Serve on a bed of mustard and cress in a round glass dish. Serves 6.

FARMHOUSE EGGS

Cover the bottom of a casserole with stale breadcrumbs, then cover the crumbs with a layer of grated cheese, Cheddar or Cheshire. Break six or more eggs into the dish, depending on how many to be served. Cover with another layer of bread-crumbs and cheese. Carefully pour over 1 pint of cream. Sprinkle with a thick layer of breadcrumbs and cheese. Season each layer with salt and pepper. Place in a slow oven, 325° F., and cook till eggs are set, and the crumbs and cheese are browned. Serves 6.

HIGHLAND EGGS

½ *lb. Finnan haddock*　　　　　2 *hard-boiled eggs*
½ *oz. butter*　　　　　　　　　*beaten egg and breadcrumbs as*
milk as required　　　　　　　　*required*
½ *oz. flour*　　　　　　　　　　*frying fat or oil*
1 *dessertspoon minced parsley*

Wash and trim haddock. Place it in a frying pan with the butter and ¼ pint of milk. Simmer haddock gently till flesh is creamy. Lift from pan, and remove skin and bone. Flake fish finely. Measure the milk in which it has been boiled. Make up to ¼ pint with additional milk. Mix flour to a cream with some of this milk. Heat remainder in a saucepan. Stir into creamed flour, then return mixture to pan. Stir till boiling. Allow to boil for 1 minute, stirring constantly. Add fish and parsley. Mix well. Leave on a plate until cold. Shell eggs and divide fish mixture into two equal portions. Place an egg in the centre of each and mould the fish round them. Egg and crumb. Fry in deep hot fat or oil until golden brown. Drain on absorbent paper. Serve with mushroom sauce. Serves 2.

POTATO OMELETTE

3 *eggs*
1 *teaspoon minced parsley*
1 *tablespoon breadcrumbs*
1 *tablespoon mashed potatoes*
1 *tablespoon grated cheese*
1 *tablespoon milk*
salt and pepper to taste
1 *tablespoon butter*

Beat eggs until frothy. Stir in parsley, breadcrumbs, potatoes, cheese, milk, and salt and pepper to taste. Melt butter in an omelette pan. Pour in mixture. Fry for about 1½ minutes, then brown under grill. Fold in two. Serve at once. Serves 2.

SCOTCH EGGS

3 *hard-boiled eggs*
3 *oz. sausagemeat*
beaten egg
4 *oz. dried breadcrumbs*

To make certain the yolks of the eggs remain in the centre of each egg, make a cross on one side of each with an indelible pencil. Place eggs in a saucepan. Cover with cold water and bring to the boil, then turn at once on to their other sides, and boil for 10 minutes. Remove to a large basin of cold water. Leave till cool, then shell carefully. Divide the sausagemeat into 3 equal portions. Dry eggs carefully, then dip in seasoned flour. Mould a portion of sausagemeat round each egg till they are all evenly covered with the meat. Brush with beaten egg and dip in dried breadcrumbs. Fry in deep smoking hot fat to cover till golden brown. Drain on absorbent paper. When cold, halve crosswise.

SCOTTISH EGG SCALLOPS

$\frac{3}{4}$ cup flaked Finnan haddock
$\frac{3}{4}$ cup well-seasoned parsley
  sauce

5 eggs
salt and pepper to taste
2$\frac{1}{2}$ tablespoons grated cheese

Mix the haddock and sauce together in a saucepan. Stir till boiling. Boil for 3 minutes, stirring constantly. Divide equally between 5 greased ramekins or scallop shells. Break an egg into each. Season with salt and pepper to taste. Sprinkle with grated cheese. Bake in a moderate oven, 350° F., until eggs are set in about 10 minutes. Serves 5.

FINNAN HADDOCK SOUFFLÉ

$\frac{1}{2}$ lb. flaked boiled Finnan
  haddock
1 oz. butter
3 separated eggs

salt and pepper to taste
grated nutmeg to taste
$\frac{1}{4}$ pint cream

Place haddock and butter in a mortar. Pound until smooth, then rub through a hair sieve into a basin. Beat in egg yolks, one at a time, till all three are incorporated. Season with salt, pepper and nutmeg. Whip cream and fold into mixture, as lightly as possible, then fold in stiffly beaten egg whites. Pour into a buttered soufflé or fireproof dish. Bake in a slow oven, 325° F., for 45 to 60 minutes until a knife inserted in centre comes out clean. Serves 3.

SAUCES

A good sauce should be smooth and perfectly flavoured or seasoned. If to be served in a sauceboat, the sauceboat should be hot for hot sauces, and cold for cold sauces. When I learned to cook a little white wine was generally added to a white sauce to serve with fish, and a little red wine to a brown sauce to serve with game. I hope that now all ingredients for making good food are available again, housewives will remember this when sauce is wanted.

ANCHOVY SAUCE

1 *oz. butter*
1 *oz. flour*
½ *pint milk*
salt and cayenne pepper to taste

½ *teaspoon lemon juice*
1 *teaspoon anchovy essence*
a few grains of carmine
½ *gill cream*

Melt butter in a saucepan. Stir in flour. When frothy, stir in milk. When smooth and boiling add salt and cayenne pepper to taste. Boil slowly for 3 minutes, stirring constantly, then stir in lemon juice, anchovy essence, carmine, and cream. When piping hot, pour into a heated sauceboat. Serve with boiled or steamed fish. *Yield:* Fully ½ pint.

BÉCHAMEL SAUCE

1¼ pints milk
1 small peeled onion or
    shallot
12 peppercorns
1 bouquet garni
½ bay leaf

½ blade of mace
2 oz. butter
1½ oz. flour
salt and cayenne pepper to taste
finely grated nutmeg to taste

Pour milk into a saucepan. Add onion or shallot, and the pepper-corns, bouquet garni, bay leaf and mace tied in a small muslin bag. Simmer very gently for 15 minutes. Remove bag. Melt butter in another saucepan. Add flour. When frothy, strain in milk, stirring constantly, until boiling. Keep on stirring or whisking while simmering for 10 minutes, then pass through a scalded tammy cloth or fine strainer and reheat. Add salt and cayenne pepper and finely grated nutmeg to taste. *Yield:* Fully 1¼ pints.

BREAD SAUCE

3 or 4 cloves
1 shallot or small onion
½ pint milk
¼ blade mace
6 peppercorns

3 oz. sieved white breadcrumbs
1 teaspoon butter
2 tablespoons cream
salt to taste

Stick the cloves into the peeled shallot or onion. Pour milk into a saucepan. Add shallot or onion, mace and peppercorns. Heat slightly. Stand in warm place on the stove with lid on pan for 30 minutes. Strain milk into another saucepan. Add crumbs. Stir till boiling, and of a dropping consistency. Stir in butter and cream. Season with salt to taste. Serve in a hot sauceboat. *Yield:* About ½ pint.

TO VARY: Add ½ oz. butter and omit cream, or knead the teaspoon of butter with a teaspoon of flour and bring sauce again to boil. Simmer for a minute, stirring constantly, then add a knob of butter and 2 tablespoons of cream. Do not reboil. *Yield:* Fully ½ pint.

BROWN SAUCE

This is a sauce sometimes used when making a piquant or other savoury sauce.

2 teaspoons vinegar	1 tablespoon chopped tomato
¾ oz. butter	¾ oz. flour
1 dessertspoon chopped onion	¾ pint stock
1 oz. chopped bacon	½ blade mace
2 or 3 slices carrot	6 peppercorns
1 small slice turnip	bunch of herbs
1 chopped celery stick	salt to taste

Pour vinegar into a small saucepan. Heat until it is almost evaporated, then add butter and onion. Fry slowly till onion is clear, then add bacon and fry till fat is clear. Stir in vegetables, in order given, then the flour. When thoroughly blended, stir in stock, mace, peppercorns, herbs and salt to taste. When boiling, cover and simmer gently for about 45 minutes, stirring occasionally, then strain and use. *Yield:* about ¾ pint.

PIQUANT SAUCE I: Stir in 2 or 3 chopped gherkins, 1 chopped, peeled shallot, 1 tablespoon chopped capers and cayenne pepper and vinegar to taste, after simmering for ½ hour.

PIQUANT SAUCE II: Cook 2 tablespoons capers and 2 tablespoons minced shallot slowly in 2 tablespoons vinegar, until shallot is soft, then stir in the Brown Sauce and bring to boil. When boiling, season with salt and pepper if necessary.

PIQUANT TOMATO SAUCE: Increase tomato to ¼ pint, using tinned tomatoes.

BROWN SAUCE FOR FISH

2 tablespoons butter	2 teaspoons Worcester sauce
2 tablespoons flour	2 tablespoons red currant jelly
2 teaspoons ketchup	2 tablespoons sherry

Melt butter slowly in a small saucepan. Add flour. Stir till brown, then stir in ketchup, Worcester sauce, and red currant jelly. Stir till boiling. Simmer gently for 5 minutes, then strain. Just before serving, stir in the sherry and a teaspoon of butter, and reheat, but do not allow to boil. *Yield:* ½ cup.

CAPER SAUCE

2 *oz. butter*
2 *oz. sifted flour*
½ *pint mutton stock*

½ *pint milk*
1 *tablespoon capers*
1 *teaspoon caper vinegar*

Melt the butter in a saucepan. Add the flour. Stir over low heat for a minute or so until frothy, then gradually stir in the mutton stock. Stir till smooth and boiling, then gradually stir in the milk. Bring to boil and cook, stirring constantly, until thick enough to coat the back of the spoon, then stir in the capers, vinegar, and salt and pepper to taste. *Yield:* About 1 pint.

CELERY SAUCE

1 *large prepared head of*
   celery
walnut of butter
flour as required

1 *cup cream*
salt and pepper to taste
ground mace to taste

Cut celery into thin slices. Boil gently in salted water to cover till tender. Drain off all the stock except 4 tablespoonfuls. Dish up celery. Roll butter in flour. Add to stock. Stir till boiling. Gradually stir in cream, heated until tepid. When boiling, stir in celery and reheat. Season with salt and pepper to taste and ground mace. Serve with fried, grilled or roast veal, or boiled chicken, turkey or any game. *Yield:* About ½ pint.

CURRY SAUCE

1 *oz. butter*
1–2 *tablespoons chopped*
  onion
½ *cooking apple*
1 *or 2 teaspoons curry*
  powder

½ *oz. rice flour*
salt to taste
1 *or 2 teaspoons chutney*
½ *pint stock*
¼ *teaspoon curry paste*
squeeze of lemon juice

Melt butter in a saucepan. Add onion. Fry slowly till slightly coloured. Chop and add apple with curry powder, rice flour, salt to taste, chutney and stock, in order given. Stir till boiling. Dilute the curry paste with a little of the sauce and stir into remaining sauce in pan. Cover. Simmer very gently for at least 1 hour, uncovering and stirring frequently, then add lemon juice, and a little cream if liked. Use white stock or half white stock and half milk when making curry sauce for white meat, and brown stock for dark meat. *Yield:* About ½ pint.

FAST-DAY SAUCE

This is a sauce my mother used to serve with boiled fish on Good Friday.

1 *sliced onion*
1 *head celery*
1 *sliced carrot*
2 *sprigs parsley*
2 *pints water*

¼ *lb. butter*
3 *small tablespoons flour*
squeeze of lemon juice
salt and pepper to taste

Place onion in a saucepan. Trim celery. Slice. Rinse and add to saucepan, with carrot, parsley and water. Cover and simmer gently until the vegetables are tender, then strain and measure off 1½ pints. Melt butter in a saucepan. Add flour. When frothy, add half the stock gradually, then stir till boiling. Cook for 2 or 3 minutes, stirring constantly and thin with remaining stock to taste. Add lemon juice and salt and pepper to taste. *Yield:* 1 pint.

FENNEL SAUCE

1 *oz. butter*   1 *tablespoon chopped fennel*
½ *oz. flour*   *salt and pepper to taste*
1½ *gills fish stock*

Melt the butter. Stir in flour. When smooth, stir in stock. Stir
till boiling. Add fennel and salt and pepper to taste. Sometimes
the sauce is made with only 1 gill of stock and ½ gill of cream,
added at the last moment. Serve in a hot sauce boat. *Yield:* 1½ gills.

HOLLANDAISE SAUCE

1 *tablespoon lemon juice*   2 *oz. butter*
2 *egg yolks*   *salt and cayenne pepper to taste*

Pour the lemon juice, or a dessertspoon wine vinegar if preferred,
into a small basin. Stir in egg yolks. When blended, lower into a
pan of hot water. Stir in the butter, bit by bit. Keep stirring till
thick, but do not allow to boil or the sauce will curdle. Season
with salt and cayenne pepper to taste. Serve with boiled asparagus,
fish, etc. For 3 persons.

ECONOMICAL HOLLANDAISE: When required for asparagus, stir 2
tablespoons of cold water into the lemon juice before starting to
make sauce, reduce lemon juice to ½ tablespoon and add to it the
same amount of tarragon vinegar. If to serve with fish, substitute
fish stock for the water.

RICH HOLLANDAISE: Use 3 or 4 yolks, 1 teaspoon vinegar, 2 oz.
butter and ½ gill cream. Stir all ingredients over hot water till
sauce thickens, then season with salt and cayenne pepper.

LEMON SAUCE

1 *oz. butter*   2 *egg yolks*
1 *oz. flour*   ½ *teaspoon lemon juice*
¾ *pint fish stock*   *salt and cayenne pepper to taste*

Melt butter. Stir in flour. When frothy, stir in fish stock. Stir till smooth and boiling, then place pan over boiling water. Beat egg yolks. Stir in a little of the sauce. When blended, stir into sauce in pan. Stir till piping hot but do not allow to boil. Remove from top of hot water, and gradually stir in lemon juice. Season to taste. *Yield:* ¾ pint.

MELTED BUTTER SAUCE

2 oz. butter	*½ pint cold water*
¾ oz. flour	*salt and pepper to taste*

Melt butter in a saucepan. Stir in flour. When frothy, gradually stir in the water. Bring to boil, stirring constantly. Simmer gently for about 6 minutes, stirring occasionally. Season with salt and pepper. *Yield:* About ½ pint.

PARSLEY BUTTER: Follow above recipe, but add 1–2 teaspoons minced parsley according to taste.

MELTED BUTTER: When melted butter is required to serve with boiled asparagus or globe artichokes, melt butter very gently over hot water then season with salt and pepper and skim before serving.

MINT SAUCE

2 heaped tablespoons chopped	*½ tablespoon moist brown*
fresh mint	*sugar*
2 tablespoons hot water	*5 tablespoons vinegar*

Place the mint in a sauce boat. Add sugar and hot water. Stir till sugar is dissolved. Leave until cool, then add vinegar. *Yield:* About ½ cup.

TO VARY: If a sweeter sauce is required, increase sugar to 2 tablespoons. If a stronger sauce, omit water and use ½ pint malt vinegar. Stand either sauce for 2 or 3 hours before serving.

MUSHROOM SAUCE

8 *oz. mushrooms*
½ *pint white stock*
1 *small peeled onion*
1 *oz butter*

1 *oz. flour*
¼ *pint milk*
salt and pepper to taste
1 *egg yolk*

Wash and peel mushrooms, then cut them up finely. Heat the stock in a saucepan. Add mushrooms. Simmer gently with the onion till soft, then rub through a sieve. Melt butter in another saucepan. Stir in flour. When frothy, gradually stir in milk. Bring to boil, stirring constantly, then add the mushroom purée and salt and pepper to taste. Simmer very gently for 15 minutes, then cool slightly and stir in the egg yolk. Cook over boiling water till thick, but do not allow to boil. Serve with boiled or roast chicken or turkey, etc. *Yield:* ¾ to 1 pint sauce.

ONION SAUCE

6 *large peeled onions*
¼ *lb. butter*
1 *oz. flour*
½ *pint milk*

½ *pint white sauce*
salt and pepper to taste
pinch of sugar
cream to taste

Cut the onions in very thin slices. Melt butter in a small shallow saucepan. Add onion. Fry very slowly, stirring occasionally, until tender, but not discoloured. Sprinkle in the flour. Stir till smooth and frothy. Add the milk to the white sauce. Stir into the onion mixture. Stir constantly until boiling, then cook over boiling water with lid on pan for about 20 minutes, stirring only occasionally. Season with salt and pepper. Add sugar. Rub through a sieve into a clean saucepan. Add cream to taste and stir till piping hot. The sauce should be rather thick, but not pasty. Serve with boiled or roast mutton. *Yield:* 1 pint.

OYSTER SAUCE

9 *bearded oysters*
1½ *oz. butter*
1 *oz. flour*
salt and pepper to taste

¼ *pint fish stock*
¼ *pint milk*
½ *gill cream*
1 *teaspoon lemon juice*

When you open the oysters, pour liquor into a small saucepan. Add the oyster beards. Bring to boil and strain. Melt butter in another saucepan. Stir in flour. When frothy, add salt and pepper to taste, stock, oyster liquor and milk. Stir till smooth and boiling, then simmer gently for 3 minutes. Remove pan from stove. Gradually stir in cream, then add oysters and lemon juice. Stir till piping hot, but do not allow to boil. Serve with boiled turbot. For 4 persons. *Yield:* About ¾ pint.

PARSLEY SAUCE

1 *oz butter*
1 *oz. flour*
½ *pint milk*

salt and pepper to taste
2 *tablespoons thick cream*
1 *tablespoon minced parsley*

Melt butter in a saucepan. Stir in flour. When frothy, stir in milk. Stir till smooth and boiling. Season with salt and pepper. Stir in cream and parsley, and simmer, stirring constantly, for three minutes. *Yield:* Fully ½ pint.

RAVIGOTE SAUCE

(SIMPLE)

½ *pint thick Béchamel sauce*
¼ *pint cream*
1½ *teaspoons chopped parsley*
1½ *teaspoons chopped tarragon*

1½ *teaspoons chopped chervil*
1½ *teaspoons chopped chives*
white vinegar to taste

Beat a little of the hot sauce into the cream, then gradually stir the cream into the remainder of the sauce. Stir till piping hot, then add the herbs. When blended, gradually stir in white vinegar to taste, from 1 to 1½ dessertspoons. *Yield:* About ¾ pint.

ROBERT SAUCE

2 oz. butter	½ bay leaf
2 sliced peeled onions	6 peppercorns
1 tablespoon flour	salt and cayenne pepper
½ pint brown stock	made mustard to taste
bouquet garni	1 teaspoon wine vinegar

Melt butter in a saucepan. Add onion. Fry over low heat until pale yellow. Add flour. When frothy, stir in stock. Bring to boil, stirring constantly. Add bouquet garni, bay leaf and peppercorns, tied in a muslin bag. Cover and simmer gently for about 30 minutes, then remove bag of herbs, and stir in from 1 to 2 teaspoons of mustard according to taste, then the vinegar. Add more salt if required. Serve with roast beef, goose, fried or grilled kidneys, roast pork or veal, and fried or grilled steaks. *Yield:* About ½ pint.

SAUCE SUPRÊME

Perhaps it is owing to the French influence that Sauce Suprême and Chaudfroid Sauce figure in high class Scottish menus. As I use both sauces frequently, I pass on the versions that were taught me in Dundee.

1½ oz. butter	12 button mushrooms
1 oz. flour	juice of ½ lemon
½ pint white stock	salt and pepper to taste

Melt butter. Stir in flour. When frothy, stir in stock. Cook until boiling, stirring constantly, then chop the mushrooms and add. Simmer gently, stirring constantly, until mushrooms are tender, then add the lemon juice and salt and white pepper to taste. Strain into a heated sauceboat. *Yield:* About ¾ pint.

CHAUDFROID SAUCE

Use Brown Chaudfroid Sauce for coating brown meats and white for poultry and veal, etc.

BROWN CHAUDFROID SAUCE: Heat up ½ pint Brown Sauce (page 102), and ¼ pint aspic jelly separately, then gradually stir the liquefied jelly into the sauce. Remove pan from stove. Soften ¼ oz. powdered gelatine in 2 tablespoons cold water. Stir into sauce. When dissolved, add 1 dessertspoon lemon juice. Bring to boil, stirring constantly. Simmer very gently for 5 minutes, then pass through a fine strainer. Gradually stir in ¼ pint cream, then use. *Yield:* About 1 pint.

WHITE CHAUDFROID SAUCE: Follow the recipe for Brown, but substitute Sauce Suprême (page 109) for Brown Sauce.

WHITE CHAUDFROID SAUCE
(WITHOUT ASPIC)

¾ *pint milk*	¼ *oz. powdered gelatine*
2 *slices carrot*	1¼ *oz. butter*
2 *slices onion*	1¼ *oz. flour*
pinch of celery seed	¼ *pint cream*
pinch of salt	

Measure off 1 tablespoon milk. Pour remainder of milk into a saucepan. Add carrot, onion, celery seed and salt. Heat very slowly till nearly boiling, then remove from stove. Soak the gelatine in the tablespoon of milk for 5 minutes. Melt butter. Add flour. When frothy, gradually strain in the milk. Stir till smooth and boiling. Simmer gently, stirring constantly for 2 or 3 minutes, then remove from stove. Stand for a minute, then stir in gelatine. When dissolved, strain through butter muslin. Stir in cream very lightly.

TO COAT COOKED CUTLETS: Trim neatly. Decorate each with a tiny wheel or flower of thyme and truffle. Coat with melted aspic, then trim with chopped aspic. Serve in a silver entrée dish on a mound of chopped aspic, piled up high.

STIRLING SAUCE

½ *pint black treacle*
1 *quart vinegar*
½ *pint mushroom ketchup*
½ *oz. cayenne pepper*
1 *small lemon*

½ *oz. salt*
½ *oz. garlic*
½ *oz. ground cloves*
½ *oz. ground ginger*

Mix the treacle with the vinegar, mushroom ketchup, and cayenne pepper. Slice lemon, and add with salt, garlic, cloves and ginger. Turn into a fresh basin. Stir 4 times a day with a wooden spoon for 5 days, then strain twice. Bottle and cork securely. Serve with steaks or cold meat when a piquant sauce is wanted. *Yield:* 3 pints.

TOMATO SAUCE

1 *oz. butter*
1 *small sliced peeled onion*
2 *slices of carrot*
1 *cup sliced, peeled tomatoes*
½ *oz. rice flour or cornflour*

½ *pint stock*
salt and pepper to taste
1 *or* 2 *cloves*
½ *teaspoon sugar*

Melt the butter slowly. (If a richer sauce is wanted, use only half the butter and add ½ oz. of chopped bacon. Fry for a moment or two.) Add onion and carrot. Fry slowly for about a minute without browning onion. Add tomatoes. Mash with a spoon. Simmer for 4 or 5 minutes, stirring constantly. Stir in rice flour, then gradually stir in the stock. (If preferred, half stock and half tomato juice can be used.) Bring to boil. Skim if required. Add salt and pepper to taste and cloves. Simmer gently for about ½ hour, stirring occasionally, then rub through a hair sieve. Return to saucepan. Stir till piping hot, then add sugar. *Yield:* About ½ pint.

VENISON SAUCE

1 *small sliced onion*
1 *tablespoon chopped celery*
1 *sprig thyme*
½ *bay leaf*
2 *oz. lean bacon*
2 *cloves*
6 *peppercorns*
2 *oz. butter*

½ *tablespoon flour*
1 *pint brown stock*
walnut of meat glaze
pinch of sugar
1 *teaspoon tomato catsup*
2 *teaspoons red currant or*
  rowan jelly
¼ *pint claret*

Place the onion, celery, thyme and bay leaf in a saucepan. Cut up the bacon into small pieces, and add with the cloves, peppercorns and butter. Fry slowly until the onion is pale yellow and soft, stirring occasionally, then stir in flour and stock, made from venison bones and trimmings. Stir till boiling. Cover and simmer very gently, stirring occasionally, for 1 hour. Strain into another saucepan. Add a walnut of glaze, a pinch of sugar, 1 teaspoon tomato catsup, 2 teaspoons red currant or rowan jelly, and a ¼ pint of claret boiled down till glazed. Stir till boiling. Simmer gently for 30 minutes. *Yield:* About ½ pint.

WHITE SAUCE

There are three versions of white sauce, but all are made with butter, flour and milk. Allow 1 oz. butter and 1 oz. flour and ¼ pint of milk when making a thick sauce for binding ingredients together such as when making cutlets or rissoles. Allow 1 oz. butter and 1 oz. flour to ½ pint milk when a coating sauce is wanted for fish or vegetables, and the same amount of butter and flour to 1 pint of milk when a pouring sauce is required for serving in a hot sauceboat or pouring round food.

METHOD: Melt the butter in a saucepan. Stir in the flour. Cook till frothy, but do not allow to brown. Gradually stir in a little of the milk, then add the remainder. Bring to boil, stirring constantly, and simmer for 3 minutes, still stirring. Season with salt and pepper.

Use ½ pint white sauce, either coating or pouring, for making the following sauces.

CELERY: Substitute chicken or veal stock for half the milk. Sieve 2 boiled celery sticks. Add purée to sauce with a pinch of sugar and 2 tablespoons cream.

CHEESE: Stir 2 tablespoons grated cheese into sauce. Cook till melted, stirring constantly

EGG: Add 1 chopped hard-boiled egg, or add the white only and garnish dish with the sieved yolk. Serve with boiled salt fish or chicken.

FISH: Substitute fish stock for half the milk.

MUSTARD: Stir 1 tablespoon made mustard and 1 dessertspoon vinegar into sauce. Serve with grilled herring.

ONION: Chop 2 large boiled onions and add to sauce. Serve with boiled chicken, mutton or rabbit.

PARSLEY: Stir 2 teaspoons finely chopped parsley into sauce.

WHITE CHICKEN SAUCE

Melt 1½ tablespoons chicken fat in a saucepan. Stir in 2 rounded teaspoons flour and salt and pepper to taste. When blended, stir in ¾ cup chicken stock and ¾ cup milk. Stir till smooth and boiling. If mushroom sauce is wanted, add ½ cup chopped fried mushrooms.

SAUCE FOR WILD FOWL

½ pint gravy
1 small peeled onion
1 snippet lemon peel

1 tablespoon rowan or red
    currant jelly
salt and cayenne pepper to taste

Simmer the gravy with the onion and lemon peel very gently for 15 minutes then strain. Return to pan. Add jelly. Stir till piping hot, then season with salt and cayenne pepper to taste.

MRS ANDERSON'S SALAD DRESSING

1 teaspoon mixed mustard
1 teaspoon caster sugar
2 tablespoons salad oil

4 tablespoons milk
2 tablespoons vinegar
cayenne pepper and salt to taste

Mix the ingredients very gradually, then beat until blended, when the dressing should have a soft, creamy appearance. The texture is better if the yolk of 1 hard-boiled egg is blended with the mustard before stirring in the remaining ingredients. *Yield:* ½ cup.

CREAM SALAD DRESSING

3 hard-boiled egg yolks
1 teaspoon caster sugar
1 teaspoon made mustard
1 teaspoon salt

½ teaspoon white pepper
¼ pint thick cream
3 tablespoons malt vinegar

Place the yolks in a basin. Mash with a spoon until quite smooth, then beat in sugar, mustard, salt, pepper, and cream by degrees, and lastly the vinegar. *Yield:* 1½ gills.

FRENCH DRESSING

1 teaspoon caster sugar,
    if liked
1 teaspoon salt

pinch of paprika, if liked
3 tablespoons wine vinegar
¾ cup olive oil

114

Mix sugar, salt and paprika together. Stir in vinegar and oil. Mix till well blended with a wooden spoon, or shake in a bottle. *Yield:* 1½ *gills*.

TO VARY: 1. Omit sugar, and add 1 teaspoon French mustard or ½ teaspoon English made mustard to seasonings, or add as well as sugar.

  2. Add 2 teaspoons minced onion and 2 teaspoons minced chives or parsley to dressing.

MISS BRECHIN'S MAYONNAISE

3 *raw egg yolks*   1 *teaspoon mixed mustard*
½ *pint olive oil*   1 *teaspoon salt*
1 *teaspoon tarragon vinegar* *dash of cayenne pepper*
3 *tablespoons malt vinegar*   *pinch of sugar*
a few drops of Chili vinegar

Place the yolks in a basin (I learned to make this on a sweltering August day, so the basin was imbedded in a bowl of cracked ice). Stir the oil in with a wooden spoon, drop by drop. When showing signs of thickening add a little more at a time. When all the olive oil is incorporated, stir in vinegars gradually, then the seasonings, and beat well. *Yield:* About 2½ gills.

SAUCE TARTARE

3 *teaspoons chopped capers*   ½ *teaspoon chopped tarragon*
1 *tablespoon chopped gherkin* 2 *dessertspoons chopped parsley*
1 *teaspoon chopped chervil*   ½ *pint mayonnaise*

Mix all the ingredients thoroughly till blended. Stand for about an hour. Serve in a cold sauceboat with boiled, fried or steamed fish, etc. *Yield:* About ½ pint.

BRANDY SAUCE

This is the sauce my father always insisted on me making to serve with his plum pudding.

1 *teaspoon cornflour*
¼ *pint milk*
1 *teaspoon caster sugar*

1 *beaten egg yolk*
about 2½ *tablespoons brandy*

Cream the cornflour with a little of the milk and bring remainder of milk to a boil. Draw pan to side of stove. Stir in creamed cornflour. Boil, stirring constantly, for 4 to 5 minutes, then add sugar. Remove from heat. When slightly cooled, stir in egg yolk and brandy, then stir sauce over boiling water till thick, but do not allow to boil. Serve hot. *Yield:* Fully ¼ pint.

CUSTARD SAUCE

1 *dessertspoon caster sugar*
1 *egg*

½ *pint hot milk*
vanilla essence to taste

Place sugar and egg in a basin. Beat till blended. Gradually stir in the hot milk. Strain into the top of a double boiler. Stir over boiling water until thick but do not boil. Add vanilla essence. Serve in a hot sauceboat. If wanted cold, cover. Stir occasionally while cooling to prevent skin forming on top. *Yield:* Fully ½ pint.

JAM SAUCE

¼ *pint water*
2 *tablespoons apricot or*
  raspberry jam
4 *or* 5 *lumps of sugar*

½ *lemon*
1 *teaspoon cornflour*
2 *or* 3 *drops carmine*
Madeira or Sherry if liked

Place the water, jam, sugar, thinly peeled lemon rind and strained juice in a saucepan. Bring to boil, then skim carefully. Cover and stand in a warm place for 8–10 minutes, then strain into a warm saucepan. Dissolve cornflour in a dessertspoon of water and stir into sauce. Stir till boiling. Simmer for a moment or two, then add carmine and 1 tablespoon of Madeira or sherry if liked. For 2 persons. *Yield:* Fully ¼ pint.

MARMALADE SAUCE

¼ *oz. cornflour*　　　　　　½ *tablespoon caster sugar*
1 *dessertspoonful lemon juice*　1 *tablespoon marmalade*
¼ *pint water*　　　　　　　*a drop cochineal*
1 *strip thinly peeled lemon rind*

Mix the cornflour with the lemon juice. Pour water into a saucepan. Add lemon rind. Boil for 3 or 4 minutes, then rapidly stir in the cornflour. Stir till boiling and boil for 1 minute, stirring constantly. Mix the sugar with marmalade. Add to sauce. Stir till sugar is dissolved, then remove from stove and stir in cochineal. Pour over or round dished up steamed sponge or batter pudding. *Yield:* ¼ pint.

SWEET WHITE SAUCE

¼ *oz. cornflour*　　　　　*caster sugar to taste*
½ *pint milk*　　　　　　*flavouring to taste*

Cream the cornflour with a little of the milk and bring remainder to a boil. Stir in creamed cornflour. Simmer for 5 minutes, stirring constantly, then add sugar, and flavouring to taste. Stir in a pat of butter. *Yield:* About ½ pint.

If lemon flavouring is wanted, boil a snippet of lemon rind with the milk, then remove it before adding the cornflour. If vanilla flavouring is preferred, place a vanilla pod in the milk before bringing it to the boil and remove it before adding cornflour.

PUDDIN'S AND PIES

The proof o' the puddin' is the preein' o' it.

When I was young we served all kinds of pudding in Angus, plain baked, boiled or steamed during the week in cold weather and fruit and curds or custard sauce, jellies and other simple cold sweets in the summer. We also had apple tarts in the winter, rhubarb in the spring and soft fruit tarts in the summer.

For Sunday dinner for which most of the food was prepared on the Saturday to save work on Sundays, we rose to greater heights with jellies flavoured with port wine or sherry, and whipped cream. My mother used to turn a packet of jelly into a quart measuring jug, add water to bring the amount up to fully ¾ pint, then port wine or sherry to make the quantity up to a pint. In midsummer we often had Hydropathic Pudding or curds and cream with fresh berries. A rich trifle was a standby all the year round. It was only when the weather was very cold that a pudding was left steaming by the fire while we were at Church.

BAKED PUDDINGS

APPLES WITH DUNFILLAN CRUST

2 *lb. cooking apples*	1 *egg spoon baking powder*
brown or caster sugar to taste	1 *egg*
3 *oz. butter*	2 *oz. caster sugar*
4 *oz. flour*	4 *tablespoons milk*

Peel, core, slice and stew apples with only enough water to prevent burning and brown or caster sugar to taste. Place in a pie

118

dish. Rub butter into flour. Stir in baking powder. Beat egg. Add sugar and milk. Stir till blended, then stir into the flour. Pour over the top of the apples. Bake in a moderate oven, 350° F., for about 30 minutes. Serve with cream or custard sauce. Serves 4.

BATTER PUDDING (1851)

Mix 3 or 4 oz. of sifted flour with milk until creamy, then stir in 1 pint of milk. Pour into a saucepan. Add a piece of butter the size of a small egg. Stir constantly over moderate heat until thick, then remove pan from stove. When cold, stir in the beaten yolks of 4 eggs and ground ginger and grated lemon peel to taste. Pour into a buttered basin. Cover with greased paper, then steam. Serve hot with a sweet sauce. (This batter pudding can also be served with meat.)

OBSERVATION: A little orange marmalade or conserve is a great improvement to this and all other batter puddings. Arrowroot, ground rice or potato flour can be substituted for the flour.

BAKED CHOCOLATE BREAD PUDDING

¼ lb. grated breadcrumbs	2 oz. caster sugar
fully ½ pint hot milk	few grains salt
1 oz. chocolate	2 eggs

Sprinkle the crumbs into the milk. You need just as much milk as the crumbs will 'take up'. Stir in chocolate, sugar and salt. When both are dissolved, beat in 1 egg at a time. Beat till thoroughly blended. Place in a greased pie dish. Bake in a hot oven, 450° F., until set, in about ½ hour. Serve with cream or custard sauce. Serves 3.

BAKED COCONUT PUDDING

3 *oz. desiccated coconut*
1 *pint milk*
2 *oz. butter*
1 *tablespoon caster sugar*

3 *separated eggs*
3 *tablespoons sponge cake crumbs*
½ *teaspoon vanilla essence*

Line a small pie dish thinly with shortcrust. Prick well with a fork. Ornament the rim with a fork or thumbs and forefingers. Simmer the coconut in the milk for 15 minutes. Cream butter. Add sugar. When blended, drop in egg yolks, cake crumbs and vanilla essence. Beat well, then stir in the milk and coconut. When blended, beat 1 egg white to a stiff froth. Stir into mixture. Pour into prepared dish. Bake in a moderate oven, 350° F., for about 30 minutes. Beat the remaining egg whites till stiff, then gradually beat in 4 oz. caster sugar. Pile over the pudding. Bake for about 15 minutes until meringue is set and tinged with gold. Serves 5 or 6.

DATE AND APPLE PUDDING

2 *oz. sieved breadcrumbs*
2 *oz. caster sugar*
4 *chopped, stoned dates*
1 *sliced, peeled and cored apple*

grated rind ½ *lemon*
2 *separated eggs*
¾ *pint milk*

Mix half the crumbs with half the sugar and dates. Place in the bottom of a greased pie dish. Sprinkle with the apple slices and lemon rind. Beat the egg yolks. Gradually stir in the milk. Cover the apple with the remainder of the crumbs mixed with sugar and dates, and pour the yolk mixture gently over the filling. Bake in a moderate oven, 350° F., until the apple is tender in about 1 hour. Whisk the egg whites to a stiff froth. Stir in remainder of sugar. Pile over the pudding. Dust with caster sugar. Bake in a moderate oven, 350° F., till crisp in 15 to 20 minutes. Serve with cream. Serves 3.

BAKED GROUND RICE PUDDING

¼ lb. ground rice
2 pints milk
½ small lemon rind
2 oz. caster sugar

1 oz. butter
1 tablespoon brandy
2 beaten eggs

Mix the ground rice to a cream with a little of the milk. Place remainder of milk in a saucepan. Add lemon rind. Simmer gently for 5 minutes, then strain. Stir in the ground rice. When boiling, simmer gently until thick, stirring constantly, then add the sugar and butter. Stir till dissolved. Turn into a basin. When cool, stir in the brandy and eggs. When blended, pour into a greased 2½ pint size pie dish. Bake in a moderate oven, 350° F., for about 20 minutes until set and lightly browned. Serves 6.

CARNOUSTIE QUEEN OF PUDDINGS

¾ pint milk
1½ oz. butter
3 oz. sieved breadcrumbs or
  sponge cake crumbs
5 oz. caster sugar

grated rind ½ lemon
2 separated eggs
3 tablespoons apricot or
  raspberry jam

Bring milk and butter almost to boiling point. Pour over the crumbs. Soak for 10 minutes, then stir in 2 oz. sugar and lemon rind. Cool slightly, then beat egg yolks and stir into the mixture. Bake in a moderate oven, 350° F., for about 30 minutes, or at 300° F. for about ¾ hour, until set. Spread either with apricot or raspberry jam. Beat the egg whites with a few grains of salt till frothy, then gradually beat in remaining sugar. Beat until stiff. (Sometimes I add ½–1 oz. ground almonds to the mixture.) Pile on pudding. Dredge with caster sugar before baking at 350° F. for about 15 minutes till meringue is crisp. Serve with cream. Serves 3 or 4.

BAKED RICE PUDDING

2 heaped tablespoons rice
4 tablespoons caster sugar
¼ teaspoon salt

2 pints milk
1 tablespoon butter
½ teaspoon vanilla essence

Rinse the rice. Drain and sprinkle over the bottom of a buttered pie dish. Stir in sugar, salt and milk. Break up butter into small pieces and add. Stir in vanilla essence. Bake in a slow oven, 300° F. Leave for about 30 minutes until a slight skin begins to appear over the milk. Stir well. Stir every 20 minutes or ½ hour until the rice is soft and nearly cooked, and the milk is thick and creamy, then allow to bake till brown. The whole process takes about 3 hours. Dust with grated nutmeg if liked. Serves 6.

BAKED SEMOLINA PUDDING

2 dessertspoons semolina
1 pint milk
pinch of salt

1 separated egg
1 tablespoon brown sugar
½ teaspoon vanilla essence

Soak semolina in the milk in a rinsed saucepan for 10 minutes. Bring to boil, and simmer for 10 minutes, stirring constantly all the time. Remove pan from stove. Cool slightly, then stir in salt, egg yolk, sugar and essence. Beat egg white till stiff. Fold into mixture. Bake for about 20 minutes in a moderate oven, 350° F., till faintly browned. Dredge with caster sugar. Serves 2.

STEAMED PUDDINGS

CLOOTIE DUMPLING

6 oz. flour
3 oz. shredded suet
3 oz. cleaned currants
1 oz. cleaned sultanas
2–3 oz. caster sugar

1 teaspoon ground cinnamon
½ teaspoon bicarbonate of soda
about ¾ cup buttermilk or sour milk

Mix the flour with the suet, fruit, sugar, cinnamon and soda. Stir in enough buttermilk or sour milk to make a rather soft batter. Dip a pudding cloth into boiling water. Sink it in a basin large enough to hold the batter. Dredge it lightly with flour, and spoon in the batter. The bowl gives it a round shape. Draw the fullness of the cloth together evenly, then tie it tightly with string but leave enough room for the dumpling to swell. Place a saucer or a plate in the bottom of a large saucepan. Lift the dumpling into the pan. Pour in enough boiling water to cover. Simmer for fully 2 hours, then untie. Turn out carefully on to a hot serving dish. Dredge with caster sugar. Serve with hot custard sauce. Serves 4 to 6.

TO VARY: If preferred, pour the batter into a greased mould to within an inch of the rim. Cover tightly with buttered paper. Steam for about 3 hours.

STEAMED COCONUT PUDDING

¼ *lb. shredded suet*
¼ *lb. sieved breadcrumbs*
2 *oz. desiccated coconut*
2 *oz. caster sugar*

2 *beaten eggs*
½ *gill milk*
2 *tablespoons apricot jam*

Mix all the ingredients in order given until thoroughly blended. Three-quarter fill a greased pudding mould. Cover with greased paper. Steam for 3 hours. Remove from pan. Turn out on to a hot plate. Coat with Lemon Sauce. Serves 3 or 4.

CORTACHY PUDDING

6 *oz. sieved breadcrumbs*
6 *oz. shredded suet*
6 *oz. cleaned currants*
6 *oz. caster sugar*
6 *oz. chopped cooking or tart apples*

6 *eggs*
½ *nutmeg*
pinch of salt
1 *oz. minced, candied peel*
1 *minced lemon rind*

Mix the breadcrumbs, suet, currants, sugar, apples and eggs until blended. Grate in nutmeg. Add salt, peel and lemon rind. Mix well. Three-quarter fill a greased basin. Cover with greased paper and a pudding cloth. Steam 3 hours. Serve with lemon sauce. Serves 6.

FEATHER CRUST PUDDING

4 *large cooking apples*   1 *egg*
½ *lb. flour*   ¾ *cup milk*
2 *teaspoons baking powder*   *sugar to taste*
2 *tablespoons butter*

Peel and core the apples, then slice thinly. Sift the flour with the baking powder. Rub in butter. Beat egg, then stir in the milk. Add to flour with sugar to taste, about 2 ozs. Stir in the apple. Three-quarter fill a greased pudding basin. Cover with greased paper. Steam for about 1¼ hours. Turn out gently. Coat with custard sauce or serve with cream. Serves 3.

FREE KIRK PUDDING

2 *tablespoons stoned raisins*   3 *tablespoons shredded suet*
2 *tablespoons cleaned currants*   ½ *teaspoon mixed spice*
2 *tablespoons caster sugar*   ½ *teaspoon bicarbonate of soda*
2 *tablespoons sieved*   1 *tablespoon minced candied*
  breadcrumbs   *peel*
2 *tablespoons ground rice*   *pinch of salt*
2 *tablespoons flour*   *milk as required*

Mix the raisins with the currants, sugar, breadcrumbs, ground rice and flour. Stir in suet, spice, and bicarbonate of soda dissolved in 3 tablespoons milk, then the peel and salt. Stir in enough additional milk to make a dropable batter. Three-quarters fill a greased mould. Cover with greased paper. Steam for 2 hours. Serve with custard sauce. Serves 2.

HIELANT BONNETS

washed peel of 1 lemon
1 cinnamon stick
½ pint boiling water
3 tablespoons flour

1 large walnut of butter
tiny pinch of salt
2 beaten egg yolks

Place the lemon peel and cinnamon in a saucepan. Add the water.
Simmer for 10 minutes, then put through a fine strainer. Mix
water, when slightly cooled, with the flour. When smooth, turn
into saucepan. Cook over moderate heat for 2 or 3 minutes,
stirring constantly. Add walnut of butter. Stir till melted. Add
salt. Leave until cool. Beat in egg yolks, one at a time. Drop
dessertspoons of this batter into hot lard, a few at a time, and fry
till golden, turning with draining spoon to ensure even browning.
Drain on an absorbent paper. Dredge with caster sugar. Serves 3.

STEAMED LEMON PUDDING

1 cup sieved breadcrumbs
3 oz. caster sugar
1 washed lemon

1 pint milk
2 egg yolks
2 stiffly beaten egg whites

Mix the crumbs with the sugar. Grate the lemon rind into the
milk. Mix with crumbs and sugar. Beat yolks and whites of eggs
separately. Extract the lemon juice. Strain into crumb mixture,
then beat in egg yolks. Fold in egg whites. Three-quarters fill a
greased pudding basin. Cover with greased paper. Steam for 3
hours. Turn out on to a hot serving dish. Serve with cream. Serves
2 or 3.

MARMALADE SUET PUDDING

one 2 lb. loaf
½ cup moist brown sugar
pinch of salt
½ teaspoon ground mace
2 tablespoons marmalade

1 small teaspoon bicarbonate of
  soda
¼ lb. shredded suet
1 cup milk or butter milk

Remove crusts from loaf. Rub the bread into crumbs. Mix all the ingredients together in order given. Beat well. Three-quarter fill a buttered pudding basin. Cover with greased paper and a pudding cloth. Steam for 3 hours. Turn out on to a hot dish. Coat with custard sauce. Serves 6.

MY MOTHER'S PLUM PUDDING

½ lb. sieved breadcrumbs	1½ teaspoons mixed spice
½ lb. sieved flour	1 teaspoon salt
1 lb. moist brown sugar	½ grated nutmeg
1 lb. shredded suet	8 well-beaten eggs
1 lb. cleaned currants	grated rind 1 lemon
1 lb. roughly cut raisins	2 tablespoons brandy
1 lb. cleaned sultanas	1 grated carrot
1 lb. chopped mixed candied peel	stout or old ale

Mix all the ingredients in order given, and stir in enough stout or old ale to make a dropable batter. Three-quarters fill a very large pudding basin, greased, and lined in the bottom with a greased round of paper, if wanted for a large number, otherwise use 2 or 3 basins, according to number to be served. Cover. Steam large pudding for 8 hours and smaller puddings for 6 hours. Resteam on Christmas Day for 2 hours, then turn out. Remove paper gently if clinging to pudding. Sprinkle with heated brandy or whisky and set a match to it. Serve with Brandy Butter or Sauce.

SAGO PLUM PUDDING

4 tablespoons sago	6 oz. cleaned sultanas
½ pint milk	2 oz. cleaned currants
½ pint sieved breadcrumbs	grated rind ½ lemon
¼ lb. caster sugar	1 small teaspoon bicarbonate of
2 oz. shredded suet	soda
1 teaspoon ground cinnamon	1 beaten egg

Sprinkle the sago into the milk. Soak for 12 hours. Stir in remaining ingredients in order given, dissolving the soda in an additional

126

tablespoon of milk. Add egg. Beat well. Steam in a covered greased basin, filled only three-quarters full, for 2½ to 3 hours. Unmould on to a hot plate. Serve with custard sauce or Toffee Sauce. Serves 4.

TOFFEE SAUCE: Melt ¼ lb. butter or margarine. Add ½ lb. golden syrup and ½ lb. Demerara sugar. Stir till sugar is dissolved. Boil for 15 minutes, stirring constantly until beginning to thicken, then pour quickly over pudding.

SCOTCH PLUM PUDDINGS (1954)

½ lb. cleaned currants
½ lb. cleaned sultanas
½ lb. muscatel raisins
¼ lb. glacé cherries
¼ lb. seedless raisins
2 oz. glacé pineapple
¼ lb. angelica
¼ lb. blanched almonds
¼ lb. candied orange peel
2 oz. candied citron peel
2 oz. candied lemon peel
2 oz. dried apricots
9 oz. stale breadcrumbs
6 oz. flour
1 saltspoon grated nutmeg
½ teaspoon ground cinnamon
½ teaspoon mixed spice
¼ teaspoon ground mace
¾ lb. shredded suet
10 oz. moist brown sugar
1 orange
½ lemon
3 oz. grated carrot
½ lb. cooking apples
5 eggs
1 saltspoon salt
2 tablespoons black treacle
2 tablespoons ginger syrup
1 teaspoon Noyeau
4 tablespoons brandy or rum
sherry as required

Place currants and sultanas in a basin. Split and stone muscatel raisins, then halve or chop them and add to currant mixture. Halve or quarter cherries. Clean raisins if necessary. Chop pineapple, angelica and almonds. Mince peel and apricots. Stir in crumbs, then add all this mixture to the currants, sultanas and muscatel raisins. When blended, sift flour with the spices, then stir in the suet and sugar. Grate in orange and lemon rinds and add carrot. Mix with the currant mixture. Peel, core and chop apples then weigh (there should be 6 oz.). Stir into mixture.

127

When blended, beat eggs with the salt. When light, stir into prepared ingredients. Strain orange and lemon juice into treacle. Stir in ginger syrup, Noyeau and brandy or rum. Stir till thoroughly blended, then add to the pudding mixture and mix well. Now stir in from $\frac{1}{4}$ to $\frac{1}{2}$ pint of sherry, just enough to make mixture of a dropable consistency. Fill up 3 prepared basins to within about $\frac{3}{4}$ inch of rims (to make certain that the puddings will turn out perfectly, it is a good idea to place a greased circle of greaseproof paper smoothly over the bottom of each before adding the mixture). Cover with greased circles of paper, pleating each carefully round the rim to allow rising. Fix in place with strong rubber bands. Brush tops with melted fat. Cover with pudding cloths, tied securely under the rims.

TO COOK PUDDINGS: Place a little apart on a rack in a large stockpot or fish kettle in a pan containing enough boiling water to come half-way up the sides of basin. Cover closely. Adjust heat so that water boils steadily but not rapidly, and replenish with boiling water as required. Steam, allowing 9 hours for 2 quart puddings, and 7 hours for the pint pudding. When ready, either store on a shelf or suspend from a hook in a cool, dry, airy cupboard. Re-steam for 2 hours on Christmas Day.

REGENT'S PUDDING WITH RUM SAUCE

2 oz. stoned raisins
2 oz. cleaned currants
2 oz. flour
2 oz. stale breadcrumbs
2 oz. caster sugar

2 oz. coconut
4 oz. shredded suet
2 eggs
$\frac{1}{2}$ gill milk

Mix all the ingredients together, using either desiccated or freshly grated coconut. Beat well for 10 minutes. Three-quarters fill a greased mould. Cover with greased paper and a pudding cloth. Steam for 3 hours. Turn on to a hot dish. Coat with Rum Sauce. Serves 3.

RUM SAUCE: Beat 1 oz. caster sugar with 1 egg yolk, 10 drops vanilla essence and 1 tablespoon rum till blended, then gradually fold in $\frac{1}{4}$ pint whipped cream.

ROTHESAY PUDDING

2 oz. sieved breadcrumbs
3 oz. shredded suet
4 oz. flour
2 tablespoons raspberry or
  bramble jam

$\frac{1}{2}$ oz. caster sugar
about $\frac{1}{4}$ pint milk
$\frac{1}{2}$ teaspoon bicarbonate of soda
$\frac{1}{2}$ teaspoon vinegar

Mix the crumbs with the suet, flour and sugar. Stir in the jam. When blended, stir in enough of the milk to make a dropable batter. Moisten the soda with the vinegar. Stir into the batter. Three-quarter fill a greased basin. Cover with a greased paper. Steam for 2 hours. Unmould on to a hot dish. Coat with lemon custard sauce. Serves 4 or 5.

CREAM PANCAKES

3 oz. sifted flour
3 tablespoons milk
3 separated eggs
$\frac{1}{2}$ pint cream

lemon and vanilla essence
1 teaspoon caster sugar
jam or marmalade

Mix the flour to a creamy paste with the milk. Beat in egg yolks, one at a time, then stir in cream and 3 drops of lemon and vanilla essence. Stand in a cool place for an hour. Beat egg whites to a stiff froth. Fold into batter. Fry in enough melted butter to cover bottom of pan till lightly browned below. Brown tops under grill. Spread lightly with heated apricot or raspberry jam or orange marmalade. Roll up. Dredge with caster sugar. Serves 3.

COLD PUDDINGS

FLOATING ISLANDS

1 *pint milk*	2 *egg whites*
2 *oz. loaf sugar*	$\frac{1}{4}$ *lb. caster sugar*
$\frac{1}{4}$ *teaspoon vanilla essence*	4 *egg yolks*

Heat milk and loaf sugar slowly in a shallow saucepan until sugar is dissolved. Bring to boil. Add vanilla essence. Beat egg whites until stiff. Stir in caster sugar. Fill a dessertspoon with mixture and drop into the boiling milk. Repeat. Poach them slowly, turning carefully until evenly coated. Remove carefully. Drain on a sieve. Beat egg yolks. Strain 2 or 3 tablespoons of the milk into egg yolks, then strain remainder of milk into the top of a double boiler. Gradually stir in egg yolks. Stir over almost boiling water until custard coats the back of the spoon. Remove from heat. Leave until quite cold. When required, pour the custard into a glass or silver dish, and arrange egg white islands on top. Serves 4 or 5.

APPLE FLOATING ISLAND

8 *large cooking apples*	2 *teaspoons rose water*
caster sugar as required	*rind of 1 lemon*
6 *or 7 eggs*	$\frac{1}{2}$ *pint top milk or thin cream*

Bake the apples in a fireproof dish until tender, but unbroken. Leave until cold, then carefully peel and core them. Rub the pulp through a hair sieve. Beat with caster sugar to taste. Beat the whites of 4 or 5 of the eggs with the rose water, then very slowly mix with the apple pulp. Beat until light and fluffy. Heap on top of a rich custard, served in a shallow glass dish, and made in the following way:

Infuse the thin rind of the lemon in the top milk or cream for 30 minutes, then remove rind. Add 4 to 6 oz. caster sugar. Beat the yolks of 4 eggs and the remaining whites. Gradually stir in the sweetened milk or cream. Cook in the top of a double boiler, over boiling water, stirring constantly until the custard coats the back of a spoon, but do not allow to boil. Serves 6.

BEN NEVIS

2 *quarts chestnuts*
1 *tablespoon caster sugar*
½ *gill Marsala*

1 *teaspoon vanilla essence*
1 *pint thick cream*

Blanch and shell chestnuts. Place in a saucepan. Cover with boiling water. Simmer until tender enough to rub through a sieve, then drain and sieve. Whip lightly with a fork for a moment or two, then beat in sugar, and when blended, gradually stir in the Marsala and the vanilla essence. Pile up in a crystal dish. Whip cream till fluffy, then sweeten it to taste and flavour delicately with Marsala or rum. Pile fluffily on top. For 8 persons.

BRAMBLE AND APPLE FOOL

1 *lb. brambles*
1 *lb. cooking apples*
1 *lemon*
6 *oz. loaf sugar*

½ *cup water*
custard sauce
½ *pint thick cream*

Pick over brambles. Peel, core and slice the apples. Place the fruit in an enamel saucepan. Add the rind and lemon juice, sugar and water. Stir gently till sugar is dissolved. Bring to boil. Simmer gently for 5 minutes. Rub through a sieve. If pulp is sweet enough thin to the consistency of thick cream with custard sauce. If not sweet enough, dissolve a little more sugar in it before adding custard. Pour into a shallow glass dish. Whip cream. Sweeten and flavour with vanilla essence. Pile on top. Sprinkle with pink sugar or a few blanched pistachio nuts. For 6 persons.

THE LAIRD'S CREAM

1 *packet lemon jelly*
1½ *oz. caster sugar*

½ *gill sherry*
½ *pint thick cream*

Dissolve jelly according to instructions on packet and thinly line a fancy mould with it. Leave until set. Meanwhile dissolve the sugar in remainder of jelly and stir in the sherry. When about to set, beat cream till fluffy and fold into mixture. Pour or spoon into mould. When set and chilled, unmould carefully. Decorate to taste with whipped cream and fresh berries. Serves 6 or 7.

CALEDONIAN WHIP

2 *egg whites*
2 *tablespoons sifted icing sugar*
2 *tablespoons strawberry jam*
2 *tablespoons red currant jelly*

Beat all these ingredients together with a wooden spoon until the mixture is so thick that the spoon will stand in it, then turn into a glass dish. Serve with thick or whipped cream. Serves 2.

CARRAGEEN PUDDING

½ *oz. carrageen (sea moss)*
1¾ *pints milk*
1 *piece lemon rind*
1 *pinch salt*
1 *tablespoon granulated sugar*

Wash carrageen and put in a saucepan with milk, lemon rind and salt. Simmer gently till thick. (It will set in a jelly if tested on a plate.) Add sugar and stir till dissolved. Strain the mixture into a rinsed mould or individual moulds. When set, unmould. Serve with cream. Serves 6.

CHOCOLATE MILK JELLY

1¼ *pints milk*
2 *oz. loaf sugar*
1 *lemon rind*
1½ *oz. chocolate*
¾ *oz. powdered gelatine*
¾ *gill water*
a few drops vanilla essence

Pour milk into a saucepan. Add sugar and the thickly pared lemon rind. When sugar is dissolved, bring to boil, then simmer gently until flavoured with lemon to taste. Now remove the rind. Grate chocolate. Bring milk to the boil and add chocolate. Stir until boiling. Meanwhile, soak the gelatine in the water for 10 minutes, then dissolve it slowly over boiling water. Strain into the milk, stirring constantly, then add the vanilla essence. Stir occasionally off stove until the mixture shows signs of thickening, then pour into a wet mould. When set and chilled, turn out gently. Decorate with whipped cream and chocolate shot. Serves 6.

COVENANTER'S CREAM

(R. Russell Steele's recipe)

1 *cup oatmeal*   1 *oz. powdered gelatine*
milk as required   *butterscotch sauce*

Soak the oatmeal over night in a pint of milk. Strain and measure. Make up to a pint again with fresh milk. Melt gelatine over hot water, then stir it into the milk. Pour into a glass dish or glasses. Serve with Butterscotch Sauce. Serves 4.

BUTTERSCOTCH SAUCE: Melt 1 oz. butter. Add 1 tablespoon flour. When frothy, stir in 1 cup of milk. Stir till smooth and boiling, then add 2 tablespoons brown sugar. Stir over low heat till sugar is dissolved. Leave until cold. When required, whip in a tablespoon of cream.

CURDS

1 *quart milk*   2 *teaspoons rennet*
a few grains of salt

Heat the milk to blood heat, 98.4° F. Pour into a shallow glass dish. Stir in the salt and rennet. Allow to set at room temperature. Serve with cream. For 6 persons.

TO VARY: Stir in ½ teaspoon vanilla essence with the rennet.

CURRANT SOLID

4 dessertspoons blackcurrant
  purée
1 tablespoon powdered gelatine

2 tablespoons cold water
4 dessertspoons caster sugar

To make the purée place ½ cup blackcurrants in a saucepan with water to cover. Cover. Stew gently until soft, then rub through a sieve. Soak gelatine in the cold water in a pint measure, for 5 minutes. Stir in purée, sugar and enough water just off the boil to make a pint of mixture. Pour into 4 individual wet moulds or 1 large wet mould, pint size. Chill. Unmould. Decorate with whipped cream and a blob of blackcurrant jam or jelly. Serves 4.

CUSTARD CAKE

1 lemon jelly
angelica and glacé cherries
1 oz. powdered gelatine
¼ pint water
1 pint custard sauce

½ teaspoon vanilla essence
¼ pint cream
½ oz. chopped citron peel
2 crumbled sponge cakes

Line a large wet mould thinly with lemon jelly dissolved according to instructions and about to set. Decorate with sprays of flowers made with angelica stems and glacé cherries. Coat with a thin layer of the jelly. When set, melt the gelatine in the water. Stir into custard sauce. Sweeten to taste. Stir in vanilla essence. Whip cream until stiff. Gradually fold into custard, then lightly stir in citron peel and the sponge cake. Pour into prepared mould. Leave until set and chilled. Unmould. Decorate with whipped sweetened cream and the remainder of jelly, set and chopped. Serves 8 or 9.

SLIGACHAN CUSTARD CREAM

1 oz. powdered gelatine
2 cups water
6 separated eggs

6 oz. caster sugar
2 dessertspoons sherry
strawberry jam as required

Soak gelatine in ½ cup of the water for 5 minutes. Bring remainder of water to the boil. Add to soaked gelatine. Stir till dissolved. Leave till cool. Beat the yolks till honey coloured with half the sugar. Beat egg whites till stiff with remainder of sugar. Stir the dissolved gelatine gradually into the yolks. Fold in egg whites, then slowly stir in the sherry. Pour into a shallow glass dish. Leave until set. Spread with strawberry jam. Decorate with whipped cream. Serves 6.

TO VARY: Substitute brandy for sherry and apricot for strawberry jam.

FAIRY CREAM

1 *pint water*
rind and juice of 1 *lemon*
3 *tablespoons caster sugar*

1½ *tablespoons cornflour*
2 *egg whites*
vanilla sauce

Pour the water into a saucepan. Add thinly peeled lemon rind and strained juice, then the sugar. Stir till dissolved, then bring to boil. Meanwhile, cream the cornflour with cold water. Strain the lemon water. Gradually stir into the cornflour, then pour into pan and stir till boiling. Boil for 4 minutes, stirring constantly. Beat 2 egg whites to a stiff froth. Fold into cornflour mixture. Pour into a wet mould. Chill. Unmould into a glass dish. Pour the sauce round.

VANILLA SAUCE: Mix 1 teaspoon cornflour with ¾ pint milk and 2 egg yolks. Stir in the top of a double boiler over hot water till thick, but do not allow to boil. Sweeten to taste, then flavour to taste with vanilla essence. Chill before using.

YARROW FRUIT CREAM

1 *lb. red currants*
½ *lb. raspberries*
caster sugar to taste

1 *tablespoon cornflour*
vanilla essence to taste

Extract the juice from the currants and raspberries. Pour into a saucepan. Sweeten to taste, then bring to boil. Mix cornflour to a cream with cold fruit juice or water. Stir into fruit juice in pan. Boil from 7–10 minutes, stirring constantly, then add vanilla essence. Pour into a wet mould. Unmould when cold. Decorate with whipped cream and raspberries. Serves 3.

CARSE OF GOWRIE FRUIT SALAD

¼ *lb. wild raspberries*
½ *lb. stemmed red currants*
¼ *lb. stoned cherries*
3 *sliced apricots*
1 *sliced peach*
1 *sliced orange*
3 *sliced bananas*
wine fruit syrup

Place all in a fruit salad bowl. Cover with wine-flavoured syrup. Chill in refrigerator or on ice before serving with thick or whipped cream. Serves 6.

WINE FRUIT SYRUP: Dissolve 1 lb. loaf sugar in 1 pint boiling water. Leave until cold. Strain in the juice of 2 lemons. Add 1 wineglass of claret, a sweet liqueur, such as Curaçao or Cointreau, to taste and a wine glass of sherry.

MIDSUMMER FRUIT SALAD

½ *lb. picked raspberries*
½ *lb. picked strawberries*
½ *lb. stoned cherries*
2 *oz. red currants*
2 *oz. white currants*
ginger or raisin syrup

Rinse all the fruit after picking out the hulls from the berries, and stemming the currants. Drain thoroughly. Place in a glass dish. Cover with ginger or raisin syrup. Chill and serve with whipped cream, flavoured if liked by soaking scented red rose petals in the cream for 30 minutes to 1 hour until delicately flavoured before whipping and sweetening. Serves 6.

GINGER OR RAISIN SYRUP: Stir 12 lumps of sugar in ½ pint water over low heat till dissolved, then boil slowly for 10 minutes. Chill.

Add 1 tablespoon of a sweet liqueur, and ½ pint ginger or raisin wine.

GROSERT FOOL

¼ *pint cold water*   1 *lb. green gooseberries*
8 *oz. lump sugar*   ½ *pint cream*

Pour water into a saucepan. Add sugar. Stir over low heat till dissolved. Bring to boil. Simmer for 10 minutes. Top and tail berries. Add to syrup. Stew gently till tender. Rub through a wire sieve. Whip cream. Fold into the purée. Serve in glasses. *Yield:* 6 glasses.

'HATTED KIT': FORT WILLIAM WAY

There are several ways of making this but I am giving you a simple modern version I enjoyed when caravanning near Fort William.

1 *pint milk*   *thick cream to taste*
1 *pint fresh buttermilk*   *stewed blaeberries*

Bring the milk to the boil. Pour it into the buttermilk and it will curdle at once. Turn into a colander lined with butter muslin, and let the curd drain until all the whey has gone. Turn the curd into a glass dish. It should be solid. Chill. Serve with thick cream and stewed blaeberries.

TO STEW BLAEBERRIES: Rinse berries. Turn into the top of a double boiler with 3 tablespoons water to a pound of fruit. Add sugar to taste. Cover. Cook gently over boiling water till soft and sugar is dissolved, then turn out and chill.

HIGHLAND MIST

Crush 1½ dozen macaroon biscuits into fine crumbs with a rolling pin. Mix to a paste with 2 or 3 tablespoons thin cream. Place a layer in a trifle dish. Cover with a layer of sweetened whipped cream, flavoured with vanilla essence. Repeat layers till crumbs are all added, making the last layer of cream. Chill. Serve with pineapple. For 6 persons.

HYDROPATHIC PUDDING

This is a sister of the English Summer Pudding.

½ *lb. black currants*	½ *lb. caster sugar*
½ *lb. red currants*	*stale white bread or sponge cake*
½ *lb. raspberries*	*custard sauce and cream*

Stalk and pick over the fruit before weighing. Place in a sieve. Lower into a basin of cold water then remove and drain well. Place in a shallow saucepan with the sugar. Stir gently over moderate heat till sugar is dissolved, then simmer gently for about 4 minutes. Line a pudding basin or plain mould with stale bread or with thin slices of sponge cake, arranged so that the pieces fit into each other. Gently pour in the fruit. Place a round of bread or cake, cut to fit, over the fruit. Lay a plate on top and weight it down. It is better to place the basin in a soup plate before weighting it so that if any of the juice overflows the basin it can be returned to pudding. Stand in a cold place for 24 hours before serving. Turn out gently into a trifle dish. Coat with vanilla custard sauce. Serve with cream. Serves 6.

MARY ROSE CREAM

8 *oz. ratafias*	¾ *pint thick cream*
½ *gill brandy*	1 *oz. caster sugar*
4 *oz. apricot jam*	½ *teaspoon vanilla essence*
¼ *oz. powdered gelatine*	2 *oz. maraschino cherries*
½ *gill milk*	

Oil a plain oval, round or oblong mould. Place a row of ratafias in the mould, flat side upwards. Now dip some remaining biscuits in the brandy and put a spot of apricot jam on flat side of each and arrange a row above the first, jammed side downwards, but in between the joins of the biscuits in first row so as to form a basket effect. Continue jamming and adding biscuits in this way until the last row reaches the top of mould. Soak the gelatine in the milk for about 20 minutes, then stir in a small pan over boiling water till gelatine is dissolved. Whip cream. Remove a fourth of it to a small basin. Stir into remainder the gelatine-milk, sugar and vanilla essence. When the cream begins to thicken, place a layer in a mould. Add a few of the cherries and a little of the jam. Continue adding cream and cherries and jam till mould is full. Chill. Unmould carefully into a glass dish. Serves 4 to 6.

MOONSHINE

FROM LANARKSHIRE

$\frac{3}{4}$ oz. powdered gelatine	$\frac{1}{2}$ lb. loaf sugar
1 pint boiling water	2 washed lemons

Soak gelatine in 2 tablespoons cold water, then dissolve in the boiling water. Add sugar and the thinly peeled rind of 2 lemons. Cook over low heat for 10 minutes without boiling, then strain through a hair sieve. Strain in lemon juice. Leave until nearly cold, then whisk till it looks like snow. Chill in a wet mould. Unmould. Decorate with whipped cream and fresh fruit Serves 6.

PINEAPPLE FROST

(Alma's Recipe)

16 marshmallows	3 teaspoons vanilla essence
1 cup milk	$\frac{2}{3}$ cup crushed pineapple
1 beaten egg	1 cup thick cream
pinch of salt	crushed meringue

Heat marshmallows and milk in the top of a double boiler over boiling water until marshmallows are melted. Stir into egg. Return to top of double boiler. Cook, stirring constantly, for 4 to 5 minutes. Remove pan from above hot water. Leave mixture until cool, then stir in salt and vanilla essence. Drain pineapple

139

thoroughly before measuring then fold in. Whip cream until stiff. Fold lightly into mixture. Chill until beginning to set. Serve in sundae glasses. Garnish with whipped cream and crushed meringue. Serves 6.

PORT WINE JELLY

rind and juice of 1 *lemon*
½ *pint cold water*
1 *inch cinnamon stick*
2 *oz. loaf sugar*

1 *dessertspoon red currant jelly*
½ *oz. powdered gelatine*
½ *pint port wine*

Wash and dry lemon. Peel off the rind thinly and extract and strain the juice. Place in a wet enamelled saucepan. Add water, cinnamon, sugar, red currant jelly and gelatine. Stir over low heat until the sugar and gelatine are dissolved, then draw pan to the side of the stove. Cover and stand for 15 minutes. Add port wine. Strain through butter muslin into a jug. When cool, pour into individual glasses. Decorate with whipped cream. Serves 4.

STEWED PRUNES

When we had stewed prunes on Sunday at Memus, they were flavoured when cold with ½ gill of port wine, and served with cream. On weekdays water was substituted for the port and custard sauce for the cream.

1 *lb. prunes*
1 *strip lemon rind*

¼ *lb. caster sugar*
½ *gill port wine*

Wash prunes thoroughly in a basin of cold water. Drain and place in a basin. Add ½ pint cold water. Soak for 12 hours. Turn into a saucepan. Add lemon rind. Cover. Stew very gently till tender in about 1 hour. Sweeten to taste. Cool then add port wine. Serves 6.

RATAFIA CREAM (1851)

Gradually stir two glasses of brandy into a quart of cream. Heat over boiling water, stirring constantly, until hot but not boiling, then gradually stir into 4 or 5 well-beaten egg yolks. Return to the top of double boiler, and stir over hot water until thickened, but do not allow to boil. Flavour to taste with ratafia or noyeau. If liked, the strained juice of a lemon or a Seville orange can be stirred in as well before reheating. Serve in glasses after chilling.

SCOTCH MIST

½ pint cream
caster sugar to taste
¼ teaspoon vanilla essence

2 tablespoons sieved, boiled
   chestnuts

Beat the cream till fluffy. Sweeten to taste with sugar and add vanilla essence. Moisten the chestnuts with a tablespoon of thick cream, then fold in half the whipped cream. Pile in a small glass dish. Coat with remainder of cream. Dip in sherry the ends of enough sponge fingers to encircle the cream. Place fingers, dipped ends downwards, round the cream. Serve with compote of orange or tangerine fingers. Serves 4.

SEA-MOSS MILK JELLIES

If you live by the sea-side where moss is obtainable, you can make jellies from fresh moss when in season. If you've dried the moss it will have to be soaked in the milk for a few minutes before cooking. This moss, which is useful for making moulds suitable for dyspeptics and invalids suffering from chills, is obtainable at health food stores and some general food stores.

There are two ways of making sea-moss jelly. Either pour boiling milk over the moss and let it stand in a warm spot on the stove, or over hot water for 2 hours, or after soaking in the milk, allowing in each case 1 heaped tablespoon to each quart of milk, turn into a saucepan and simmer until thick, then strain into a basin and leave till set, before serving with cream.

LEMON SEA-MOSS JELLY

½ oz. sea-moss
1 pint milk

1 teaspoon sugar
thinly pared lemon rind

Wash and soak moss in cold water to cover for 2 hours. Pour milk into a saucepan. Add sugar, and the rind from ½ a lemon. Simmer very gently for 30 minutes. Pour through a fine strainer into another saucepan. Strain milk over. Simmer for 10 minutes, then pour into serving dish. Leave till set and chilled. Serve with cream.

SEA-MOSS BLANCMANGE

½ oz. sea-moss
1 quart milk
3 strips lemon rind

2 eggs
1 small tablespoon caster sugar

Trim, wash and soak moss in cold water to cover for 2 hours. Place in a saucepan. Add milk and lemon rind. Bring slowly to boil. Separate yolks and whites of eggs. Add sugar to the yolks and beat till blended, then strain the moss over it. Stir till blended, then pour into the top of a double boiler. Cook over boiling water, stirring constantly, till thick like a custard, but do not allow to boil. Remove from heat. Beat egg white till stiff. Fold into mixture. Cool slightly, then pour into a glass dish. Serve with cooked fruit and cream. Serves 8.

SHIVAREE

1 packet orange jelly
1 can apricots
macaroons and ratafias

½ pint thick cream
vanilla essence to taste
rose water to taste

Dissolve jelly according to instructions on packet. When beginning to congeal, stir in half the well-drained apricots. Pour into a glass serving dish. When set, stuff remaining apricots with equal quantity of macaroons and ratafias, crushed and bound with a little of the apricot syrup, and lay on top of jelly, stuffed sides uppermost. Whip cream till stiff. Flavour with vanilla essence to taste and sweeten to taste. Add a few drops of rose water as well. Pile in swirls over the apricots. Decorate with glacé cherries and angelica. For 6 persons.

SLOE GIN JELLY

2½ oz. powdered gelatine   ½ pint sloe gin
½ lb. loaf sugar   1 tablespoon Noyeau
2 pints cold water   whipped cream
3 egg whites   purple grapes

Put the gelatine, sugar, water and egg whites into an enamel saucepan. Stir over slow heat till sugar is dissolved, then whisk until boiling. Simmer gently for 5 minutes, then strain through a jelly bag. Leave until cold. Stir in the sloe gin and Noyeau, then pour gently into a wet mould. Chill. Unmould. Decorate with whipped cream and purple grapes. Serves 8.

STONE CREAM

apricot jam   1 teaspoon vanilla essence
juice of 1 lemon   ½ oz. gelatine
1 wineglass sherry   2 tablespoons water
1 pint cream   ¼ pint hot milk
2 oz. caster sugar

Spread the bottom of a glass dish with apricot jam. Pour in the lemon juice and sherry. Bring the cream to a boil. Stir in caster sugar and vanilla essence. When sugar is dissolved, leave until cool. Soften the gelatine in the water. Add milk. Stir till dissolved. Cool slightly, then stir in the cream. Leave until nearly cold, then pour carefully over the jam. Serves 6.

Note: In some parts of Scotland, ½ lb. apricot jam is used, and only 2 oz. is spread over the bottom of dish. Cover with a layer of the cooled cream, then chill till set. Spread with 2 oz. more of the jam, then cover with another layer of cream. Repeat layers.

TAPIOCA CREAM

1 *pint milk*	3 *tablespoons tapioca*
2 *large tablespoons caster sugar*	½ *pint whipped cream*
vanilla essence to taste	

Heat milk in the top of a double boiler over boiling water. Add sugar when nearly boiling. Stir till dissolved, then add vanilla essence. When boiling, stir in tapioca. Cook until thickened, stirring constantly, then cover and cook until clear in about 15 minutes. Cool in a basin. Fold in the cream. Chill. Ornament with glacé cherries, and angelica, and chopped blanched almonds.

TO VARY: When cold, stir in 2 or 3 tablespoons raspberry jam before folding in the cream, but reduce the sugar to only 1 tablespoon.

TIPSY LAIRD

1 *unfilled sponge roll*	½ *gill Curaçao*
¼ *lb. apricot jam*	1 *oz. ratafias*
1 *tablespoon caster sugar*	2 *oz. blanched almonds*
½ *pint Madeira*	1 *pint rich custard sauce*
½ *gill brandy*	

Cut the roll in 5 equal-thick slices crosswise. Remove top slice. Spread one side of remaining slices with apricot jam. (If preferred, spread 1 slice with apricot, another with greengage, another with strawberry, and the last with marmalade.) Stir the sugar into the Madeira, then stir in the brandy and Curaçao. Place the ratafias flat in a glass trifle dish. Lay the bottom slice of cake on top. Sprinkle with a little of the wine. Build the cake together again in this way until the cake is finished and the wine is used. Spike with the almonds, split in two. Add 1 teaspoon vanilla essence to the custard. Pour custard round. (If preferred, spread the built up cake thinly with melted apricot jam, flavoured with brandy, then spike with the almonds. Another way is to cover with the custard before spiking with the almonds.) Decorate with ½ pint whipped cream. Serves 5.

A TRIFLE OF A ROLL

1 *large sponge roll*   ½ *tablespoon caster sugar*
½ *pint sherry*   ½ *oz. angelica*
½ *pint thick custard sauce*   ½ *oz. crystallized rose petals*
½ *pint thick cream*

Soak roll in the sherry until all is absorbed. Coat roll with the custard. Whip cream till stiff. Sweeten with the sugar. Place half the cream in a second basin and tint it a pale pink. With an icing bag and a rose pipe, ornament first with white roses then with pink. Decorate with rose petals and angelica foliage. Serves 6.

TURFACHIE LEMON SOUFFLÉ

3 *separated eggs*   ½ *pint whipped cream*
6 *oz. caster sugar*   ½ *oz. powdered gelatine*
2½ *lemons*   1 *tablespoon cold water*

Place the egg yolks, sugar, grated lemon rind and strained lemon juice in the top of a double boiler. Whisk over hot water till nearly boiling. (The water should be well below boiling point.) Strain into a basin. Leave until cold, then fold in the cream. Soften gelatine in the water, then dissolve over boiling water. Strain into mixture. Beat egg whites to a stiff froth. Fold into mixture. Leave until into a cream then pour into a dainty soufflé dish with a band of paper tied round. When firm, peel off paper carefully. Strew ratafia crumbs over the top. Serves 4.

TURFACHIE ORANGE SOUFFLÉ: Follow above recipe, substituting orange rind and juice for the lemon and halving the amount of sugar.

VENUS PUDDING

lemon or lime jelly
pistachio nuts
2 *sponge cakes*
a little jam
2 *tablespoons sherry*
6 *ratafias*
¼ *pint thick cream*

½ *pint milk*
caster sugar to taste
¼ *teaspoon vanilla essence*
1 *teaspoon lemon juice*
½ *oz. powdered gelatine*
5 *tablespoons cold water*

Line a jelly mould thinly with liquid lemon or lime jelly. Decorate with a design of chopped blanched pistachio nuts. Set with a thin layer of jelly. Cut each sponge cake into 5 or 6 slices, and spread thinly with apricot, raspberry or strawberry jam. Place in a basin with the ratafias. Sprinkle with the sherry. When all the sherry is absorbed, beat cream till almost stiff, then stir in the milk, sugar, vanilla and lemon juice. Dissolve the gelatine in the water over low heat and stir into mixture. Half fill the prepared mould. Chill until beginning to set. Place the sponge cake and ratafias on top, then fill up with the remainder of cream mixture. Chill. Unmould carefully. Decorate with chopped lemon or lime jelly. Serves 4.

WARRENDER PUDDING

½ *lb. rice*
2 *quarts cold water*
1 *pint milk*
4 *oz. butter*
4 *oz. sugar*

pinch of salt
2 *eggs*
2 *egg yolks*
switched cream as required

Rinse and drain rice. Place in a saucepan. Add water. Stir occasionally till boiling, then boil till soft. Drain on a sieve. Place in a shallow saucepan with the milk, butter, sugar and salt. Bring to boil over moderate heat, stirring frequently. Cover. Simmer very gently, stirring occasionally, for 1 hour. Remove from heat. Cool slightly. Stir in eggs and yolks. When blended, press over the bottom and round the sides of a plain buttered mould to the thickness of about an inch. Chill. Dip mould for a moment into warm water, then fill with switched cream, flavoured with vanilla essence. Turn out quickly. Coat with Marmalade Sauce. Serves 6.

ROSALIE NEISH'S WHITE BONNETS

You can make this dessert either with damsons, red wine and brown sugar or with greengages, white Burgundy and caster sugar.

1 *lb. stone fruit*   2 *oz. sugar*
¼ *pint wine*   1½ *gills thick cream*

See that all the fruit is quite sound. Slit with a silver knife then remove and discard the stones, though half a dozen can be cracked and the kernels added to the fruit if liked. Pour wine into a small shallow saucepan. Add sugar. Stir till dissolved, then add fruit. Cover pan closely. Simmer very gently for 10 minutes. Cool slightly. Turn carefully into a basin. When chilled, spoon into individual glasses. Top each with whipped sweetened cream, flavoured with vanilla essence. Serve 6 or 7.

WHIPT COFFEE-CREAM (1851)

Make ½ pint of strong coffee from 2 oz. of coffee. Whip a quart of sweetened cream and lay aside the froth as it rises on a sieve to drain. (If the froth does not rise well add the white of an egg, lightly beaten, and continue to beat the mixture.) When all the froth has been removed, bring remainder of cream to a boil. Beat three or four egg yolks. Gradually stir in the hot cream, and the coffee. Serve in a glass dish. Cover with the whip.

Note: Whips will be more easily made if the cream can be whipped over ice.

WHIPT SYLLABUB

Grate the rind from a lemon, then extract the juice. Strain juice. Mix the rind and the juice gradually with 1 pint thick cream, then stir in ½ pint white wine. Sweeten with caster sugar if liked. Whip it up well, then put it through a sieve. Pour a little more wine, red or white, into the bottom of the serving glasses. If not using a very sweet wine, add a little sugar. Pour the cream into the glasses. Chill slightly and serve with teaspoons.

SWEET PASTRIES AND PIES

DUNDEE FLAKY PASTRY

½ lb. sieved flour
5 or 6 oz. butter
pinch of salt

1 egg yolk
1 teaspoon lemon juice
cold water as required

Sift flour into a basin. Place butter in a cloth and press out the water with a wringing motion. Sprinkle pastry board with a very little of the flour. Roll out butter in 3 equal-sized thin strips, using more of the flour as required to prevent butter sticking to board. Add salt to flour remaining in basin. Mix well then stir in egg yolk, lemon juice and just enough cold water to form a firm paste. Turn on to floured board. Roll into a long strip. Place a strip of butter on the centre. Fold in three, then turn half round. Seal edges with a rolling pin. Repeat operation twice. Roll out and use as required.

PUFF PASTRY

½ lb. butter
½ lb. flour
¼ teaspoon salt

½ teaspoon lemon juice
about ¼ pint ice cold water

The butter must always be firm. Place on the corner of a floured cloth and roll up like a Swiss roll. Gather one end in your hands and get someone to gather the opposite ends. Now both turn to the right. Keep on turning until moisture shows through the cloth. Sift flour with salt. Stir in lemon juice mixed with enough cold water to make a soft but firm dough. Turn on to a lightly floured board or slab. Knead until smooth. Chill for about 10 minutes, then roll out the dough into a thin rectangle. Mould the butter into an oblong nearly half the size of rectangle and lay on the centre of dough. Fold the ends of the dough over it, making a fold of three. Chill for 15 minutes. Press edges together with rolling pin, then turn the dough half-way round so as to have the folded edge at one side. Press with rolling pin at nearest edge, opposite edge and centre, then roll into an oblong about 18 inches long. Take care to keep the edges as straight as possible and the corners square. Repeat folding, chilling, turning and rolling until pastry has had seven rolls and folds. Chill for 10–15 minutes before using. Bake at 500° F. unless the recipe you are following suggests another temperature.

AMBER PUDDING (1851)

Sift ¼ lb. of fine sugar into a basin. Melt ¼ lb. of butter and add to sugar. Beat six egg yolks. Mix the sugar, butter and egg yolks thoroughly, then season with half a grated nutmeg. Pour into a pie dish lined with puff pastry. Bake in a moderately hot oven for half an hour.

LEMON PUDDING (1851)

Melt ½ lb. of sugar in 6 oz. of unsalted butter. Remove from heat. Leave until cold, then stir in three well-beaten eggs and three well-beaten egg yolks, the strained juice of one lemon and the grated rind of two. When blended, pour into a pie dish lined with puff pastry neatly ornamented round the edges, and bake.

MARMALADE MERINGUE FLAN

8 oz. shortcrust	1 small tablespoon cornflour
1½ heaped tablespoons orange marmalade	1 egg yolk
	caster sugar to taste
1½ cups cold water	1-egg meringue

Line a 9-inch pie plate or open tart tin neatly with the pastry. Prick the centre well and bake in a hot oven, 450° F., until brown. Turn the marmalade into a saucepan. Add 1 cup of the water. Stir over low heat till marmalade is dissolved. Cream cornflour with the remaining water. Stir into the marmalade. Stir till boiling. Remove from stove. Cool slightly. Stir in egg yolk and caster sugar to taste. Cook over boiling water, stirring constantly till thick but do not allow to boil. Remove from heat. Beat egg white till stiff with 2 oz. caster sugar. Pour the marmalade mixture into case. Pile meringue on top. Bake in a slow oven, 325° F., for about 20 minutes till gold-tipped. Serves 6 persons.

ORANGE PUDDING (1851)

Place the grated rind of a large Seville orange, 4 oz. of unsalted butter and 6 oz. of fine white sugar in a mortar. Beat with a pestle till blended, then gradually beat in eight well-beaten eggs. Grate a raw apple into this mixture then put it in a dish lined with pastry, neatly scalloped round the edge. Cross-bar with pastry straws and bake till the pastry is done. The mixture may have three sponge biscuits, soaked in milk, added to it.

OBSERVATION: The quantities given make a very large pudding. Use half quantities for a pudding for three of four persons.

ALMOND CHEESECAKES

PASTRY

6 oz. flour
pinch of salt
3½ oz. butter

1 oz. sieved caster sugar
1 egg yolk

FILLING

raspberry jam as required
2 egg whites
2 oz. caster sugar

2 oz. ground almonds
2 drops ratafia essence

Line 12 patty tins with pastry made as follows. Sift flour and salt. Rub in fat. Stir in sugar and egg yolk. Knead till pliable, then roll out. Place a teaspoon of raspberry jam in bottom of each case. Beat egg whites till stiff. Add sugar. Beat for 10 minutes. Stir in almonds and ratafia essence. Half fill cases. Brush filling lightly with slightly beaten egg white. Bake in a moderately hot oven, 375° F., for about 30 minutes.

TO VARY: Reduce almonds to 1 oz. and stir in 2 teaspoons ground rice. Flavour mixture with almond essence or orange flower water in place of ratafia essence.

APPLE TARTLETS

Line small tartlet tins thinly with shortcrust. Prick well with a fork. Mix 1 chopped apple with 1 dessertspoon cleaned currants or raisins, 2 tablespoons stale breadcrumbs, 1 large tablespoon orange marmalade or golden syrup, the grated rind and juice of a lemon and 1 tablespoon brown or caster sugar. Fill cases with mixture. Cut out covers of pastry to fit top of cases. Brush edge of linings with cold water, and place a pastry lid on each. Bake in a moderately hot oven, 400° F., for about 30 minutes.

APRICOT CHEESECAKES

scraps of pastry (about ¼ lb.) *weight of 1 egg in flour*
1 egg *pinch of baking powder*
weight of 1 egg in butter *3 drops almond essence*
weight of 1 egg in caster sugar

Line greased patty tins thinly with puff, rough puff or flaky pastry. Prick with a fork. Put an eggspoonful of apricot jam in each. Cover with a teaspoon of the sponge mixture. Bake in a moderately hot oven, 425° F., for about 20 minutes.

SPONGE MIXTURE: Beat egg. Cream butter. Add sugar. Beat till creamy, then stir in egg, topped with the flour. Add baking powder and almond essence. Beat for a moment or two.

BALMORAL CHEESECAKES

¾ lb. shortcrust
¼ lb. butter
½ lb. caster sugar
2 beaten eggs
1 oz. stale sponge cake crumbs

¼ oz. cornflour
1 oz. glacé cherries
1 oz. candied peel
1 teaspoon brandy
1 stiffly beaten egg white

Line patty tins thinly with rich shortcrust. Prick the bottoms with
a fork. Beat the butter till softened. Gradually beat in sugar, then
beat in eggs, crumbs and cornflour. Quarter the cherries and
mince the peel. Stir into the batter with the brandy. Fold in egg
white. Half fill cases. Bake in a moderately hot oven, 400° F., for
about 20 mintues.

BRAMBLE TARTLETS

PASTRY

¼ lb. flour
pinch of salt
1 small ½ teaspoon of baking
   powder

3 oz. butter
1 oz. caster sugar
1 egg yolk
½ gill milk

FILLING

½ lb. sweetened steamed
   brambles

¾ gill thick cream

Sift flour with salt and baking powder into a basin. Rub in butter.
Add sugar. Beat egg yolk with the milk till blended, then stir into
flour mixture. When into a smooth dough thinly line tartlet tins
with the pastry. Prick well with a fork. Bake in a hot oven, 450° F.,
until golden brown. Cool on a wire rack. Fill with the brambles.
Decorate with whipped sweetened cream. *Yield:* 20 tartlets.

Note: When blaeberries are in season you can make them into
tartlets in the same way.

ORANGE CHEESECAKES

6 oz. flaky pastry
about 1½ tablespoons orange
   marmalade or apricot jam
1½ oz. butter
1½ oz. caster sugar

½ teaspoon grated orange rind
1 egg
3 oz. sifted self-raising flour
1 tablespoon milk

Make pastry in the usual way and roll into a thin sheet. Line deep patty tins with pastry, pressing in smoothly. Spoon a little jam into each. Cream butter, sugar and orange rind and beat in egg. Stir in flour and milk. Spoon this batter into pastry cases. Cover each with a cross of pastry strips. Bake in a hot oven, 425° F., for 10–15 minutes.

THRUMS CHEESECAKES

8 tartlet cases
apricot or raspberry jam as
   required
1½ eggs

¼ lb. caster sugar
1 oz. rice flour
4 drops almond or vanilla
   essence

Line 8 round tartlet tins thinly with shortcrust. Prick well with a fork and chill in refrigerator. Place an eggspoonful of apricot or raspberry jam in each. Beat eggs. Beat in sugar, rice flour and almond or vanilla essence. Divide the mixture equally between the cases. Dredge well with caster sugar. Place on a baking sheet. Bake in a moderately hot oven, 400° F., for 20 to 25 minutes.

CHOCOLATE ÉCLAIRS

2 oz. butter
¼ pint boiling water
4 oz. sifted flour
4 eggs

whipped cream or confectioner's
   custard (see p. 340)
chocolate icing

Place the butter and water in a small saucepan. Bring to boil. Add flour. Stir till smooth, then continue to stir over slow heat until a smooth ball is formed, leaving the sides of the pan clean. Remove from stove. Beat eggs lightly. When the flour mixture is

153

slightly cool, beat in a little egg at a time, adding just enough to give you a paste that would be easy to pipe, and yet retain its shape when piped. Beat thoroughly. Place in a large forcing bag, fitted with a nozzle, half or ¾ inch size. Pipe on to a greased baking sheet in strips about 4 inches long, taking care to keep the strips of equal size, and placing them about an inch apart. Bake in a moderately hot oven, 400° F., for about 35 minutes until puffy and golden brown. Remove from baking sheet. Make a slit at once down the side of each to allow the steam to escape. Cool on a wire rack. Fill with whipped cream or confectioners' custard. Coat tops with chocolate icing.

CHOCOLATE ICING: Melt 1 oz. grated chocolate in a tablespoon of warm water in the top of a double boiler. Boil for 2 minutes, then cool until tepid. Stir in ¼ lb. sieved icing sugar and 1 teaspoon vanilla essence or rum to taste. Stir only till the sugar is dissolved. Use at once.

FLORENTINES

rounds of puff pastry, 2 inches
   across
raspberry jam as required
2 egg whites

4 oz. caster sugar
2 or 3 drops vanilla essence
1½ oz. blanched almonds

Bake the rounds of pastry on a lightly greased baking sheet in a hot oven, 500° F., till risen and set, then lower to moderate, 350° F., and cook till very pale golden. Remove from oven at once. Cool on a wire rack. Spread each with raspberry jam. Beat egg whites till stiff. Gradually beat in sugar. Stir in vanilla essence. Pile over the jam. Sprinkle with roughly chopped almonds. Bake in a moderate oven, 325° F., Reg. 2, for about 20 minutes, till crisp.

MINCE PIES

Roll out puff, rough puff, flaky or short pastry and cut into rounds. Gather the remainder of pastry together and roll out slightly thinner than the first rounds, and cut into the same number of rounds. Either place the thin rounds a little apart on a lightly greased baking sheet, or line patty tins with them. Place as much mincemeat (*see p.* 324) on the centre as possible. Brush the edges with cold water, and place a remaining thick round on top of each. Make a hole in the top with a skewer, or a slit. Glaze. Bake in a hot oven, 475° F. if using puff, rough puff or flaky pastry, or 450° F. if using shortcrust. Allow 20 minutes.

VANILLA CUSTARD SLICES

½ *lb. puff pastry*
confectioners' custard as
  required
raspberry jam as required

whipped cream as required
6 *oz. glacé icing*
pistachio nuts

Roll pastry on a lightly floured board into a rectangle about a ¼ inch thick. Cut into strips 2½ inches long, and 1 inch wide. Bake in a hot oven, 500° F., till pastry is risen and set, then lower to moderate, 350° F., and bake until crisp and golden. When cool, sandwich in four layers in the following way. Spread one thinly with confectioners' custard. Cover with another layer. Spread this thinly with raspberry jam. Cover with another layer, then with lightly-whipped cream stiffened with gelatine in hot weather. Top with a fourth layer. Spread lightly with the glacé icing, coloured a delicate green. Decorate icing with chopped blanched pistachio nuts.

DATE AND APPLE TART

¼ *lb. dates*
1¾ *lb. apples*
¼ *lb. moist brown sugar*
1½ *teaspoons ground cinnamon*
½ *lb. butter*

½ *lb. flour*
½ *teaspoon baking powder*
8 *oz. caster sugar*
1 *separated egg*
½ *cup milk*

Stone and cut each date in three. Peel, core and slice apples. Place dates and apples in a saucepan with the brown sugar, 1 teaspoon of the cinnamon and half the butter. Cover and stew gently till apples are tender. Cool on a plate. Butter a flan tin. Sift flour, baking powder, 2 oz. of the caster sugar and remainder of cinnamon into a basin. Rub in remainder of butter. Mix to a rather stiff paste with egg yolk and as much of the milk as is required. Divide into two portions, one-third and two-thirds in size. Roll larger portion into a round to fit the tin. Lower it into tin and smooth over the bottom and sides, pushing it well down into the base. Prick well with a fork. Spread the fruit mixture evenly in place, then roll remainder of pastry into a lid. Brush edge of pastry lining with cold water and lay lid on top. Press gently round the edge. Bake in a hot oven, 450° F., for about 30 minutes, then cool. Mix the remainder of caster sugar with the beaten egg white. Spread over the tart. Leave until set. Cut in wedges. Serves 6 or 7.

ABOYNE FRUIT TART

Pick ½ lb. red currants, ½ lb. black currants, ½ lb. cherries and ½ lb. raspberries. Prepare fruit. Place in a pie dish. Sprinkle with 3 tablespoons light brown sugar and ½ cup water. Rub 2 oz. butter and 2 oz. lard into 6 oz. flour sifted with ½ teaspoon baking powder. Mix to a dough with ice-cold water. Roll out thinly. Cover the pie dish with this paste and decorate. Make a hole in the centre. Bake in a hot oven, 450° F., for about 30 minutes. Leave until cold. Dredge with caster sugar. Serve with cream.

MEMUS TART

¼ *lb. flour*   3 *oz. butter*
¼ *lb. cornflour*   1 *separated egg*
¾ *teaspoon baking powder*   ½ *cup milk*
1 *tablespoon caster sugar*

Mix the flour and cornflour with the baking powder and sugar. Rub in butter. Beat up egg yolk with milk. Stir into dry ingredients. Roll out pastry. Butter a shallow pie dish, or plate. Line smoothly with the pastry. Prick well with a fork and ornament the edge. Bake in a hot oven, 450° F., for 15–20 minutes until biscuit colour. Remove from oven and leave until cold. Fill with either cooked fruit or seedless or stoneless jam. Beat egg white till stiff with a heaped tablespoon of caster sugar. Froth lightly over filling.

Return to oven, reduced to 350° F. in temperature. Bake for about 15 minutes. Serve with cream. Serves 4.

AUNT JANE'S PIE

2 *tablespoons caster sugar*
1 *tablespoon butter or*
  margarine
1 *tablespoon cornflour*

2 *tablespoons self-raising flour*
1 *tablespoon plain flour*
1 *egg yolk*
fresh fruit, jam or mincemeat

Cream the sugar with the fat. Sift the cornflour with the other flours. Beat the egg yolk into the fat and sugar then stir in a little of the flour mixture. When blended, gradually knead in remaining flour. Press the pastry on to a greased plate. Prick all over the centre with a fork. Bake in a moderately hot oven, 400° F., until pale brown. Spread with fresh fruit, jam or mincemeat. Beat an egg white till frothy. Sprinkle with a few grains of salt. Beat till stiff, then gradually beat in 2 oz. caster sugar. Beat until smooth and the mixture forms peaks. Pile lightly over the top of the fruit, jam or mincemeat. Bake in a moderately hot oven, 325° F., until the meringue is crisp, in about 20 minutes. Serves 4.

HEAVENLY PIE

This pie should be made 48 hours before it is disturbed. Beat four egg whites with three-quarters teaspoon cream of tartar until stiff but not dry. Gradually beat in $\frac{1}{2}$ lb. caster sugar. Spread evenly in a greased pie plate. Bake in a slow oven, 275° F., for twenty minutes, then increase heat to 350° F. and bake till pale gold. Remove from oven and cool. Beat four egg yolks, $\frac{1}{4}$ lb. caster sugar and the juice of four lemons and grated rind of one till blended. Cook in the top of a double boiler over hot water, stirring constantly until thick, but do not allow to boil. Remove from heat. Cool slightly. Beat $\frac{1}{2}$ pint of cream till fluffy, then gradually beat into the lemon custard. Chill. Fill the meringue case with the custard. Beat $\frac{1}{2}$ pint of cream until fluffy. Sweeten with caster sugar to taste and flavour with vanilla essence. Pile on top in swirls. Serves 6.

VEGETABLES

There is in every cook's opinion no savoury dish without onion and
add for the benefit of youthful gourmets—
> *'But lest your kissing should be spoil'd*
> *The onion must be thoroughly boil'd.'*—1851

Vegetables I have often found a problem in Scotland. The long
hard winters play havoc in the kail-yard. When fresh vegetables
are available my experience is that little imagination is shown in
their preparation for the table. The preparation of root vegetables
is the exception. I was once told that if you want a good helping
of vegetables in Scotland you should order Hotch Potch or Scotch
Broth, or stewed meat and vegetables. The Scottish housewife
seems to spend so much time in preparing her vegetables for
soups and stews that she has little left for preparing them for
accompanying the meat course.

In the Western Isles and on the Western rocky mainland, and in
Orkney and Shetland, certain sea weeds rich in potassium iodide,
and sea moss are often served as a vegetable. Although a trouble
to prepare, they are all very wholesome.

CARROT AND POTATO PIE

6 *large potatoes*	1 *teaspoon salt*
6 *medium-sized carrots*	$\frac{1}{4}$ *teaspoon pepper*
2 *separated eggs*	2 *tablespoons flour*

Peel and grate potatoes. Scrape, wash and grate carrots. Beat egg
yolks with salt and pepper. Gradually stir in the flour. When
smooth, stir into the potato and carrot mixture. Beat egg whites

to a stiff froth. Fold into mixture. Turn into a greased fireproof dish. Bake in a moderate oven, 350° F., for about 40 minutes till golden brown. Serves 4.

MASHED CURLY GREENS

Place a chopped marrow bone or 1 lb. shin of beef in a large saucepan. Cover with cold salted water. Bring to boil. Fill up pan with thoroughly washed curly greens. Boil for 2 hours, then drain thoroughly, and reserve stock for broth. Chop the greens, then mash them. Return to pan. Stir in butter and salt and pepper to taste. Beat until smoothly blended, then turn into a hot vegetable dish. Serves 4.

KAIL, KAIL OR CURLY KALE

There are few Scottish gardens in which kail does not thrive. Even in the hardest winter you see kail runts defying the fiercest gales. It also stands up to severe frost. The greater the frost, the more delicate its flavour.

In bygone days the word kail could be interpreted in two ways— either a green vegetable of the cabbage family or dinner, depending on how it was used. When you asked someone to have kail with you this was a friendly way of giving an invitation to dinner.

Carefully wash a sieveful of kail, then drain thoroughly. Remove any coarse outer blades, then strip the leaves from the stalks. Discard stalks. Throw into plenty of rapidly boiling salted water. Boil briskly, uncovered, until tender, then drain. Season with pepper, and toss in melted butter. Serve with any brown meat. To vary, chop it when boiled and rub through a sieve. Return to pan. Add 2 tablespoons stock, 1 tablespoon unsalted butter, 1 tablespoon cream, and salt and pepper to taste. Stir over moderate heat for a minute or two. Serve with boiled salt beef or roast beef.

In some parts of Scotland, a little oatmeal is sprinkled over kail before serving, and in other parts it is served with bannock or oatcake, and eaten with a spoon.

HEBRIDEAN LEEK PIE

6 *large peeled potatoes*	1 *pint milk*
6 *large leeks*	2 *oz. grated cheese*
2 *oz. butter*	*salt and pepper to taste*
1 *oz. flour*	

Slice potatoes. Line a greased casserole with the potatoes. Cut leeks into inch slices and add. Cover with remainder of potatoes. Melt butter. Stir in flour. When frothy, stir in milk. Stir till smooth and boiling. Stir in salt and pepper to taste and cheese. Pour over vegetables. Cover. Bake in a moderate oven, 350° F., for about 1 hour. Remove lid. Cover the top with a thin layer of wheat flakes. Place a few nobs of butter over flakes. Return to oven. Bake for 15 minutes. Serves 4.

NETTLE HAGGIS

This is a 'Border' dish popular in Dumfries in olden days, but it is sometimes served also South of the Tweed. It is more like porridge than a haggis.

1 *panful of young nettle tops*	3 *tablespoons medium oatmeal*
1 *pint boiling water*	*salt and pepper to taste*
2 *or 3 rashers of bacon*	

Wash nettles thoroughly. Drain and place in a saucepan. Add the boiling water. Bring again to boil. Boil rapidly, with pan uncovered, for about 10 minutes until very tender, then strain, reserving some of the water. Chop as you would spinach. Remove rinds from bacon and any pieces of bone, then fry rashers. Pour the fat from bacon over the nettles, returned to saucepan. Pour ½ pint of the nettle water into another pan. Bring to boil, then sprinkle in the oatmeal, taking care not to allow the water to go off the boil, and stirring constantly. Season with salt and pepper. Stir with a spurtle or theevil until quite thick over low heat, then place over boiling water and cook for about ½ hour, stirring occasionally. Stir in the nettles. Re-season if necessary. In some parts of Scotland the bacon is chopped and added last of all, but in Dumfriesshire the bacon is sometimes served as an accompaniment.

NETTLE TOPS

When winter greens are scarce in early spring, the Highlanders often have to resort to young nettle tops. Pick them with gloved hands. Wash in several changes of salted water, then lift them out of the last 'water', into a saucepan. Do not add any water to the pan. They will cook in the water clinging to the tops. Cover and boil, stirring occasionally, until tender. Add a little butter and pepper and salt as required. Toss lightly. Serve as a vegetable or as a luncheon or supper dish with a poached egg on top of each portion.

GREEN PEA CAKES

2 *cups cooked dried peas*   1 *cup milk*
1 *teaspoon butter*   ¼ *lb. flour*
salt and pepper to taste   ½ *teaspoon baking powder*
2 *well-beaten eggs*

Rub peas while hot through a sieve. Mix with the butter, salt and pepper and eggs. Beat well. Stir in flour sifted with baking powder. Fry in rounds, dropped from a jug into a frying pan containing enough hot fat to cover bottom of pan, till bubbles form on top, then turn and fry on other side. Serve with fried sausages for breakfast. Serves 4.

PEASE PUDDING

½ *pint split peas*   *pinch of sugar*
½ *oz. butter*   1 *small beaten egg*
salt and pepper to taste

Rinse peas thoroughly then soak all night in plenty of cold water. Tie loosely in a piece of butter muslin or a pudding cloth. Place in a saucepan. Add enough boiling water to cover them by about 2 inches. Cover and simmer for 3 to 4 hours till quite soft. Drain thoroughly, then rub through a wire sieve. Beat the butter, salt and pepper to taste, sugar and egg into the purée. Return to the muslin or pudding cloth. Tie up tightly. Simmer for 20 minutes. Serve with boiled pickled pork.

TO BOIL PICKLED PORK: Wash a piece of pickled pork, cut from the leg, allowing 3 to 4 lbs. to the amount of pudding. Cover with lukewarm water. Bring to boil. Skim. Cover and simmer till tender, allowing 25 minutes per lb. and 25 minutes over. Dish up. Pour a ¼ pint of the stock over. Serve with boiled parsnips and pease pudding.

ANGUS POTATOES

6 *baked potatoes*	*pepper to taste*
2 *cups dried, smoked haddock*	*milk to moisten*
1 *teaspoon salt*	6 *pats of butter*
2 *tablespoons butter*	

Cut a slice from the top of each potato and remove the inside. Mash. Flake the fish. Add to potatoes with salt, butter, pepper and milk to moisten to the consistency of mashed potatoes. Beat till light. Refill potato shells with the mixture. Place a dab of butter on top of each. Sprinkle with pepper. Heat thoroughly in the oven. Top each with a pat of butter. Serves 6.

BOILED NEW POTATOES

1 *lb. new potatoes*	½ *oz. butter*
boiling water as required	1 *teaspoon minced chives or*
salt as required	*parsley*

Wash and scrape potatoes, taken if possible straight from the garden to the sink. Place in a saucepan. Add boiling water to cover, then salt, in the proportion of 1 dessertspoon to a quart of water. Boil for 15–20 minutes till soft. Drain. Steam for a moment or two, then remove the lid. Add butter. Toss gently in the butter. Dish up. Sprinkle with chives or parsley. Serves 3 or 4.

A BANFFSHIRE WAY WITH
JACKET POTATOES

7 *jacket potatoes*	$\frac{1}{2}$ *teaspoon minced parsley*
1 *oz. butter*	$\frac{1}{4}$ *teaspoon crushed herbs*
$\frac{1}{2}$ *beaten egg*	*salt and pepper to taste*
3 *oz. sieved breadcrumbs*	*about $\frac{1}{2}$ cup milk*

Scrub, wash and dry potatoes. Cut one end off each so that they can stand on their ends. Remove a slice from each top. Carefully scoop out the inside, leaving a very thin wall of potato. Cream the butter. Stir in egg, breadcrumbs, parsley, herbs, salt and pepper and milk as required. Pack in potato shells. Brush the cut side of the lids with beaten egg white. Place one on each stuffed potato. Bake in a hot oven, 450° F., for about 1 hour until soft. Serve on a hot dish lined with a napkin.

SMALL POTATO PIES

I had forgotten the small potato pies we used to have as children until when lunching just before the war in a hotel in Laghwat in the Sahara they were offered to me.

Remove the peel, very thinly, from large kidney shaped potatoes of equal size. Cut off a slice from the side of each, then scoop out the potato until the lining is $\frac{1}{2}$ inch thick. Fill with minced cooked meat mixed with chopped parboiled onion to taste, seasoned with salt and pepper and flavoured either with a pinch of curry powder or a few drops of ketchup and moistened with gravy. Replace the lids. Place in a shallow greased fireproof dish. Cover and bake for 1 hour in a moderate oven, 350° F., basting occasionally with melted butter or dripping, then uncover, and bake for about 15 minutes till lightly browned. Serve with a sauceboat of hot browned gravy.

CHAPPIT TATTIES

(MASHED)

1 *lb. potatoes*   *½ oz. butter*
½ gill milk   *salt and pepper to taste*

Boil, drain and mash potatoes till smooth. Heat milk and butter till butter melts. Beat into potato with salt and pepper to taste. Beat over the stove till fluffy. Serve in a hot vegetable dish. Ornament the top with a fork.

POTATOES FOR GARNISHING: Add to Chappit Tatties, prepared as above, enough sieved, boiled fresh or frozen peas, or drained canned peas to make the potato green, or boiled spinach can be substituted for peas. Use for piping or for making an oval or circular border when potato piping or border is required.

CHAMP

BASIC. This is a potato dish, equally popular in Northern Ireland. It is a variation of Chappit Tatties.

1½ *lb. potatoes*   *salt and pepper to taste*
½ pint hot milk   *butter to taste*

Peel and boil potatoes in salted water till tender. Drain, then steam for a moment or two. Tilt the lid till the potatoes 'dry off'. Mash with a beetle or wooden spoon until perfectly smooth, then beat in the milk. Season with salt and pepper to taste, then dish up on hot individual plates. Pass the butter round, so that each person can make a hole in the centre of the Champ and pop the butter in. To eat Champ, you dip a forkful of potato into the butter melting in the centre, or 'dunk' it as you please.

CHIVE OR ONION CHAMP: Pick over chives and discard any that are yellow. Rinse, dry and cut in quarter inch lengths. Simmer for 5 minutes in the milk before adding to the Champ, allowing ½ cup to 1½ lb. potatoes. Trim 6 spring onions. Wash thoroughly and chop all the white and green. Cover with rapidly boiling salted water, then drain, and cook in the milk for 5 minutes before adding to the Champ. In some parts of Scotland, both the chives and spring onions are added without cooking.

NETTLE CHAMP: Boil nettle tops in the milk for 10 minutes after chopping. Beat into the mashed potatoes with the milk, then season and serve Champ.

PARSLEY CHAMP: Boil 2 heaped tablespoons chopped, rinsed parsley in milk for 3 minutes, then stir with the milk into the Champ.

PEA CHAMP: Add 1 cup of boiled green peas, cooked in the milk, to the Champ and beat well, then gradually beat in the milk. If preferred, you can sieve the green peas and the milk before adding.

PEA AND ONION CHAMP: Add the peas as given in last recipe and the onion as given in the first variation to the Champ.

RED CHAMP: Boil and mash $\frac{1}{2}$ lb. of potatoes with 1 tablespoon hot milk, 2 oz. butter and salt and pepper to taste. Carefully boil 3 small, young beetroots, then remove skin and mash beetroot. Rub through a sieve. Gradually beat the purée into the potato and re-season as necessary. In the Borders this Champ is usually served with ornaments of sliced, boiled beetroot as a garnish.

In Scotland, potatoes are frequently mashed and mixed with other root vegetables in the following ways:

CLAPSHOT (Orkney): Mash 1 lb. boiled, peeled potatoes with 1 lb. boiled turnips. Add dripping to taste and 1 dessertspoon minced chives. Season generously with pepper and add salt to taste. Beat over the stove till thoroughly blended. Serves 6.

COLCANNON: Crush 1 lb. cold boiled potatoes with a fork. Mash until smooth. Chop 1 lb. cold boiled cabbage. Stir into the potato. Turn into a saucepan. Beat in 2 oz. butter or dripping, $\frac{1}{2}$ teaspoon pepper and $\frac{1}{2}$ teaspoon salt. Stir over low heat till fat is melted and blended with the vegetables. In some parts of Scotland, Colcannon is served with no further cooking. In other parts, the mixture is baked in a greased pie dish in a hot oven for about 25 minutes, then turned out. It goes well with cold lamb or mutton. Serves 6.

Note: In the Highlands, 2 or 3 scraped, medium-sized boiled carrots and 2 peeled boiled turnips are mashed till smooth, and added to the potato and cabbage with a tablespoon of brown gravy and a dash of pepper.

KAILKENNY (East of Scotland): This is simply Colcannon made with 2 lb. potatoes and 2 lb. cabbage and salt and pepper to taste, but no fat is added, only about a cup of cream.

RUMBLEDETHUMPS: This is what my father used to call a simple dish of Colcannon, made of equal quantity of boiled cabbage and potato, flavoured with chopped chives or the green of spring onions, moistened with plenty of butter and seasoned with salt and pepper.

POTATO FRITTERS

8 *large kidney potatoes*
2 *eggs*
1 *tablespoon minced lean ham*

1 *tablespoon grated breadcrumbs*

This is an adaptation of one of Lady Harriet St Clair's famous recipes. Parboil potatoes, then drain and cut in slices about ½ inch thick. Beat the eggs with the crumbs and ham. Dip each potato slice in the egg mixture and fry in hot deep olive oil.

POTATO AND SPINACH DUMPLINGS

3 *tablespoons sieved boiled spinach*
1 *beaten egg*
3 *tablespoons melted butter*

1 *lb. grated potatoes*
salt and pepper to taste
sifted flour as required

Mix the spinach with the egg, butter, potato and salt and pepper to taste till thoroughly blended. Stir in enough flour to make a light dough. Shape small equal-sized portions into balls about the size of a golf ball. Place in a saucepan of boiling salted water to cover. Cover pan. Boil steadily but not rapidly for 15 to 20 minutes. Serve for breakfast coated with hot bacon fat and garnished with chopped crisply fried bacon, or cook in boiling stock when boiling salt beef. Serves 4.

POTATO AND SWEDE CAKES

2 *cups mashed potatoes*   *salt and black pepper to taste*
1 *cup mashed swede*   *pinch of grated nutmeg*
1 *teaspoon chopped onions*   *beaten egg to moisten*
2 *teaspoons chopped parsley* *seasoned flour*

Mix all the ingredients except the flour in order given. Shape into flat cakes about 3 inches across. Dip in seasoned flour. Fry in shallow hot beef dripping until golden brown below, then turn and brown on other side. Serve with meat loaf or fried or grilled chops or steaks. Serves 4 or 5.

STOVED POTATOES

cooked roast beef bones or   10 *or* 12 *sliced potatoes*
    scraps of lamb or mutton   ·2 *or* 3 *sliced, peeled, medium*
    cutlets   *onions*

Boil bones in water to cover for 2 hours. Add sliced potatoes, onions and plenty of pepper and salt to taste. Cover. Simmer for 1 hour. Serve with cold meat. Serves 4.

STOVED POTATOES FROM SCRATCH

1 *oz. butter, dripping or*   ½ *lb. onions*
    margarine   ½ *pint hot water or mutton stock*
2 *lb. potatoes*   *salt and pepper to taste*

Melt fat in a saucepan. Wash, peel and slice potatoes into pan. Peel, slice and add onions. Toss in the fat for about a minute, then add water or stock and salt and pepper. Cover. Bring slowly to boil. Simmer gently for fully 1 hour, stirring occasionally to prevent burning. When ready, the potatoes should be tinged here and there with brown. Serve with cold, boiled or roast mutton or cold roast lamb. Serves 6.

TURNIP PURRY

Clean and peel small yellow turnips, taking care to cut off all wooden or stringy portions below the peel. (If large turnips are preferred, quarter them.) Boil in plenty of salted water till tender. The time required depends on the age of the turnips and their size. When tender, drain thoroughly, then mash into a purée. Sometimes they are squeezed through a colander or potato masher. Reheat with unsalted butter to taste, then season with salt, white pepper and with a little ground ginger if liked. I prefer grated nutmeg to ginger. Serve with boiled chicken, rabbit or veal.

SCOTTISH WAY WITH VEGETABLE MARROW

1 *cup chopped, cooked lamb*
stock or water as required
1 *teaspoon cornflour*
1 *cup canned or stewed*
  tomatoes
3 *chopped onions*

salt and paprika to taste
1 *cup boiled rice*
1 *medium-sized vegetable*
  marrow
¾ *pint cheese sauce*

Place meat and stock or water to cover in a saucepan. Cover and simmer for 10 minutes. Cream cornflour with water, and add. Stir till boiling. Add tomatoes, onion, salt and paprika to taste, and rice. Halve and peel marrow. Remove any seeds and pith. Parboil in salted water to cover for 10 minutes. Drain. Place half the marrow in the bottom of a greased, fireproof dish. Stuff. Cover with remaining half of marrow, then with cheese sauce. Sprinkle slightly with sieved breadcrumbs. Bake in a moderate oven, 350° F. for ¾ hour. Serves 4.

SEA WEED

When I was in the Hebrides a short time ago, I asked an old fish wife what she was picking along the shores of one of the sea lochs. She winked at me, and said, 'I am gathering my dinner.' It was not until I visited a farm house on the shores of Loch Drynoch in Skye that I learned about the uses of Tangle, Sloke and Dulse, as well as of sea moss, known also as carrageen. To many of the Islanders, sea weeds take the place of spinach in their diet.

DULSE

This is equally popular cooked or raw in Isle of Barra. If you have a peat fire, and an old-fashioned Scottish brander, you could cook it as you would cook a chop or a steak, over the hot embers.

BOILED: Wash freshly gathered dulse thoroughly in sea water for preference, otherwise in salt water, then drain well. Simmer in water to cover till very tender, then strain thoroughly and chop. Melt enough butter to cover the bottom of the saucepan. Add dulse and stir till hot and coated with the butter. Season with salt and pepper to taste.

FRIED: Wash thoroughly in sea water, then drain. Fry in melted butter till it turns colour. Season with pepper.

STEWED: Wash thoroughly as before to remove all sand and grit. Drain and place in a saucepan. Add milk to cover, and butter and salt and pepper to taste. Simmer very gently till tender, in between 3 and 4 hours. Serve with brown bread or oatcakes.

SLOKE

Sloke should not be gathered except after a spell of frost. Wash it in several changes of salt water until all the grit and sand are removed, then drain thoroughly. Pour enough water into a sauce-pan to cover the bottom. When boiling, add sloke, and stir until the water boils again. Simmer for 3 to 4 hours until tender, then season with salt and pepper to taste. Add butter and cream to taste. In the Western Isles this is sometimes served as a supper dish with oatcakes, or as a second vegetable for dinner when mutton is the main course.

In Barra, it is soaked after thorough washing in fresh cold water containing a pinch of bicarbonate of soda, before cooking, then it is cooked with only enough sea water to cover the bottom of pan and mashed frequently with a wooden spoon or beetle while cooking, until reduced to a pulp. It must not be allowed to boil, or even simmer. Season with salt and pepper when ready, and toss in butter to coat. Serve piping hot in a ring of mashed potatoes.

TANGLE

Wash thoroughly in several changes of sea water, then toss in a cloth till dry and serve raw with a French dressing if liked.

SEA WEED CAKES

Take any boiled sea weed and mix it to taste with butter and cream, and season with salt and pepper. Stir in enough medium oatmeal to stiffen. With floured hands, shape into small flat cakes. If preferred, toss in oatmeal. Fry in hot bacon fat. Turn when brown and brown on the other side. Serve for breakfast.

SEA MOSS (CARRAGEEN)

Sea moss is gathered in April and May. Before cooking it, wash it very thoroughly in three or four changes of cold salted water, then clip off the roots and dark stems with scissors. Rinse and drain moss and dry in one of the following ways:

1. Spread out on the grass. Leave for several days while it changes from brown to a creamy white. It is best to bleach sea moss in showery weather. If the weather is dry, keep sprinkling it with fresh water while it changes colour.

2. Spread it on the rocks, or on a wide window-sill with a tray below, and let it bleach till creamy white.

When perfectly dry, place in paper bags, or in aluminium foil and suspend from a hook in a dry place.

EGG MAYONNAISE SALAD
(Chef Alexander Guild's recipe)

Grate up carrot, radishes, spring onions and turnip to taste. Sprinkle with lemon juice and stir in mayonnaise to taste. Shell and chop hard-boiled eggs. Bind them with a little salad cream, then stir in chopped, peeled, firm tomato and chopped, peeled cucumber to taste. Arrange on a bed of crisp lettuce leaves. Coat with the vegetable mayonnaise.

DUNDEE POTATO SALAD

½ *lb. sliced cold potatoes*
1 *dessertspoon minced parsley*
2 *egg whites*
freshly ground pepper to taste

mustard to taste
4 *tablespoons vinegar*
2 *tablespoons cream*

Place the potatoes in a salad bowl. Sprinkle with the parsley. Beat the egg whites till stiff. Beat in pepper and mustard to taste, then vinegar. Beat till thick, then lightly stir in the cream. Pour over the potatoes. Serve immediately. Serves 3.

MEAT

Mickle meat, mony maladies

Nowhere in all the world can you find better beef and mutton than in Scotland. Scottish beef is universally famed, and the small mountain wether mutton is delicious.

Pork is not so popular as it is across the Borders. It was rarely met with until towards the end of the nineteenth century. In early days, beef hams, haggis, potted heid, sheep's head, minced collops, reisted mutton hams and venison graced the Scottish board when meat was wanted.

BEEF OLIVES AND SAUSAGES

1 *lb. lean stewing beef*
herb stuffing (see below)
2 *tablespoons flour*
½ *teaspoon salt*
½ *teaspoon pepper*

1 *tablespoon dripping*
½ *lb. beef sausages*
1 *teaspoon chopped parsley*
about ¾ pint beef stock or water

Cut beef into thin slices about 3 inches long and 1½ inches wide. Divide stuffing between the strips, placing a portion at one end of each, then roll up. Tie in place with boiled string. Mix the flour with the salt and pepper. Dip olives in flour. Fry in dripping till brown. Scald and cold-dip sausages, then dry and skin. Divide each in 3 equal portions. Arrange half the olives in the bottom of a greased casserole. Cover with the pieces of sausage then with remainder of olives. Sprinkle with remaining flour and the parsley. Cover with beef stock, or water flavoured with meat extract. Cover closely. Cook in a slow oven, 300° F., for about 2½ hours. Serve with mashed potatoes and a green vegetable. Serves 4 or 5.

STUFFING FOR BEEF OLIVES: When I learned to make the olives I had not met garlic. Now I rub the mixing bowl with a cut clove of garlic before preparing stuffing in this way: fry a chopped medium-sized onion in 1 tablespoon butter till clear. Stir in 1 cup chopped celery and ½ pint of beef stock. Pour into bowl. Add ½ pint sieved breadcrumbs, 1 teaspoon chopped parsley, ½ teaspoon crushed thyme, and mix well. Turn into saucepan. Stir well till mixture leaves the sides of the pan clean, then cool slightly and use.

BEEF-STEAK WITH CUCUMBERS (1851)

Pare and slice three large cucumbers and as many onions. Fry them in butter, and when brown, add a ½ pint of gravy. Beat and season some rump steaks and fry them. Place them in a very hot dish. Pour the cucumber sauce over them.

SCOTCH BRAISED BEEF

¼ lb. carrot	4 *allspice berries*
½ lb. celery	10 *peppercorns*
¼ lb. turnip	1 *blade mace*
½ lb. Spanish onions	1 *sprig marjoram*
¼ lb. streaky bacon	1 *sprig parsley*
2 oz. butter	1½ *pints stock*
1½ lb. topside of beef	2 *oz. flour*

Wash and prepare vegetables before weighing, then cut into inch-square dice. Remove rind from bacon and cut to the same size. Melt butter in a shallow saucepan. When smoking hot, add vegetables and bacon. Fry all until light brown, stirring frequently, then remove from pan. Drain off a little of the butter, and fry the meat until brown all over in what remains. Remove from pan. Pour off remainder of butter, leaving only the meat essence in the pan. Place the vegetables, bacon and spices and herbs tied in a muslin bag in the pan and lay meat on this bed. Pour in stock.

173

Cover closely with greased paper, then with a lid. Simmer very gently on top of the stove till meat is tender. (If preferred, place bacon, vegetables and meat in a casserole, after browning, then pour the stock into pan. Boil up and pour over meat, and cover with paper and lid. Braise in a slow oven, 300° F., until tender, turning occasionally, in about 2½ hours.) Dish up beef when cooked on a hot ashet. Remove spice and herb bag. Mix flour to a cream with a little cold stock. Strain into the gravy. Stir till smooth and boiling, adding more stock if necessary. Stir in, if liked, ½ oz. of glaze. Season to taste. Strain over the meat and arrange the vegetables round. Garnish if liked, with a few boiled green peas. Serves 4.

TO DRESS A BREAST OF MUTTON (1851)

Cut off the fat, parboil the meat, egg it and strew over it shredded parsley and breadcrumbs. Stick pieces of butter all over it. Brown it in the Dutch oven, and serve with Caper or Robert Sauce, or with stewed cucumbers.

ROAST GIGOT OF MUTTON

Wipe a leg of mutton with a damp cloth. Make slits with a sharp knife here and there over the skin. Tuck a sliver of garlic into each. Place on a trivet in a baking tin. Roast in a moderate oven, at 350° F., allowing 15–20 minutes per lb. Place on a hot ashet with the thickest part upwards, and the bone to the left. Place before the carver in this position. Serve with Onion Sauce, brown gravy, roast potatoes and mashed turnip or swede, or boiled haricot beans, tossed in butter, and red currant jelly if liked.

TO STUFF LEG OF MUTTON BEFORE ROASTING: Mix 2 oz. minced bacon with 2 finely-minced shallots, 1 teaspoon minced parsley, ½ teaspoon crushed herbs, then rub 2 tablespoons margarine or shredded suet into 4 tablespoons of breadcrumbs, and stir in the bacon mixture. Season with salt, pepper and paprika. Moisten with milk or stock. Press into the cavity of a boned leg, then sew up and roast.

PROSEN HOT POT

1 *lb. pieces of neck of mutton*   *salt and pepper to taste*
2 *peeled medium-sized onions*   *3 or 4 tomatoes*
1 *large carrot*

Wipe the mutton and cut into small pieces. Slice the onions and carrot very thinly. Place layers of mutton, onion and carrot, each seasoned with salt and pepper, alternately in a greased casserole or hot pot jar. Scald, chill and peel tomatoes. Cut into enough slices to cover the mixture in hot pot. Season with salt and pepper. Bake in a very slow oven, 300° F., until the meat is tender in 2–2½ hours. Serves 3 or 4.

SHOULDER OF MUTTON (1851)

Keep the shoulder as long as possible without spoiling. Half roast it. Score it on both sides as for broiling. Heat four anchovy fillets, finely chopped in a saucepan. Remove pan from stove. Add ½ pint rich brown gravy, ½ pint port wine, 1 teaspoonful mushroom catsup, 1 teaspoonful walnut catsup, pepper to taste, a pinch of cayenne pepper and salt if necessary. Stir till blended. Pour into a small, shallow baking dish. Baste the joint with this sauce, then slip the container under the joint and continue roasting so that the drippings fall into the sauce. Baste the mutton every fifteen minutes till ready. Rub a hot ashet with garlic. Place shoulder on dish. Skim the dropt gravy. Pour it over the mutton.

BRAISED SHOULDER MUTTON CHOPS

4 *shoulder chops*   *½ cup diced parnsip or turnip*
salt and pepper to taste   *½ cup sliced celery*
½ cup minced onion   *1 cup mutton stock*
1 *cup diced carrot*

Melt enough butter to cover a frying pan, large enough to take 4 chops. Heat slowly, then add chops. Fry till brown below, then turn and brown on other side. Season with salt and pepper. Mix the vegetables together and place in the bottom of a casserole. Lay the chops on top. Add stock. Cover closely. Bake in a slow oven, 300° F., until tender in about 1½ hours. Serve from casserole with boiled new potatoes, or mashed potatoes. Serves 4.

MUTTON AND POTATO PIE

1 *lb. neck of mutton*	*salt and pepper to taste*
2 *small black puddings*	6 *large peeled potatoes*
1 *large sliced peeled onion*	*cold water as required*

Wipe mutton with a damp cloth and cut into neat pieces. Place in the bottom of a greased fireproof dish. Halve each black pudding and lay on top of the mutton. Add the onion. Season with salt and pepper to taste. Slice potatoes on top. Season with salt and pepper to taste. Add enough cold water to come three-quarters of the way up the side of dish, and baste the seasoning into the meat. Cover and cook in a slow oven, 300° F., for about 2½ hours, uncovering after 1¾ hours to allow potato to brown on top. Serves 4.

PORK CHOPS À LA REINE

¾ *lb. loin pork chops*	3 *lumps sugar*
3 *medium-sized apples*	*salt and pepper to taste*
1 *large peeled onion*	2 *tablespoons sherry*

Trim the chops neatly, then wipe with a damp cloth. Peel, core and slice the apples into a small saucepan. Chop and add the onion. Add sugar, salt and pepper to taste, and the sherry. Cover and simmer very gently, stirring occasionally, until the apples are tender. Meanwhile, braise, fry or grill the chops. Serve with brown gravy, the apple sauce, creamed potatoes and green peas. Serves 2.

SADDLE CAKES

GARELOCH RECIPE

1 *lb. pork sausage meat*　　6 *poached eggs*
dripping as required　　*salt and pepper to taste*
6 *rounds of fried bread*

Divide the sausage meat, well-seasoned, into 6 equal portions. Shape each into a flat round cake. Fry in dripping on both sides. Place each on a round of fried bread. Top each with a poached egg. Season with salt and pepper. Dredge lightly with finely minced parsley. Serves 6.

VINEGAR CURRY

1 *oz. dripping*　　1 *large teaspoon curry powder*
1 *lb. meat*　　½ *pint stock*
3 *large peeled onions*　　*salt to taste*
3 *dessertspoons desiccated*　　1 *tablespoon malt vinegar*
　coconut　　1 *teaspoon chilli vinegar*
½ *teaspoon ground allspice*

Melt the fat slowly in a shallow saucepan. Cut up the meat into small pieces and fry slowly until brown all over, then add all the ingredients in order given, except the vinegars. Cover and simmer very gently for 2 hours, stirring occasionally, then stir in the vinegars. Cook for a minute or two, stirring constantly, then pile in the centre of a ring of boiled rice. Serve with chutney. Serves 4.

ROAST KID

In the eighteenth century, roast kid was considered a delicacy in the Hebrides and Highlands.

1 *young kid*　　½ *pint lamb or mutton gravy*
marinade as required　　1 *wineglass claret*
　(*see p. 344*)　　*seasoned flour as required*
strips of bacon　　1 *tablespoon red currant jelly*

177

Soak kid in marinade, basting it frequently for about 4 hours, then drain well and dry. Bind it with strips of bacon. Place on a rack in a baking tin. Cover with greased paper. Roast for 2–2½ hours in a slow oven, 300°–325° F. Half an hour before dishing up, dissolve jelly in gravy. Add claret. Remove paper and bacon from kid. Dredge it all over with seasoned flour and baste with the dripping. Heat sauce. Serve in a hot sauceboat. Serve kid with roast potatoes and French beans or cauliflower or spinach. Serves 6–8.

AYRSHIRE BEEF GALANTINE

½ lb. sieved breadcrumbs
¼ teaspoon ground mace
½ teaspoon meat extract
½ teaspoon salt
black pepper to taste

1 lb. minced steak
1 lb. minced Ayrshire bacon
¼ pint stock
2 beaten eggs
2 shelled hard-boiled eggs

Mix the crumbs with the seasonings, adding ¼ teaspoon grated nutmeg if liked. Stir in steak and bacon, then add stock to eggs. Stir well and mix with the crumbs and meat. When thoroughly blended, knead lightly into an oblong. Halve eggs and place end to end along centre of meat. Shape carefully into a roll with floured hands. Tie in a buttered cloth. Place in a saucepan half full of boiling stock. Bring to boiling point. Add a slice or two of carrot and onion to stock and season if necessary. Cover. Simmer gently for 2 hours. Press between 2 plates. When cold, brush with brown or tomato glaze. Garnish with parsley or watercress. Serves 6 to 8.

ROLLED, CURED PORK. Usually boiled and served cold, or sliced and fried or grilled.

CURRIED MEAT

½ lb. rump steak   ½ pint beef stock
4 large peeled onions   1 teaspoon vinegar
3 oz. butter   salt and pepper to taste
1 teaspoon curry powder 1 tablespoon disiccated coconut
¼ teaspoon allspice   boiled rice

Wipe steak with a damp cloth. Cut into dice. Slice onions. Melt butter in a shallow saucepan. Add steak. Fry slowly till brown, then slice in onions. Fry for a moment or two, then stir in curry powder, allspice and stock. Stir till boiling. Add vinegar. Season with salt and pepper. Add coconut. Simmer gently, stirring occasionally, for 2 hours. Serve on a hot, flat dish. Arrange boiled rice round, allowing 1 teacup of rice before boiling. Serves 3.

FINKADELLA

½ lb. lean minced beef   beef stock
½ oz. butter   salt and pepper to taste
1 slice bread ¼ inch thick 1 tablespoon grated onion
thin cream   5 oz. shredded suet

Pound the beef in a mortar with the butter until smoothly blended. Remove crusts from bread. Moisten with equal quantity of thin cream and weak beef stock until it is like a thick sauce. Gradually beat into the meat. When blended, season with salt and pepper, then stir in the onion and suet. Mix thoroughly, then shape into small equal-sized balls with lightly-floured hands. Place in boiling weak beef stock or soup. Cover and boil for 45 minutes. Serves 2.

POTTED HOUGH

2 lb. hough   4 whole cloves
1 nap bone   salt and pepper to taste

Place the hough, bone and cloves in a large saucepan. Well cover with cold water. Bring slowly to the boil. Skim, then simmer gently but steadily for 6 hours. Strain the stock into a clean saucepan. Remove all the meat from the bones, then remove any gristle or fat from the meat. Mince the meat and add it to the stock. Bring again to the boil. Season with salt and pepper. Stand for a ½ hour. Stir, then pour into small wet moulds. Turn out as required. Serve with salads. This potted hough keeps well.

MINCE (SCOTCH COLLOPS)

1½ lb. minced steak	¾ pint beef or bone stock
1½ tablespoons beef dripping	1 tablespoon oatmeal
2 small peeled onions	salt and pepper to taste

Use meat from the topside or shoulder. Melt dripping in a shallow saucepan. When smoking hot, add finely chopped onions. Fry slowly till onion is clear, then add steak, and brown, stirring constantly to prevent lumping. Stir in stock, oatmeal, and salt and pepper to taste. Cover and simmer gently for about ½ hour. Serve garnished with sippets of toast or in a circle of mashed potatoes. serves 4–6.

TO VARY: 1. Substitute 2 handfuls of breadcrumbs for the oatmeal when the dish is almost ready. Add a dash of mushroom ketchup or Worcester sauce if liked. Garnish with sippets of fried bread.

2. Fry 1 dessertspoon curry powder with the meat. Omit oatmeal and thicken the gravy slightly with cornflour creamed with water before dishing up.

3. Add small dumplings, 6 or 12, depending on how many are wanted per person, and upon the size, or 1 oatmeal pudding per head, pricked with a fork, about 20 minutes before dishing up.

4. Serve each portion of 'collops' thickened only slightly, with a poached egg on top.

MUTTON SAUSAGE CAKES

1 lb. lean mutton	freshly ground black pepper to taste
½ lb. fat pork	
½ teaspoon salt	½ teaspoon crushed herbs

Remove any bone from mutton before weighing, then put mutton and pork through a meat grinder. Stir in salt, pepper and herbs. When blended, pack into a straight-sided jar, 2½ inches in diameter. Store in a cool larder, or refrigerator, until required. When required, slice and fry like pork sausage-meat. Garnish with fried apple slices, or grilled halved tomatoes. Serves 6.

BREAKFAST OR HIGH TEA: Serve with grilled, halved tomatoes, or fried mushrooms.

LUNCH OR SUPPER: With fried mushrooms and potato cakes.

DINNER: With creamed or scalloped potatoes and green peas. Garnish each with a fried apple slice.

POLONI

½ lb. minced steak	salt and pepper to taste
½ lb. minced, lean ham	1 dessertspoon ketchup
1 cup stale breadcrumbs	1 beaten egg

Mix all ingredients in order given. Pack into a well-greased, straight sided jam jar. Steam for 2 hours. Cool slightly, then carefully turn out. Leave until cold. Brush with melted glaze. If you haven't a straight-sided jam jar, steam in a covered basin.

TO MAKE GLAZE: Dissolve ¼ oz. powdered gelatine in 1 cup hot water. Add salt and pepper to taste, 1 tablespoon ketchup and 1 teaspoon browning. Leave until almost cold before using.

PORRIDGE MEAT LOAF

½ lb. minced steak	½ teaspoon crushed herbs
½ cup minced leek	salt and pepper to taste
½ cup minced onion	½ cup beef stock
2 cups oatmeal porridge	

Mix all ingredients till blended. Pack evenly into a well-greased loaf tin dredged with flour. Stand tin in a baking tin, containing hot water coming 1 inch up the side of loaf tin. Bake in a slow oven, 325° F., for about 1 hour. Serve hot or cold with salad and pickles, or use cold for sandwiches.

SCOTCH COLLOPS (1790)

Cut collops from the leg or best end of the neck of veal in rounds rather larger than a crown piece. Mix one egg with one tablespoon of creamed butter, half a clove of garlic minced and bruised, minced parsley and herbs to taste, and minced peeled mushrooms to taste. Dip collops in seasoned flour, then in the egg mixture. Fry in hot butter till brown below, then turn and fry on the other side. Serve with Celery Sauce.

GRANNY CRAIG'S SAUSAGES

1 *lb. pork sausages*
1 *tablespoon butter*
2 *tablespoons flour*
1 *pint beef stock*

1 *finely minced medium-sized onion*
salt and pepper to taste

Put the sausages into a pan of cold water and bring to boil. Drain and cover with cold water. Chill for 2 or 3 minutes, then skin carefully. Melt butter in a shallow saucepan. Stir in flour. When frothy, stir in stock. Bring to boil, stirring constantly, then add onion, salt and pepper to taste and sausages. If liked, stir in a drop or two of Worcester sauce. Cover and simmer for about 20 minutes. Place a mound of hot mashed potatoes on a flat, hot dish and lean the sausages, equal distance apart, up against the potato. Pour the sauce round.

HAGGIS

Fair fa' your honest, sonsy face,
Great chieftain o' the puddin' race.

ROBERT BURNS

If you wish to be initiated into the mysteries of a haggis, take the stomach bag of a sheep. Wash it till perfectly clean with cold water. Turn it outside in. Scald and scrape it with a knife, then steep in salted water until required. Now parboil heart, lights and liver of sheep. Grate liver. Put other parts through a meat grinder with ½ lb. of mutton suet. Toast 1 lb. of pinhead oatmeal before the fire, or in the oven. Mix ingredients together with 3 chopped onion, parboiled before chopping. Season to taste with salt and pepper, then fill the bag and, before sewing, add a little of the water in which the onions were parboiled. Some cooks add only the onion water for flavouring and throw away the onions. Sew up bag, taking care it is not too full, so as to allow oatmeal to swell. Prick the bag all over with a long needle to prevent bursting. Put on an enamel plate in a saucepan with enough boiling water to cover. Boil for 4 or 5 hours, keeping the haggis constantly covered with water. Place on a hot flat dish. Remove the threads. Serve with a spoon accompanied by hot mashed potatoes, and whisky.

WITH HIGHLAND HONOURS: When haggis is served at Scottish functions, a Highlander, kilted and plaided and all, is usually engaged to carry in the lordly pudding. Before him, kilted and plaided to match, walks a piper screeching out an eldricht air like 'Where ha'e ye been a' the day, bonnie laddie, Hielant laddie?' or some such national air. Then, when the haggis arrives at the head of the table, with a great flourish of pipes it is laid before the host and served by him, or lifted again after he has cut the thread and carried round so that the diners can help themselves.

THE ROYAL TOAST: It is usual to serve small glasses of whisky with haggis. It is sipped neat in between mouthfuls. Some there are who pour it over the haggis. In times gone by we used to leap on our chairs as the haggis was piped in, put our right foot on the table, toss off the fiery whisky and throw our glasses over our shoulders onto the floor. Such was the royal toast with which haggis was welcomed. Nowadays we sip delicately.

PASTIES AND PIES

BACON AND POTATO ROLY POLY

¼ *lb. bacon*
4 *large potatoes*
1 *heaped teaspoon minced*
  parsley

1 *large onion*
salt and pepper to taste
pinch of crushed herbs
½ *lb. suet crust*

Remove rind from bacon and chop bacon. Peel potatoes and onion, and cut both into dice. Stir in parsley, salt and pepper to taste, then bacon and herbs. Roll out pastry thinly into a rectangle. Spread the filling evenly over to within ½ inch of edge. Roll up. Tie in a floured, scalded cloth. Steam for at least 2½ hours. Serve with brown gravy and cabbage or kail. For 3 persons.

FORFAR BRIDIES

J. M. Barrie, who was a native of Kirriemuir, affectionately called 'Thrums', a little country town in Angus near my old home, mentions these pasties in his famous book *Sentimental Tommy*. They are a cousin of Cornish Pasties.

1 *lb. tender steak*
salt and pepper to taste
3 *oz. shredded suet*

2 *tablespoons minced onion*
1 *lb. shortcrust*

Beat the steak with a meat bat or rolling pin, then cut it into narrow strips. Divide these in inch lengths. Season with salt and pepper. Divide into 3 equal portions. Divide the shortcrust into 3 ovals. In olden days, I am told, the crust was made without any fat, simply from flour seasoned with salt and water. Roll each portion of shortcrust out into an equal-sized oval, about ¼ inch thick. Cover the half of each oval with the meat to within half inch of edge. Sprinkle each with a third of the suet and onion.

Fold in two. Either notch the edges with thumbs and forefingers, or press edges together with the prongs of a fork. Nip a tiny piece of pastry from the centre of each. Bake in a hot oven, 450° F., till pastry is risen and set, and then lower to moderate, 350° F., and bake for about 1 hour until steak is tender when tested with a skewer. Serve hot, allowing 1 per person.

SAUCHIEHALL LAMB PIE

Line a well-greased cake tin, nine inches across, with plain shortcrust. Press it well round the base. Peel three large onions. Soak in boiling water to cover for five minutes, then chop. Remove skin from 2 lb. of lean lamb and cut up lamb into small pieces. Stir in the onion. Pack into the pastry case. Season with salt and pepper. Sprinkle with a teaspoon of chopped mint and a dessertspoon of rich, brown beef gravy, or diluted meat extract. Brush edges of case with cold water and cover with remaining shortcrust. Make two parallel slits on the centre. Start baking in a hot oven, 450° F. When risen and set, in about 10 minutes, lower quickly to 300° F., and bake from 2½–2¾ hours until meat is tender when tested with a skewer through one of the slits. If the pastry seems to be getting too dry, cover with buttered paper. Turn onto a hot ashet very carefully. Serve with stoved potatoes (*p.* 167) and rich brown gravy made with lamb or mutton stock.

MUTTON PIES

These pies are popular at Balmoral Castle.

FILLING

¾ *lb. lean mutton*   *salt and black pepper to taste*
pinch of grated nutmeg or   *mutton gravy as required*
  ground mace

PASTRY

¼ *lb. beef dripping*   1 *lb. flour*
½ *pint cold water*   ½ *teaspoon salt*

Remove any bone, gristle or skin from meat. Cut meat into very small pieces. Season to taste with salt and pepper and nutmeg or mace. To make pastry, place dripping in a saucepan. Add water. Bring to boil. Sift flour into a basin with the salt. Make a hollow in the centre. Pour in boiling dripping and water. Stir till into a dough, then leave until cool enough to handle. Knead lightly for a moment. Turn onto a floured board. Knead until free from cracks. Line 6 or 9 round tins, depending on size, thinly with two-thirds of the pastry. Keep remainder warm. Place each case as made on a baking sheet. Fill with meat mixture, moistened with gravy. Cut 6 or 9 rounds from remaining pastry to make lids for pies. Brush edges of pastry cases with cold water. Lay a lid on each. Press firmly together. Trim if necessary, and scallop edges if liked with a pair of scissors. Make a small hole in centre of each. Brush tops with beaten egg or milk. Bake in a moderate oven, 350° F., for about 40 minutes. When ready, fill up each through a funnel with hot thickened mutton gravy. Serve at once. Serves 6.

MUTTON AND BARLEY PIES: Make pastry cases as described above. Remove any skin and bone from 1 lb. mutton before weighing. Cut meat into small pieces. Season with salt, pepper and ground mace. Boil 1 cup barley till soft in plenty of water. Drain and stir into mutton when cold. Moisten to taste with mutton gravy. Follow method given for preparing and baking mutton pies, but make pastry from 6 oz. beef dripping, $\frac{3}{4}$ pint cold water, $1\frac{1}{2}$ lb. flour and $\frac{3}{4}$ teaspoon salt.

PORK PIE

FILLING

$\frac{3}{4}$ lb. lean pork	pepper to taste
3 oz. Ayrshire bacon	1 sliced hard-boiled egg
$\frac{1}{2}$ teaspoon salt	1 tablespoon cold water

PASTRY

$\frac{1}{2}$ lb. flour	1 beaten egg
$\frac{1}{2}$ teaspoon salt	cold water as required
3 oz. butter	

Sift flour with salt. Rub in butter. Moisten with egg and water to a firm dough. Roll out thinly. Line a well-greased pie-dish with alternate layers of pork, bacon and egg. Season with salt and pepper. Sprinkle with the water. Cover with the pastry in the usual way. Decorate the edges and then gather the trimmings. Decorate pie round the centre with foliage made from rolled out trimmings. Make a hole in the centre. Glaze with equal quantity of beaten egg and cold water. Bake in a moderately hot oven, 375° F., until pork is tender in about 2 hours. Pour into hole in centre through a funnel ¼ pint stock, mixed with ¼ oz. gelatine, softened in 2 tablespoons cold water and dissolved in the stock. Tuck a sprig of parsley into hole. Serves 3 or 4.

HARE PIE: Follow above recipe but substitute hare for pork.

VEAL PIE

This is one of the many dishes that dates back to the Auld Alliance.

4 *veal chops or cutlets*	2 *boiled egg yolks or*
salt and pepper to taste	*sweetbreads*
pinch of crushed herbs	½ *lb. mushrooms or morels*
pinch of ground mace	*puff pastry as required*
4 *rashers of bacon*	

Trim and bone chops. (If using cutlets, choose without bone.) Make veal bones into stock. Season meat with salt, pepper, herbs and mace. Place in a pie dish, lightly greased. Remove rind from bacon, then cut rashers in two. Roll each piece up and tuck the rolls between the chops. Add the egg yolks or sweetbreads, and peeled mushrooms or morels, and a chopped truffle if liked. Barely cover with seasoned stock, then cover with puff pastry. Bake in a moderate oven, 350° F., for about an hour, until the chops are tender when tested with a skewer.

TO VARY: Substitute oysters for the bacon rolls and egg yolks.

BEEF KIDNEYS FOR THE
DEJEUNER À LA FOURCHETTE (1851)

Mince the kidneys, and season highly with salt, pepper and cayenne pepper. Fry the mince and moisten with gravy and champagne. Serve in a hot dish. The slices may be first marinated in vinegar and herbs, and catsup or lemon or walnut pickle may be used in place of the wine.

BEEF UDDER (1851)

Boil, slice and serve with tomato or onion sauce. Udder can also be salted for two days, tacked to a tongue, and boiled together. Salted udder is also simmered very slowly, then allowed to become quite cold when it is served with oil and vinegar.

CALF'S HEART (1851)

Cut down and dress as a plain stew, and season with grated lemon rind, or stuff, roll in forcemeat and roast.

TO DRESS CALVES-TAILS (1851)

Clean, blanch and cut them at the joints. Brown them in butter or in melted kidney fat. Drain. Stew them in good broth flavoured with parsley, onion and a bay leaf. Add green peas to the stew if in season, or some small mushrooms. Skim and serve the ragout. Foreigners use garlic in this dish, and dredge it with grated Parmesan cheese.

DRESSED LAMB'S HEAD

Rinse a lamb's head, split enough to enable you to remove the brains. Place in a large saucepan. Cover with cold water. Add a dessertspoon of salt. Bring to boil, and skim carefully. Cover and simmer gently for 1½ hours. Remove head to a bowl. Take out the tongue. Score the head lightly into diamonds. Brush all over with beaten egg. Sprinkle with sieved breadcrumbs and salt and pepper to taste. Dab with flecks of butter. Bake till golden brown. While baking, rinse the brains. Cover them with boiling water, then cold-dip, skin and parboil. Cold-dip again. Chop. Dress with hot, melted, parsley butter, flavoured with minced, parboiled sage, salt and white pepper, lemon juice, cayenne pepper and one minced shallot. Skin the tongue.

TO SERVE: Dish up head. Garnish with small grilled rolls of bacon and sprigs of parsley. Place the tongue in a flat, hot dish. Pour the dressed brains round. Serve with parsley butter sauce. In the nineteenth century, the meat taken from a haggis used to be egged and crumbed and browned in a Dutch oven before the fire, and used as a border for the lamb's head.

TO DRESS A BOILED SHEEP'S HEAD

There are two simple methods of dressing a sheep's head.

BAKED SHEEP'S HEAD: Place each half on a greased shallow baking tin, split side downward. Coat with brown crumbs. Dab with dripping or margarine. Bake in a moderate oven, 350° F., until golden brown. Garnish if possible with fried brain cakes and slices of fried sheep's liver, and sprigs of parsley. Sometimes a bed is made for the head with 2 tablespoons each of chopped, boiled sheep's heart and chopped boiled liver, moistened with the broth, and seasoned to taste.

BRAIN CAKES: Boil the soaked brains in salted water very gently until firm in about 12 minutes. Strain. Chop brains finely on a board, then mix with 2 tablespoons sifted breadcrumbs, 1 teaspoon minced parsley or chives and salt and pepper to taste. With floured hands, shape into small, equal-sized flat cakes. Melt a tablespoon of dripping. Fry cakes on both sides until brown. Drain on absorbent paper.

SHEEP'S HEAD WITH BRAIN SAUCE: 1 boiled sheep's head, 1 oz. butter, 1 oz. flour, ¾ pint milk, 1 sheep's brain, salt and pepper to taste.

Remove all the meat from the head. Melt the butter in a saucepan. Add flour. When frothy, stir in milk. Stir till boiling. Boil soaked brains gently for about 12 minutes in salted water, then strain, chop and add to sauce. Stir till piping hot. Season with salt and pepper to taste. Add the head and reheat, stirring constantly. Take care not to break the head. Place on a hot ashet. Garnish with chopped parsley and fried sippets of bread.

SHEEP'S HEAD BRAWN: Soak a thoroughly cleaned sheep's head for twelve hours in cold water to cover containing a large handful of salt. Drain and place the head in a large saucepan. Cover with cold water. Add six black peppercorns, two whole cloves, two sprigs of parsley and one sprig of thyme. Bring slowly to boil. Skim thoroughly. Simmer for two hours or more, depending on the age of the sheep. When meat shows signs of coming away from the bones, remove the head to a board, and let the stock simmer until reduced to about one pint. When head is slightly cooled, remove all the meat. Skin the tongue. Discard skin and any gristle on meat, then mince both meat and tongue very finely. Dissolve one tablespoon of powdered gelatine in the stock. Strain into a basin. Stir in the meat and tongue. When about to set, stir once again and pour into a wet mould. Chill before turning out.

DERACHIE POTTED HEAD

Wash a pig's head very thoroughly, then wash the trotters, all four. Prepare a chicken or rabbit as for boiling. Heat enough cold water in a large saucepan to cover the head, trotters and chicken or rabbit. Place the head, trotters and chicken or rabbit in the pan. Bring to boil. Skim if necessary, then simmer very gently, adding boiling water if required from time to time as all the meat must be constantly covered. When flesh shows signs of coming away from the bone, remove head, trotters and chicken or rabbit. Pick all the flesh from the bones. Cut meat into very small pieces. If left too large, the 'brawn' will not be easy to carve. Some Scottish housewives put all the meat through a meat grinder, but I

190

prefer it chopped up. Strain the stock into a large basin and leave overnight to set. Skim off the thickest of the fat. The liquid by this time should be a mass of jelly. Return to pan. Add the prepared meat. Bring to the boil. Season with salt and pepper. Pour into wet bowls or moulds. Chill for twenty-four hours.

SCOTCH BLACK PUDDINGS

1½ *pints pig's blood*	1 *small handful of oatmeal*
salt as required	*pinch of cayenne pepper*
1½ *gills milk*	*pinch of grated nutmeg or*
¾ *lb. belly lard*	*ground mace*
3 *peeled onions, medium-sized*	½ *saltspoon crushed herbs*

Allow the blood to run into a deep pan. Stir it constantly until almost cold, then throw in ¾ teaspoon salt and rub through a hair sieve. Stir in milk. Cut the lard into pieces about an inch square, and mince the onion. Stir the lard, onion, oatmeal and plenty of salt and cayenne pepper to taste, and ground nutmeg or mace, and herbs, into the blood. (If preferred, substitute 8–10 oz. of rice cooked in boiling water to cover for ½ hour, and well drained, for the oatmeal.) Stir in stock if required. To prepare skins: Wash carefully, then soak overnight in salt water to cover. When the filling is ready, tie one end of each skin, and turn inside out. Half-fill skins, then tie them in equal lengths, or tie in rings. Bring a panful of cold water to the boil. Add a spoonful of cold water, then the puddings. Boil for 5 minutes, then prick each with a large needle to prevent bursting. Return to pan. Simmer gently for 30 minutes, then remove from pan. Hang up in a dry, cool, place. When required, place in a pan of almost boiling water. Simmer gently for 10–15 minutes. Drain and serve, or grill them.

TO VARY: Use 3 pints of blood, mixed with ½ pint water, 1 cup oatmeal, 1 teaspoon salt, ½ teaspoon black pepper, ½ teaspoon Jamaica pepper, ½ teaspoon ground cloves, 1 tablespoon minced onion or shallot and 1 lb. shredded suet. Follow the foregoing method.

TRIPE IN OLD STYLE

This is another dish showing the French influence.

Cut clean, blanched tripe into three inch squares. Roll each up and thread the rolls on a length of strong cotton. Place in a casserole. Add a knuckle of veal or a calf's foot. Season with salt and pepper. Add water, or better still veal stock, allowing 1 pint to 2 lb. tripe. Cover closely and cook in a slow oven, 300 °F., till tender. Draw out cotton. Serve cold in its own jelly with potato salad flavoured with onion, or dip each roll in batter and deep-fry, or reheat and serve with onion sauce made half with top milk and half with the stock.

TO DRESS VEAL SWEETBREADS (1851)

Parboil them, but be sure not to boil them too much. Divide and stew them in white gravy; thicken and season this with salt, mace and white pepper, and when just ready, a little hot cream, or egg the parboiled sweetbreads, dip them in crumbs, chopped herbs and seasonings and finish them in a Dutch oven. Serve with melted butter flavoured with catsup.

LOBSCOUSE

Cut up stewing beef with a little fat into small pieces. Cut up peeled potatoes about the same size, in the proportion of 3 pieces of potato to every 2 pieces of beef. Place in an iron stewing pan. Cover with beef stock. Add a bay leaf. Bring to boil. Cover and simmer very slowly till meat is tender. Season with salt and black pepper to taste. Stir well. Turn into a deep hot dish. When serving, top each portion with a large pat of butter.

MADE-UP DISHES

BEEF MOULDS

½ lb. cooked beef	¼ teaspoon pepper
2–4 oz. boiled bacon or ham	¼ teaspoon grated nutmeg
1 dessertspoon chopped parsley	1 cup breadcrumbs
pinch of crushed herbs	1 beaten egg
¾ teaspoon salt	½ small cup jellied stock

Chop the meat quite small. If no bacon or ham is available, add
2–4 oz. more beef, and a little fat. Stir in parsley, herbs, salt,
pepper, nutmeg, breadcrumbs, egg and stock. If short of stock,
a peeled tomato may be chopped and added. Fill greased dariole
moulds with the mixture, and smooth over the top with a wet
knife. Cover with greased paper. Steam till set. Turn out gently.
Coat with tomato sauce. Serves 4.

HAM AND POTATO CAKES

¼ lb. lean boiled ham	salt and pepper to taste
1 lb. cold boiled potatoes	grated rind ¼ lemon
1 teaspoon minced parsley	1 beaten egg

Chop ham. Mash potatoes smoothly. Stir into the ham with a
pinch of crushed herbs if liked, parsley, salt and pepper and lemon
rind, then beat in the egg. Form into small flat cakes with floured
hands. Drop gently into hot deep fat. Fry until crisp and nicely
browned. Drain on absorbent paper. Garnish with parsley Serves
4.

INKY-PINKY

This is a recipe credited to Meg Dods who used to preside over an
ancient hostel in the Border country. It was a popular dish in
Angus and frequently served on washing days when roast beef
was the Sunday joint.

Cut cold roast beef in slices, then remove any skin, and cut away the outside edge. Slice boiled carrots, allowing 2 carrots to each portion of beef. Make gravy to taste from stock made of the bones, and flavoured to taste with onion. Lay the beef and the carrots in the gravy. Season with salt and pepper and sharpen with a few drops of vinegar. Thicken gravy slightly with cornflour creamed with water. When boiling, dish up. Serve with sippets of toast and mashed potatoes.

GAME AND POULTRY

Scotland has always been famous for game, and the Scots wisely prefer their young game roasted and their old game braised. In days of yore, game was usually hung until it was 'high' before it was cooked, but nowadays this is not the general practice.

Once when I was young and foolish I wanted to learn to shoot game. I could shoot a penny off a dyke at about twenty feet distance, but I had never attempted to help to fill my mother's game larder, so I asked a young gamekeeper to teach me how to bring down something for the pot . . . Dressed in a hobble tartan skirt topped with my brother's khaki army jacket and with his Scottish Horse bonnet on my head I sailed up to Glenogil feeling no end of a sport on an October afternoon and was met by Jock dressed in his kilt.

First we tramped over the lower slopes of St Arnolds with the dogs at our heels to retrieve our spoils, then we clambered back over fences with my gun at half cock, but no luck. When the light began to fail we sorrowfully turned homewards. Walking down from the Big Hoose I suddenly saw a rabbit waiting for me right in the middle of the drive. I took aim. It toppled over, and I flopped down and howled my eyes out for what I had done. Jock awkwardly wiped away my tears with his handkerchief. I had forgotten mine. He then offered me a Turkish cigarette, and told me to wait . . . while he collected my first and only kill. We buried it behind his cottage. That was the beginning and end of my sporting days. I vowed there and then that if my mother wanted something savoury for the pot somebody else would have to do the killing.

GAME JELLIES

2 *lb. game bones*   *salt and pepper to taste*
4 *cups water*   4 *tablespoons powdered gelatine*
6 *cloves*   1 *large can tomatoes*
1 *blade mace*   *shells and whites of 2 eggs*
1 *sliced, peeled onion*

Wash the bones, raw or cooked, and partly carcass if possible,
then place in a saucepan. Add water, cloves, mace and onion, and
salt and pepper to taste. Bring to boil. Skim if necessary. Simmer
very gently for 2 hours, then strain into a clean, rinsed saucepan.
Add gelatine, soaked for 5 minutes in ½ cup cold water, tomatoes,
and egg shells and whites. Allow to boil up till frothy, then draw
pan aside. Stand for 10 minutes, then strain through a hot jelly
bag into 6 wet individual moulds. Chill, then unmould. Garnish
with watercress. Serve with green salad and mayonnaise. Serves 6.

GROUSE

Of the four varieties of grouse I know, I have only met with two
in Scotland—the capercailzie or capercaillie or wood grouse and
the red grouse. In the spring when I was young, I used to walk
two and a half miles to the Cortachy Woods to listen to the love
call of the capercailzie at dusk, and liked it so much that I hated
to be asked to cook the cock of the woods. It is scarce in Scotland.
The more familiar grouse is the red grouse which many think is
the most delicious game bird of all.

ROAST RED GROUSE
(YOUNG)

Knead a teaspoon of lemon juice and salt and pepper to taste
into 1 oz. of butter for each bird. Tie a thin slice of bacon over
each breast. Place the butter inside the carcass, not in the crop.
Place on a trivet in a baking tin. Roast in a moderate oven, 350° F.,
for 30 to 35 minutes, basting frequently with melted butter. When

nearly ready, remove the bacon and dredge the breast with flour. Baste well, and finish roasting. Grouse flesh should be slightly under done, rosey I call it. While roasting, parboil the liver for 2 or 3 minutes, then pound it in a mortar and beat in a little creamed butter and salt and cayenne pepper to taste. Spread over a slice of toast for each bird. Slip in tin, one under each bird, 5 minutes before removing from oven. Dish up on the toasts. This is an old-fashioned way of serving grouse. In these days the liver is often washed and returned to the birds before roasting.

TO VARY: Stuff the birds with cranberries and tie vine leaves over the fat bacon. Bake in a hot oven, 425° F., for about $\frac{1}{2}$ hour, basting frequently. When half cooked, remove the vine leaves and bacon. Dredge the breast with flour and baste, then finish cooking.

TO SERVE GROUSE: Garnish with sprigs of watercress. Serve with potato chips or straws, crisply fried breadcrumbs, bread sauce, and cranberry or rowan jelly.

TO COOK OLD GROUSE: Either braise or cook them in a casserole, or brown them in a little butter in a saucepan. Add 2 or 3 tablespoons stock, then cover and cook over very slow heat until tender, adding more stock as required to prevent burning.

ROAST CAPERCAILZIE
(WOOD GROUSE)

This bird has to be well hung before roasting. Sometimes Scottish epicures insist on burying it for a week before plucking and cooking it.

Stuff carcass with a $\frac{1}{4}$ lb. chopped seasoned rump steak, and 2 oz. chopped bacon. Cover breast with slices of fat bacon. Roast in a hot oven, 450° F., for 10 minutes, then lower to moderate, 350° F., and roast for about 1 hour or a little longer, depending on age, basting frequently. When nearly ready, remove bacon from breast. Dredge lightly with flour and baste well, then finish roasting. Untruss. Serve on a hot ashet. Garnish with watercress, lightly coated with French dressing. Serve with gravy made with

197

cream in place of water, bread sauce, fried crumbs, potato chips or straws, and with a green vegetable if liked, or a salad.

CASSEROLE OF GROUSE

1 *brace old grouse*	$\frac{1}{4}$ *lb. mushrooms*
1 *oz. flour*	1 *medium-sized carrot*
$2\frac{1}{2}$ *oz. butter*	1 *medium-sized onion*
1 *pint beef stock*	2 *tomatoes*
salt and pepper to taste	*triangles of pastry*

Joint birds. Wipe joints with a damp cloth. Dip them in the flour. Melt butter in a large frying pan. Add joints. Fry slowly till lightly browned, turning frequently. Transfer to a casserole. Add remainder of flour to fat left in pan. Stir over low heat till brown. Remove pan from heat. Add stock and salt and pepper to taste. Peel and stem mushrooms. Wash them in salted water. Add to casserole with peeled carrot and onion, left whole. Scald, peel and chop tomatoes and add. Strain in stock. Cover casserole. Place in a slow oven, 300° F., and cook till tender, in 1–1$\frac{1}{2}$ hours, depending on age of bird. Remove carrot and onion. Dish up. Garnish with triangles of pastry. Serves 6.

GROUSE MOUSSE

$\frac{3}{4}$ *lb. raw grouse flesh*	$\frac{1}{2}$ *gill cream*
1$\frac{1}{2}$ *oz. bacon*	*about* 1 *pint Brown Sauce*
1 *oz. boiled ham*	(*p.* 102)
2 *egg yolks*	*salt and pepper to taste*

Cut the grouse into thin slices. Remove rind from bacon and chop bacon. Chop ham. Fry the bacon and the grouse lightly after the bacon fat begins to run. Place the grouse, bacon and ham in a mortar. Pound well with a pestle. When into a paste, gradually pound in the egg yolks and the cream. When blended, rub through a sieve. Stir in enough Brown Sauce made from the grouse bones to moisten mixture, then season with salt and pepper to taste. Place in a greased, plain timbale mould or soufflé dish. Cover with greased greaseproof paper. Steam gently for about 45 minutes. Unmould on to a hot dish. Coat with hot Brown Sauce, seasoned to taste. Garnish with a little chopped truffle. Serves 3 or 4.

GROUSE PIE

1 *brace young grouse*
1 *lb. lean rump steak*
1 *rasher of bacon*
3 *sliced hard-boiled eggs*

salt and pepper to taste
pinch of ground mace
¾ *lb. puff, flaky or rough puff*
   pastry

Wash, dry and joint birds. Take out and discard the lower part of the backs. Cut steak into small pieces about 1½ inches square. Remove rind from bacon and chop bacon. Slice eggs. Butter a pie dish large enough to take the birds and line with steak. Add joints of grouse. Sprinkle with bacon. Cover with slices of egg. Season with salt and pepper to taste and mace or grated nutmeg. Sprinkle with remainder of steak. Cover with pastry in the usual way. Brush with beaten egg. Bake in a hot oven, 425° F., for ½ hour. Lower to 300° F. and bake for 1 hour.

GROUSE PUDDING

1 *plump grouse*
2 *oz. streaky rashers*
salt and pepper to taste
½ *lb. flour*

4 *oz. shredded suet*
½ *teaspoon baking powder*
pinch of salt
cold water as required

Carve the grouse into suitable portions for serving. Place bones in a saucepan. Cover with cold water. Add 2 slices of onion, ½ bay leaf, three cloves, 1 small blade of mace, and 4 black peppercorns. Simmer gently for 3 or 4 hours, then strain, and cool. Remove rind from bacon and cut bacon into small strips. Mix the flour with the suet, baking powder and salt, then stir in enough cold water to make a stiff paste. Roll out thinly. Line a greased pudding basin with two-thirds of the pastry, then pack in the grouse and bacon alternately. Season the grouse with salt and pepper to taste. Sprinkle a pinch of crushed herbs over the meat if liked. Fill up nearly to the top with cold grouse bone stock. Brush edge of pastry lining with cold water. Roll remainder of pastry into a lid. Fit on the top. Cover pudding with the greased paper, then with a pudding cloth. Steam for 3 hours. To serve, remove pudding cloth and paper and tie a napkin round basin. Serve with mashed potatoes and green peas or spinach, and grouse gravy. Serves 3.

GROUSE SALAD

1 *cold, roast grouse*   1 *head of celery*
1 *heart of lettuce*   *cream dressing*
mustard and cress   4 *hard-boiled eggs*

Remove all meat from grouse carcass, and reserve carcass for soup. Cut meat into small pieces. Wash and dry the lettuce leaves and mustard and cress, and trim, scrape and wash and dry celery, then shred. Add a little chicory or the heart of a Batavian lettuce. Mix lightly together with the grouse in a salad bowl. Coat with the dressing. Garnish with the eggs shelled and cut lengthwise. Serve at once or sauce may curdle. Serves 4.

DRESSING FOR GROUSE SALAD: Mix 1 minced shallot with 1 dessert-spoon minced parsley, 1 tablespoon caster sugar, 1 teaspoon salt and $\frac{1}{4}$ teaspoon pepper. Stir in 2 egg yolks. When thoroughly blended, gradually stir in 4 tablespoons olive oil, drop by drop. When thickened, stir in very slowly 2 tablespoons chili vinegar. Beat till blended, then fold in $\frac{1}{2}$ pint whipped cream. Pour over the salad.

ROAST BARON OF HARE

1 *fresh hare* $\frac{1}{4}$ *pint thick cream*
butter as required   1 *teaspoon lemon juice*
$\frac{1}{2}$ *gill beef stock*   *salt and pepper to taste*

Wipe a fresh young hare with a damp cloth both inside and out. Remove head, then fore and hind legs, leaving only the whole of the back. Cut ribs short. Remove tendons. Place on a rack in a baking tin. Spread with butter. Bake in a hot oven, 450° F., basting every 10 minutes, for ¾ hour. Heat stock. Stir in cream, and pour over baron. Baste well. Lower temperature to moderate, 350° F. Roast for 5 minutes. Dish up. Strain liquor into a small saucepan. Skim off fat. Stir in lemon juice and salt and pepper to taste. Pour round hare. Serve with mashed potatoes and green peas. Serves 4.

SUTHERLAND HARE PATTIES

the hind legs and back of a hare
¼ lb. shredded suet

1 tablespoon minced onion
salt and pepper to taste

Remove the flesh from the hind legs and back of hare. Put through a meat grinder. Mix with the suet, onion and salt and pepper to taste. With floured hands, shape into small, equal-sized patties, 2½–3 inches across and ½ inch thick. Fry very slowly in shallow, hot dripping till brown below, then turn carefully and brown on the other side. Cover, and fry slowly for 2 or 3 minutes, then uncover and fry again for a moment or two on each side to crisp up. Serve round fried potato chips or straws. Garnish each cake with a fried mushroom and fringe with watercress. Serve with red currant jelly. Serves 4.

ROAST PARTRIDGES

The aroma given off by a roasting partridge, or pertrik as we call them, always wafts me back to the Manse kitchen, where I used to roast partridges when they were young and pot-roast them when old.

4 *young partridges*
salt and pepper to taste

fat bacon as required

Wipe cleaned birds inside and out with a damp cloth. Season insides with salt and pepper. Wash and dry livers of birds and replace. Truss. Cover breasts with fat bacon. Tie on securely. Place on a rack in a baking tin. Roast in a fairly hot oven, 425° F., basting every 5 minutes with melted butter, for 15 minutes, then baste with the bacon dripping in tin. Allow 25 minutes altogether. Untruss and dish up. Stir ¼ pint white stock into drippings in pan. Boil for 2 minutes. Season if necessary. Skim off fat. Strain into a hot sauceboat. Garnish birds with watercress. Serve with bread sauce, fried crumbs, potato chips or straws, and green peas or a lettuce salad. Serves 4.

TO POT-ROAST: Prepare birds. Melt enough butter to cover bottom of a saucepan. Add birds. Fry slowly, turning frequently, until brown all over, then add 2–3 tablespoons white stock for each bird. Season birds with salt and pepper. Cover closely. Simmer very gently until tender, time depending on age of birds. Take a look at the birds occasionally to see there is still some liquid in the pan, and replenish with a tablespoon or two more if or when necessary. Dish up. Add enough additional stock to give you fully ¼ pint of gravy. Stir in a walnut of butter kneaded with a teaspoon of flour. Stir till boiling. Season to taste. Spoon over the birds. I always cook mine in a saucepan, but to save constant watching, the birds could be transferred to a casserole with the gravy and cooked, covered, in a slow oven, 300° F. until tender.

SALMI OF PARTRIDGE
SPORTSMAN'S FASHION (1851)

Put left-over roasted partridges or partridges roasted until half done, skinned and carved, into a saucepan with a small glass of olive oil, a large glass of wine, pepper and salt to taste, and the grated rind and juice of a lemon. If left-over, just heat through. If half-roasted, cook gently until tender in the sauce. Serve with grilled crusts.

RABBITS WITH FINE HERBS (1851)

Carve two white young fat rabbits neatly, and fry the pieces in butter with some chopped bacon and a handful of chopped mushrooms, and chopped parsley, and eschalots and pepper, salt and ground allspice to taste. Dissolve a teaspoonful of flour in ½ pint of consommé. Pour into the pan. Cover and stew slowly till rabbits are cooked. Dish up rabbit. Skim and strain the sauce. Reheat. Season with cayenne pepper and a good squeeze of lemon juice and pour it round the joints.

STEWED WILD RABBIT

1 *young rabbit*	$\frac{1}{2}$ *pint boiling water*
flour as required	1 *medium-sized onion*
salt and pepper	1 *bay leaf*
1 *tablespoon butter*	6 *scraped young carrots*

Thoroughly clean rabbit. Cut into joints. Place in a basin. Cover with boiling water. Soak for a minute, then drain and dry thoroughly. Dip in flour seasoned with salt and pepper. Heat a shallow stew pan. Add butter. When smoking hot, but not discoloured, add the rabbit and fry slowly till brown on each side. Add boiling water. Thinly slice and add onion, bay leaf and carrots. Cover closely. Simmer very gently until tender in about $\frac{3}{4}$ hour, but remove the bay leaf after cooking for $\frac{1}{4}$ hour. Serve with boiled or mashed potatoes.

JOCK'S MOTHER'S STEWED RABBIT

1 *wild rabbit*	1 *blade mace*
salt, pepper and paprika to	1 *sprig parsley*
taste	4 *oz. pickled pork*
3 *small peeled onions*	1 *teaspoon butter or*
2 *oz. bacon*	*margarine*
1 *pint brown stock*	1 *tablespoon flour*
juice $\frac{1}{2}$ *lemon*	

Joint and blanch rabbit, omitting ribs. Place joints in water. Stand 1 minute, then remove and dry. Dip in flour, seasoned to taste with salt, pepper and paprika. Remove rind from bacon. Place half the bacon in a saucepan. Add joints, onions, stock, lemon juice, mace, parsley and parboiled pickled pork cut into small squares. Cover with remainder of bacon and a sheet of buttered paper. Cover pan closely. Simmer for 1 hour, or longer as required. Arrange rabbit on a hot dish. Strain liquor and skim carefully. Melt butter in a saucepan. Stir in flour. Add liquor to taste. Bring to boil and pour over rabbit. Garnish with cooked green peas. Serves 4.

ROAST HAUNCH OF VENISON

Remove the large bone and knuckle from a well-hung haunch of venison. Trim. Wash if necessary, or wipe with a damp cloth, then with a dry one. Season with salt and pepper. Roll in a sheet of well-greased paper. Make a stiff paste with flour and water and knead till smooth. Roll out till large enough to cover joint. Wrap joint in the paste, then cover with another greased paper. Tie securely with string. Bake in a moderate oven, 350° F., for 3 or 4 hours, according to size, basting well while cooking with beef dripping. When nearly ready, remove paper and chip off paste. Dredge with flour. Baste well, and bake till brown. Dish up. Serve with brown venison gravy flavoured with port wine, and with red currant jelly, roast potatoes and green peas.

VENISON PIE

1½ lb. shoulder of venison	2 medium-sized onions
salt and pepper to taste	1 sprig parsley
¼ teaspoon ground mace	½ gill red wine
¼ teaspoon allspice	½ gill vinegar
stock as required	

Beat the meat with a meat bat or rolling pin. Rub in salt, pepper, mace and allspice, then cut into 2 inch squares. Sprinkle lightly with mutton dripping. Place in a saucepan. Cover with stock made from venison bones and trimmings of the meat. Bring slowly to boil. Cover and simmer very gently for 1 hour, then add the onions and parsley. Cover and simmer gently until almost tender in about 2 hours. Remove pan from stove. Uncover and leave until quite cold, then remove the fat on top. Turn meat into a pie dish. Add the wine and vinegar mixed with equal quantity of stock, then enough stock to come almost up to the top of dish. Place a funnel in centre. Cover with puff pastry. Bake in a hot oven, 500° F., till the pastry is risen and set, then lower to moderate and bake for about 20 minutes. Fill up with remaining stock. Serve hot with mashed potatoes and green peas. Serves 5 or 6.

PIGEON AND VENISON PIE

1–1¼ lb. flaky pastry	½ teaspoon black pepper
2 prepared pigeons	1 teaspoon salt
1 lb. lean venison steak	pinch of grated nutmeg
1½ tablespoons flour	beef stock as required

Line the moistened rim of a pie dish neatly with a strip of pastry, then roll out the remainder of pastry to form a lid to fit the dish. Wipe and quarter the pigeons. Cut up the steak. Mix the flour with the black pepper, salt and nutmeg on a plate. Dip the meat and the pigeon quarters in turn in the seasoned flour. Arrange a layer of venison in the bottom of the dish, then the pigeons. Cover with the remainder of the venison. Half fill the dish with stock. Cover with the pastry lid, make a cross cut in centre and decorate the top with pastry snippets. Bake in a hot oven, 450° F., until the pastry is risen and set, then reduce heat to 325° F. and bake slowly until cooked through. The pie should take about 2 hours altogether. Just before serving, remove the centre ornament and pour more hot stock, seasoned and thickened as required, through centre cut to take the place of what has evaporated during the cooking. Replace the ornament, and bake for 2 or 3 minutes. Serves 6–8.

DEER SAUSAGES

½ lb. minced lean venison	3 oz. oatmeal
2 tablespoons minced onion or shallot	salt and pepper to taste
3 oz. shredded suet	pinch of crushed herbs

Wash deer tripe skins, then turn them inside out. Mix the venison with the onion or shallot, suet, oatmeal, salt and pepper and herbs. Leaving the fat on the inside of the skins, fill the skins loosely, then tie. Prick lightly all over. Place in a pan of boiling water to cover. Boil slowly and steadily for 45 minutes. When required, fry in a little hot lard until evenly brown or grill for 15 minutes. Serve hot for breakfast or high tea.

VENISON SAUSAGES

1 *lb. cold venison*   *salt and pepper to taste*
6 *oz. lean ham*   *ground mace to taste*
6 *oz. butter*

Remove all skin and sinew from venison before weighing. Put venison through a meat grinder with the ham. Place in a mortar. Pound with butter, adding a small piece at a time. Season with salt, pepper and mace. Tie in sausage skins. When required, fry slowly in a little hot butter or lard for ¾ hour, turning frequently. Serves 3 or 4.

GRILLED VENISON STEAKS

3 *tablespoons flour*   6 *venison steaks*
salt and pepper to taste   *melted fat or oil*

Season flour with salt and pepper. Have the steaks cut about ¾ inch thick. Dip steaks in flour. Shake gently. Place on a grill brushed with melted fat or cooking oil, and heated. Grill about 2 inches from the heat for 3 to 5 minutes, according to whether you want them rare or well done, then turn. Brush the second sides with fat or oil and grill for about the same length of time until cooked to taste. Arrange side by side on a hot dish. Top each with a slice of fried tomato or a fried mushroom, or with a slice of tomato topped with a mushroom. Garnish with watercress. Serve with chip potatoes and green peas or string beans.

MARTINMAS STEAKS

½ lb. shoulder of venison   *salt, pepper and paprika to taste*
¼ lb. pork   *1½ teaspoons fresh breadcrumbs*
1½ teaspoons minced onion   *1 slightly beaten egg*

Put meat through meat grinder three times. Stir in onion, salt, pepper and paprika to taste, breadcrumbs and egg to moisten. Shape into cakes, 1¼ inches thick. Fry for 4 minutes on each side in a little hot fat. Dish up each on a round of fried bread. Garnish with grilled tomatoes and watercress. Place a pat of maître d'hôtel butter or a fried mushroom or tomato slice on top of each. Serves 2.

POULTRY

Scottish housewives, most of whom dislike serving food dressed up so that you don't know what you are eating, seem to prefer poultry boiled or roasted. In the farmhouses, boiling fowls are usually cooked with oatmeal stuffing. In the towns, boiled fowl is generally cooked unstuffed and served with rice, stewed in the stock when the 'boiler' is nearly ready. Fancy stuffings are seldom found in roast birds. Bread and sausagemeat stuffings are most popular, sausagemeat usually in the crop, and herb in the carcass. In my youth, birds to be roasted were only stuffed in the crop. I shall never forget the horror on the face of a daughter of Thrums who had stuffed the breast of a plump yellow-skinned chicken for high tea and left the body empty. I exclaimed, 'My mother always stuffs the body as well. She says it makes the bird go further.' Deadly silence on the part of all the guests while I slowly crimsoned.

BOILED FOWL

Pluck, singe and draw bird. Cut skin around knee joints. Twist each foot and leg in turn, then remove feet, drawing out the sinews from the thighs as you pull. Wipe inside and outside with a damp cloth. If to be boiled whole, insert fingers in tail end and loosen the skin from the legs. Now place thumb against one knee joint and push the leg upwards so that it slips inside the skin. Repeat with other leg. Pull skin smoothly over bird so as to have an even surface for coating with sauce. Stuff and truss.

STUFFING: The first stuffing comes from a farmer's wife in Glenquiech on the Braes of Angus. The second I coaxed from an Edinburgh housewife. For *Oatmeal Stuffing* you need:

4 *oz. medium oatmeal*	2 *tablespoons finely chopped*
2 *oz. shredded suet*	*onion*
salt and black pepper to taste	*pinch of crushed sage if liked*

If liked, substitute butter or margarine for suet. Spread oatmeal in a baking tin. Toast in oven till crisp and dry, but it must not turn colour. Cool. Stir in remaining ingredients. If using butter or margarine, melt before adding.

For the *Edinburgh Stuffing* you need:

chicken liver	*pinch of dried herbs*
3 *oz. boiled ham*	*salt and pepper to taste*
3 *oz. pork sausage meat*	*pinch of grated nutmeg*
3 *oz. bacon*	1 *beaten egg*
1 *oz. stale breadcrumbs*	

Put the liver, ham and sausage meat through a meat grinder. Remove rind from bacon. Put bacon through grinder. Mix with breadcrumbs, herbs, salt and pepper to taste, nutmeg and egg to bind. Stuff fowl. Sew up and truss.

TO BOIL FOWL

1 *old fowl*	*salt,* $\frac{1}{2}$ *teaspoonful per lb. of*
1 *slice fat bacon*	*bird*
2 *or* 3 *whole cloves*	1 *blade mace*
1 *sliced peeled onion*	6 *peppercorns*
$\frac{1}{4}$ *lb. sliced leek*	$\frac{1}{4}$ *lb. diced turnip*
6 *oz. sliced carrot*	2 *sliced celery stalks*
1 *cut lemon*	

Dip in boiling water. Rub breast with a cut lemon to whiten it. Cover breast with a thin slice of fat bacon. Wrap in greased paper or cheesecloth. Place in a deep saucepan, breast upwards. Add enough cold water to cover the thighs. Cover. Bring slowly to simmering point. Skim well. Cover. Simmer gently for 1 hour. Add seasonings and vegetables. Cover. Simmer gently till tender, for 3 to 4 hours, depending on age and size. The breast above the stock steams till tender, while the rest of the bird simmers. Drain. Remove string and skewers. Dish up. Coat breast with caper, egg and parsley, parsley or mushroom sauce. Serve remainder in a hot sauceboat. Garnish bird with boiled young carrots, brushed with melted chicken fat, or boiled dumplings, sprinkled with chopped parsley. Serve with boiled or mashed potatoes, green peas, and boiled bacon, ham, or pickled pork if available.

TO VARY: 1. Bring quickly to the boil in new milk to cover in place of water. Serve with Parsley Sauce.

2. Garnish with sprigs of parsley and boiled sprigs of cauliflower, coated with white sauce. Sprinkle with sieved hard-boiled egg yolk.

3. Cut into joints. Coat with white chicken sauce or mushroom sauce. Serve with green peas and mashed potatoes.

EGG AND PARSLEY SAUCE: Make ¾ pint white sauce with half chicken stock and half milk. Add 1 chopped hard-boiled egg and 1½ tablespoons chopped parsley.

TO BOIL AND ROAST AN OLD HEN

1 *old hen*	5 *tablespoons melted butter*
½ *teaspoon salt*	1 *teaspoon made mustard*
½ *teaspoon ground ginger*	1 *teaspoon vinegar*
pepper to taste	*paprika to taste*
boiling water as required	¾ *cup breadcrumbs*

Dress, clean and joint bird, or leave whole if preferred. Rub all over with salt, ground ginger and pepper. Leave for 12 hours. Place in a saucepan. Cover with boiling water. Simmer till tender. Drain. Place on a rack in a baking tin. Stir 2 tablespoons of the butter into mustard and vinegar. Season with paprika and a pinch of salt. Rub bird all over with mixture. If jointed, coat with the mixture before placing on rack. Mix crumbs with remainder of butter. Sprinkle over the hen. Bake in a fairly hot oven, 425° F., till the crumbs are golden. Serve with brown gravy, bread sauce, green peas and chip or new potatoes. Serves 6 or 7.

ROAST CHICKEN

In days gone by it was considered correct to stuff only the neck of the chicken. Now the body is stuffed as well which makes the bird go further. Use chestnut stuffing or sausage meat for the neck and celery stuffing for the body, after seasoning inside with salt.

CHESTNUT STUFFING: Mix 3 oz. sieved boiled chestnuts with 1 oz. sieved breadcrumbs, salt and pepper to taste, 1 tablespoon melted butter and giblet stock to moisten. Season with salt and white pepper to taste. Stuff neck and truss.

CELERY STUFFING: Place 10 oz. sieved crumbs in a basin. Fry 4 oz. minced celery and 2 oz. minced onion slowly in 1 oz. butter till onion is clear, stirring occasionally. Stir into crumbs. Add ½ teaspoon crushed herbs, 1 teaspoon minced parsley, salt and pepper to taste, and the minced parboiled liver of bird if liked, then the giblet stock to moisten. Stuff body and truss.

Brush rack in a shallow baking tin with melted fat. Brush bird all over with creamed butter or chicken fat. Place on one side of its breast on rack. Roast in a moderate oven, 350° F., for about 1¾ hours, turning on other side after 15 minutes, and basting with drippings. Turn and baste again in 15 minutes. Repeat turning and basting twice. After roasting for 1 hour, turn bird on its back and baste well with drippings. Roast for about another 15 minutes till the breast is golden brown. Remove any skewers and string. Place on a large hot flat meat dish. Garnish with rolls of bacon and sprigs of parsley or watercress. Serve with brown gravy, bread sauce, roast or chip potatoes, and green peas or string beans. For 6 persons.

TO VARY ROAST CHICKEN

CHICKEN WITH BROWN SAUCE: Slit the breast of a roasted fowl to let the juice flow out. Lay sliced, raw onions in the slits. Serve with Brown Sauce (*p.* 102) in the dish.

CHICKEN WITH RAVIGOTE SAUCE: Roast chickens four to six months old. Serve them with Ravigote Sauce (*p.* 108).

CHICKEN WITH SAUCE TARTARE: Serve roasted chickens, about three and a half months old, with Sauce Tartare (*p.* 115).

CHICKEN OR TURKEY CREAMS

6 oz. chicken or turkey   *2 well-beaten eggs*
3 oz. stale breadcrumbs   *¼ pint whipped cream*
1 oz. butter   *salt and pepper to taste*
¼ pint hot milk

Put the chicken or turkey through a mincer. Stir in crumbs. Add butter and milk. Stir well, then add eggs. Beat till blended. Fold in cream and salt and pepper to taste. Three-quarter fill greased dariole moulds. Cover with greased paper. Steam for 10 to 15 minutes. Turn out gently onto a hot dish. Garnish with green peas or chopped truffle. Serve with tomato or white sauce. Serves 6.

CHICKEN DUMPLINGS

½ lb. flour   *2 tablespoons butter or*
4 teaspoons baking powder   *   margarine*
1 teaspoon salt   *1½ cups diced boiled chicken*
½—¾ teaspoon curry powder   *milk as required*

Place flour in a basin. Stir in baking powder, salt and curry powder. Sift into another basin. Rub in fat. Add chicken. Stir in ¾ cup milk, and more if necessary to make a thick dropable batter. Drop from a dessertspoon into a shallow saucepan containing

211

enough boiling chicken stock to cover dumplings. Cover closely. Cook for about 12 minutes without uncovering pan. Serve coated with parsley or mushroom sauce. Serves 6.

CHICKEN ELIZABETH

2 tablespoons melted bacon fat
1 roasting chicken
salt and pepper to taste

1 tablespoon butter
2 or 3 sprigs tarragon
4 or 6 pork sausages

Pour bacon fat into the bottom of a casserole deep enough to take bird. Place bird in casserole. Season with salt and pepper to taste, then plaster with the butter, and top with the washed tarragon. (If you haven't any, sprinkle with a teaspoon of tarragon vinegar.) Cover and bake in a moderate oven, 350° F., for 1½ hours. Prick and arrange sausages down side of dish at half time. Serve with boiled or mashed potatoes and a green salad or spinach. For 4–6 persons.

CURRIED CHICKEN

1 apple
2 peeled onions
2 oz. butter
1 chopped clove of garlic
2 tablespoons curry powder
2 tablespoons flour
2 tablespoons tomato puree

¾ pint chicken stock
½ oz. chutney
½ oz. desiccated coconut
2 tablespoons sultanas
juice of ½ lemon
1 boiled chicken

Peel, core and chop apple. Chop onions. Melt butter in a saucepan. Add apple, onion and garlic. Fry slowly, stirring frequently, for 5 minutes. Add curry powder. Stir for a moment or two, over heat, then add flour, tomato purée and stock. Stir till boiling. Simmer for ½ hour. Add chutney, coconut, sultanas and lemon juice. Cover and simmer for another ½ hour. Meanwhile, remove the meat from chicken. Cut into fair-sized pieces. When sauce is ready, add chicken. Bring to boil. When hot, arrange in a hot dish with boiled rice round. Serve with a dish of mango chutney. Serves 6.

FRICASSÉE OF CHICKEN

There are several ways of making a fricassée of chicken. I like it best made with freshly cooked chicken but left over chicken can be used in the same way. This is how my mother taught me to make it:

a chicken about 4 lb. in weight   1¼ pints boiling water
2 heaped tablespoons chicken   1 oz. flour
   fat or butter   ½ pint milk
salt and pepper to taste

Prepare bird as for boiling. Cut into suitable pieces for serving. Melt fat in a shallow saucepan. When hot, add joints, and fry slowly till brown, turning occasionally. Add salt and pepper to taste and water. Cover closely. Simmer gently until tender in about 1½ hours. Dish up bird. Cream flour with the milk, and stir into stock. Stir till smooth and boiling. Season if necessary. Pour over chicken. Serve with mashed or riced potatoes and green peas. Serves 6.

If you want a white fricassée do not brown joints. Stew as described, then melt fat. Stir in flour. Add milk gradually, stirring constantly. When boiling, season to taste if required, add chopped parsley to taste, and pour over chicken.

FRICASSÉE USING COOKED CHICKEN. 1½ oz. butter, margarine or chicken fat, 1 oz. flour, ¼ pint chicken stock, ½ pint milk, salt and pepper to taste.

Melt fat in a saucepan. Stir in flour. When frothy, stir in stock, then milk. Stir till smooth and boiling. Season with salt and pepper to taste. If a rich sauce is wanted, stir a tablespoon cold water into 2 egg yolks, and stir slowly into the sauce. Reheat chicken in sauce, stirring constantly, but do not allow to boil. *To vary fricassée:* Add 1 teacup fried sliced mushrooms to sauce.

SIMPLE FRICASSÉE: Make 1 pint medium white sauce with ½ pint milk and ½ pint chicken stock, flavoured with onion. Season with salt and pepper to taste. Stir in 1 pint diced, cooked chicken and 2 or 3 tablespoons green peas or sliced fried mushrooms, and serve in one of the following ways:

CHICKEN PATTIES: Fill hot baked patty cases with hot chicken fricassée. Dredge filling lightly with paprika. Reheat in oven.

CHICKEN CANAPÉS OR TOASTS: Pile hot fricassée on rounds or squares of fried bread or toast. Dredge lightly with chopped chives, parsley or paprika.

BAKED POTATOES WITH CHICKEN FILLING: Remove a slice from the top of large potatoes baked in their jackets. Scoop out potato from the centre, leaving a shell of potato nearly ½ inch thick. Fill potato with the hot chicken mixture. Mash the potato you removed. Add hot milk, butter and salt and pepper to taste. Beat till fluffy. Pipe round filling. Bake till golden brown.

CHICKEN TURNOVERS: Roll flaky or rough puff pastry out to between ⅛ and ¼ inch thickness. Cut into rounds or squares, 4 to 5 inches across. Brush with beaten egg white. Fill centres with chicken mixture. Fold in two. Press edges together with the prongs of a fork. Prick top with a fork to allow steam to escape. Bake in a hot oven, until it is golden brown. Garnish with parsley. Serve hot or cold.

CHICKEN SCALLOPS: Pack chicken mixture into greased scallop shells. If liked, put a layer of cooked spinach, sieved and mixed with a little white sauce, in the bottom. Sprinkle lightly with equal quantity of grated cheese and dried breadcrumbs. Pipe if liked with mashed potato. Bake till brown.

HOWTOWDIE

This is a dish of stewed chicken that smacks of French influence. In the early nineteenth century, it was served with eggs poached in the stock.

1 *pullet or plump roasting chicken*
herb stuffing (see below)
4 *oz. butter*
6 *button onions*
2 *whole cloves*
1 *teaspoon salt*
6 *black peppercorns*
¾ *pint boiling stock or water*
5 *or 6 small poached eggs*
2 *lb. spinach*

214

Stuff bird. Close openings and truss. Place in a casserole with the butter and the peeled onions. Roast, in a hot oven, 450° F., for 10–15 minutes, turning frequently till lightly browned, then add the cloves, salt, peppercorns, and a blade of mace if liked. Add stock. Cover. Cook in a moderate oven, 350° F., until tender in about 40 minutes, time necessary depending on the size of the pullet. When ready, remove from oven and strain stock into a saucepan. Wash and add the liver. Simmer gently for 2 or 3 minutes. Remove liver, then poach the eggs in the stock. Boil the spinach meanwhile and rub through a sieve. Add butter and salt and pepper to taste, and a little thick cream. Dress in a circle on a hot ashet. Sieve the liver into the stock. Place bird in spinach nest. Pour sauce carefully over the bird without touching the spinach. Arrange the eggs, poached in giblet stock and neatly trimmed, on the spinach.

TO VARY: Cook 8 oz. champignons in the stock after the liver, and arrange round base of spinach. Scramble the eggs. Sometimes the sauce is thickened with a little creamed cornflour until the consistency of very thin cream.

HERB STUFFING: Mix 2 cups sieved breadcrumbs, with 2 teaspoons minced onion, $\frac{1}{2}$ teaspoon crushed mixed herbs, 1 teaspoon minced parsley, salt and pepper to taste and a pinch of paprika if liked. Melt 2 oz. butter. Stir into mixture.

SMOORED PULLETS

2 *young pullets* *flour as required*
salt and pepper to taste 3 *or 4 oz. butter*

Remove necks from birds and use them with the giblets for stock. Split the pullets down the back. Season inside and out with salt and pepper, then dredge lightly all over with flour. Melt the butter in a strong saucepan. Add the halves of the birds. Fry, turning frequently, till brown all over, then cover tightly. Simmer very gently until tender in about $\frac{1}{2}$ hour, turning at half time. Serves 4.

215

TO VARY: After dishing up, stir 1 cup of sour cream into the pan. Heat, stirring constantly, but do not allow to boil. Arrange each half pullet on a slice of buttered toast or fried bread. Coat with the cream gravy. Garnish with watercress.

A FARMHOUSE WAY OF COOKING
A DUCK

1 *duck*
3 *slices fat salt pork*
1 *sliced medium-sized carrot*
1 *sliced medium-sized onion*
2 *sprigs thyme*
1 *sprig parsley*

1 *bay leaf*
2 *tablespoons butter*
2 *cups boiling giblet stock or water*
flour

Prepare and weigh duck. Cut pork in ¼ inch slices. Fry slowly until all the fat has been extracted, then remove scraps. Add to fat the carrot, onion, thyme, parsley and bay leaf. Fry slowly, turning occasionally, for 10 minutes. Add butter. When melted, add duck. Fry until brown all over, turning frequently till evenly browned. Place on a low rack in a deep roasting tin. Sprinkle with the hot fat. Add stock or water. Cover. Bake in a moderately slow oven, 325° F., until tender, basting often, allowing 20–25 minutes per lb. Add more stock or water if required. When ready, remove bird to a hot dish. Strain gravy. Skim off fat. Thicken with flour creamed with stock or water. Stir until boiling. Season to taste. Serve in a hot sauce boat. Serves 4 or 5.

DUCK WITH ORANGE SAUCE

Melt ¼ lb. butter in a heavy saucepan. Season a young duck and add. Fry slowly, turning frequently, till brown all over. Add ¼ pint chicken or duck giblet stock, the juice of an orange, and 2 or 3 snippets of orange rind. Cover pan. Cook slowly till tender, in about ½ hour.

ROASTIT BUBBLY-JOCK

1 *hen turkey*, 12–14 *lb.*   *sausagemeat stuffing* (*see below*)
chestnut and oyster stuffing   *salt and pepper to taste*
   (*see below*)

Wash and dry bird. Rub the inside with salt. Fill crop lightly with chestnut and oyster stuffing, then fold the skin over onto the back and skewer or sew in place. Stuff body with sausage meat and sew up or skewer opening or close it with a heel of stale bread. Truss and weigh. Place bird on one side on rack in a roasting tin. Brush all over with melted butter or chicken fat. Cover with a piece of butter muslin dipped in melted fat. Roast, uncovered, in a slow oven, 300° F., until tender, allowing about 20 minutes per lb. Baste every ½ hour with drippings in pan and turn at the same time on its other side, so that the bird cooks evenly. When half cooked, sprinkle all over with salt and pepper or paprika to taste. Remove muslin ½ hour before dishing up and turn bird on its back. Baste well, and continue to cook until evenly browned. Untruss. Dish up. Garnish with watercress, and bacon and mushroom rolls, and paper frills. Serve with brown gravy, bread sauce, green peas and roast potatoes.

CHESTNUT AND OYSTER STUFFING: 1 pint sieved boiled chestnuts, ½ cup melted butter or margarine, 1 small teaspoon salt, pepper to taste, ¼ cup top milk, 1 cup dry breadcrumbs, 2 tablespoons chopped parsley, ½ cup chopped celery, 1 tablespoon grated onion, 1 pint small oysters.

Mix the chestnut purée with all the fat except 2 tablespoons, salt, pepper, top milk, crumbs, parsley, celery and onion. Chop the oysters, and simmer for 2 minutes in the remainder of the melted fat and add.

SAUSAGEMEAT STUFFING: 2½ lb. pork sausage meat, minced fried turkey liver, salt and cayenne pepper to taste, 1 tablespoon minced onion, ¼ teaspoon crushed herbs.

Mix ingredients together till blended.

BACON AND MUSHROOM ROLLS: Allow 1 rasher of thin streaky

bacon and 2 small peeled mushrooms per person. Halve the rashers. Roll a mushroom up in each portion, and run on the skewer. Grill slowly till bacon is crisp.

BROWN GRAVY: Pour off all the drippings from pan except 1½ tablespoons. Sprinkle in 3 teaspoons flour, then stir in about ¾ pint giblet stock. Bring to boil, stirring constantly, then season with salt and freshly-ground pepper and add a dash of gravy browning if necessary.

CRANBERRY SAUCE: 1 lb. sound cranberries, ¾ lb. granulated sugar, 2 teacups water.

Pick over and wash cranberries, in a colander under the cold water tap. Drain thoroughly. Place berries, sugar and water in a saucepan. Bring to boil. Cover. Simmer for about 10 minutes till skins all break, then skim and cool. Pour into sterilized small pots and seal. Use as required. This will make about 1½ lb. of sauce.

CREAMED TURKEY

3 *tablespoons butter*
2 *tablespoons flour*
1 *cup milk*
salt and pepper to taste
1½ *cups diced cooked turkey*
cayenne pepper and celery salt to taste
2 *hard-boiled eggs*
3 *tablespoons sherry*

Melt butter in the top of a double boiler. Stir in flour. When frothy, draw pan to side, and stir in milk. Return to stove. Stir till boiling. Season to taste with salt, pepper, cayenne pepper and celery salt. Add turkey and stir until boiling. Separate eggs. Mince yolks and chop egg whites. Add gradually with sherry, stirring constantly. (If preferred, substitute cream for half the wine.) Serve on croûtes of fried bread or hot buttered toast, or in hot patty cases. Serves 3 or 4.

TO VARY: Substitute 2 tablespoons sliced bottled mushrooms for the eggs.

218

BARNYARD PIE

½ lb. raw poultry
¼ lb. ham
salt and pepper to taste
pinch of grated nutmeg
1 teaspoon minced parsley
1 lb. flour

chicken or turkey stock as
   required
1 teaspoon salt
¼ lb. lard
⅓ pint milk or water
¼ lb. pork sausagemeat

Remove any bone or skin from chicken, duck, goose, guinea fowl or turkey. Weigh meat. Cut into small pieces. Cut up ham to match. Mix the poultry with the ham, salt and pepper to taste, nutmeg, parsley and stock. Hard-boil two eggs and cut them in 6 or 7 pieces. Sift flour and salt into a heated basin. Melt lard in a small saucepan. Stir in milk. Bring to boiling point. Pour into centre of flour. Mix into a paste as quickly as possible. Turn onto a floured board. Knead until smooth and free from cracks. Cut off about a quarter and keep warm for the lid, etc. Mould the larger piece at once into a raised pie mould—or cake tin, failing a mould—or round a slightly heated, straight-sided jam jar, making the bottom and walls equally thick. Roll out beforehand if liked. Trim edges with a pair of scissors. Season sausagemeat if necessary, and line the bottom of the mould thinly, drawing it up the sides as far as it will go. Half fill case with the poultry mixture. Cover with the eggs, points outwards. Pack in remainder of poultry mixture. Pat and roll out remainder of pastry into a round to form a lid. Brush the inside edge of the pie crust. Lay lid on top. Press edges together. Trim neatly with scissors, leaving a ridge about ½ inch high, standing up round pie. With a pair of scissors, snip the ridge about ½ inch apart, then bend the snipped pieces alternately outwards and inwards. Make a good hole in the middle. Brush top with beaten egg yolk mixed with equal quantity of water. Decorate round hole with foliage made from trimmings. Coat with egg glaze. Bake on a greased baking sheet in a fairly hot oven, 425° F., for 16–20 minutes. Reduce heat to 325° F. and bake until meat is tender when tested with a skewer and the pastry is golden, in about 1½ hours. Fill up pie in the centre through a funnel with liquefied jellied poultry stock. Serve cold with a salad. Decorate pie with watercress.

SCRAMBLED CHICKEN OR DUCK LIVERS

2 *chicken or duck livers*
1 *walnut butter*
seasoned flour as required
2 *eggs*

1 *teaspoon minced parsley*
salt and pepper to taste
2 *slices hot buttered toast*

Wash and dry livers. Melt butter. Chop livers. Toss in seasoned flour and fry slowly, turning occasionally, till cooked through. Meanwhile, beat eggs slightly and add parsley. Melt enough butter or margarine to cover bottom of a small saucepan. Add egg, milk and salt and pepper to taste. Stir over slow heat till egg is scrambled. Divide equally between toasts. Make a hollow in the centre of each. Fill up with fried liver and any gravy. Serve at once. Serves 2.

SAVOURIES

ABERDEEN NIPS

6 *oz. cooked smoked haddock*   *salt and pepper to taste*
¼ *pint thick white sauce*   *paprika to taste*
2 *egg yolks*

Chop the haddock finely. Place in a small saucepan. Add sauce, egg yolks and salt and pepper to taste. Stir over low heat till mixture thickens. Pile on fried croûtes of bread. Sprinkle with paprika. Serve in a circle. Garnish with sprigs of parsley. Serves 4.

ACACIA JUMBLE

1 *egg*   1 *tablespoon Worcester or*
1 *egg yolk*   *Harvey sauce*
1 *tablespoon grated Parmesan*   *cayenne pepper to taste*
   cheese   *fried bread*

Mix egg and egg yolk with the cheese, sauce and cayenne pepper to taste. Rub through a sieve into a saucepan. Stir till piping hot then spread on fried bread. Serves 1.

CANAPÉS ROB ROY

Allowing 3 per person, cut out strips of bread about 2½ inches long and from ¾ to 1 inch wide. Toast lightly and spread at once with butter. Keep hot. Season soft roes with salt and pepper. Sprinkle them with a few drops of lemon juice or vinegar. Cover strips with roes. Cook under the grill till slightly coloured. Dredge lightly with cayenne pepper.

CHEESE TOASTS

4 *oz. butter*
3 *oz. grated cheese*
3 *oz. grated bread*
1 *teaspoon made mustard*

2 *egg yolks*
salt and pepper to taste
6 *slices of bread*

Beat butter till creamy. Stir in cheese, grated bread, mustard, egg yolks and salt and pepper to taste. Beat till blended. Remove crusts from bread slices. Toast the bread. Spread with the paste. Brown under the grill. Serve at once. Serves 6.

CURRIED CHICKEN CANAPÉS

1 *cup finely chopped cooked*
   chicken
1 *cup finely chopped cooked*
   ham

½–1 *teaspoon curry powder*
¾ *cup thick white sauce*
6 *slices of bread*
fine breadcrumbs as required

Mix chicken and ham. Add curry powder and white sauce. Toast slices of bread on one side. Butter untoasted side and spread with a thick layer of curried chicken, then sprinkle thickly with fine breadcrumbs. Place in a buttered fireproof dish. Bake in a hot oven for 5 minutes. Serves 6.

SCOTCH FLIPPERS

1 *oz. flour*
salt and cayenne pepper to
   taste
½ *oz. butter*
1 *oz. grated cheese*

½ *egg yolk*
few drops lemon juice
½ *tablespoon cream*
savoury cream

Sift the flour with the salt and cayenne pepper into a small basin. Rub in butter. Stir in cheese, egg yolk, lemon juice and cream.

Roll out into a round or oval. Prick well all over. Cut into small rounds or ovals. Bake a little apart on a lightly-greased baking sheet in a moderately hot oven, 375° F. for about 10 minutes, till pale gold. Cool on a wire rack. Use as follows:

SAVOURY CREAM: Peel a scalded tomato, then rub it through a sieve. Heat slightly. Add 2 sheets of gelatine. Stir over hot water to dissolve. Mince 1 tablespoon shelled shrimps finely. Place in a basin. Strain in tomato purée, then add ¼ gill liquefied aspic jelly, ½ tablespoon mayonnaise, salt and pepper to taste and a squeeze of lemon juice, and a few drops of carmine. Half whip ½ gill cream, and gradually stir in shrimp mixture. Pour into a flat wet dish to the depth of ¼ inch and leave until set. Cut into rounds or ovals to fit biscuits and lift one with a palette knife on to each biscuit. Whip a little cream stiffly. Season to taste with salt and paprika, or with cayenne pepper, then add a drop of carmine. With an icing bag fitted with a rose pipe force a line of roses down the centre of each, or cover each with a lattice work of cream. Serve on a platter covered with a plain paper doiley.

DALMENY CANAPÉS

thin slices of bread	*2 teaspoons anchovy paste*
2 oz. butter	*squeeze of lemon juice*
2 hard-boiled egg yolks	*cayenne pepper to taste*

Stamp out rounds of bread about 2 inches across. Fry in a little butter till golden below, then turn and fry on the other side till the same shade. Beat the butter into the egg yolks, then beat in the anchovy paste, lemon juice and cayenne pepper. Place in a forcing bag. Pipe it criss-cross over the croûtons. Powder with minced parsley.

FINNAN CANAPÉS

½ oz. butter	*salt and pepper to taste*
1 tablespoon milk	*4 small squares of buttered toast*
¼ lb. cooked Finnan haddock	*1 teaspoon minced parsley*
2 slightly beaten eggs	

Place butter in a saucepan. Add milk. Heat till butter is melted, then add flaked haddock. Stir gently till smoking hot. Remove from stove. Stir in eggs. Season to taste with salt and pepper. Stir over slow heat till mixture scrambles. Pile on squares of toast. Sprinkle with the parsley. Serves 2.

FISH CRISPS

1 *cup flaked crab*	1 *tablespoon grated onion*
½ *teaspoon Worcester sauce*	¼ *teaspoon dry mustard*
1 *cup thick white sauce*	*salt and pepper to taste*
1 *tablespoon butter*	*potato crisps*

Heat all ingredients together in a saucepan, stirring constantly. Season to taste. Pile on rounds of fried bread. Sprinkle lightly with crisped potato crisps. Serve at once. Serves 3.

A GRAMPIAN WAY WITH A KIDNEY

1 *large Spanish onion*	*salt and pepper to taste*
1 *quartered sheep's kidney*	

Peel and halve the onion. Carefully cut out the heart and substitute the kidney. Season with salt and pepper. Join the two halves. Wrap in shortcrust. Bake on a well-buttered tin in a moderate oven, 350° F., for about 1¼ hours. Serves 1.

KIDNEY AND MUSHROOM TOAST

2 *sheep's kidneys*	¼ *lb. mushrooms*
¾ *oz. flour*	¼ *pint stock*
salt and pepper to taste	1 *teaspoon ketchup*
1 *oz. butter*	½ *teaspoon piquant sauce*

Skin the kidneys. Core, then cut kidneys into small pieces. Toss in the flour seasoned with salt and pepper. Melt butter. Add kidneys and mushrooms, roughly chopped, and fry slowly for

$\frac{1}{2}$ minute, then stir in remainder of flour, stock, ketchup and sauce. Simmer gently for about 7 minutes, stirring almost constantly until kidneys are tender. Pile on strips of hot buttered toast. Garnish with finely-minced parsley, mixed with a sieved hard-boiled egg yolk. Serves 2.

KIPPER SNACKS

1 *large meaty kipper*
$\frac{1}{2}$ *gill well-seasoned white sauce*
2 *oz. peeled mushrooms*

butter as required
pepper, salt and paprika to taste

Grill kipper and carefully remove all flesh. Flake into tiny pieces. Add to white sauce. Fry mushrooms in a little hot butter, then chop and add to creamed kipper. Season mixture highly to taste. Fry rounds of bread, $\frac{1}{4}$ inch thick, and 3 inches across, in melted butter till golden brown on one side only. Sandwich the rounds with the filling, keeping the fried side of the bread to the outside. Place a large fried mushroom on top of each. Garnish with parsley. *Yield:* 6 snacks.

LOCH FYNE TOASTS

8 *large mushrooms*
butter as required
salt and pepper to taste

2 *Loch Fyne kippers*
8 *rounds of hot buttered toast*
lemon juice and coralline pepper

Peel and remove stalks from mushrooms. Fry them in melted butter slowly so that they do not shrink. Dust each with salt and pepper. Grill kippers slowly, then skin them and slip the flesh off the bones. When cold, pound in a mortar with $\frac{1}{2}$ oz. of butter and pepper to taste. Have rounds of toast, $2\frac{1}{2}$ or 3 inches across, ready. Spread a layer of the kipper mixture on each, and lay a mushroom on top. Sprinkle lightly with lemon juice. Dust with coralline pepper. Heat quickly in oven. Serves 4.

MARROW TOAST

Saw the marrow bone. Remove the marrow. Cut into pieces about 3 inches long. Drop into boiling salted water for 1 minute. Drain very thoroughly on a sieve. Season with salt and pepper and sprinkle with a very little minced parsley and a squeeze of lemon juice. Mix quickly till blended. Spread on fingers or squares of hot buttered toast. Serve at once, as a breakfast or dinner savoury.

NEWHAVEN CANAPÉS

1 *fillet of cooked smoked*   3 *tablespoons minced beetroot*
  herring   *French dressing as required*
1 *peeled cooking apple*   8 *canapés*
2 *cold boiled potatoes*   8 *cooked button mushrooms*
1 *tablespoon shredded celery*

Chop herring. Core and chop apple. Slice and chop potatoes. Mix till blended. Stir in celery and beetroot, and French dressing to moisten. Divide equally between 8 canapés of toast or fried bread. Dredge lightly with paprika. Top each with a cold fried mushroom in centre. Serves 4.

RAGS AND TATTERS

3 *oz. flour*   1 *oz. grated Cheddar cheese*
pinch of salt   1 *oz. grated Parmesan cheese*
dash of cayenne pepper   *beaten egg as required*
2 *oz. butter*

Sift dry ingredients into a basin. Rub in butter with a pinch of made mustard if liked. Stir in Cheddar and Parmesan cheese and enough of the egg to make a stiff paste. Roll out thinly on a lightly floured board. Spread half the paste thinly with beaten egg then with anchovy essence or paste or chutney. (If liked, sprinkle picked shrimps evenly on top.) Brush the other half with beaten egg. Fold over the filled half. Press layers lightly together. Cut with a pair of floured scissors into small odd shapes. Bake on a greased baking sheet in a hot oven, 475° F., until golden brown if to be served at once. Dredge lightly with salt and cayenne pepper. If to be served later, bake only till pastry is risen and very pale gold, and reheat when wanted. Serve piping hot on a hot dish covered with a paper doily.

STUFFED SARDINES

6 *large sardines*
½ *tablespoon picked shrimps*
1 *teaspoon capers*

1 *oz. butter*
cayenne pepper to taste
1 *hard-boiled egg yolk*

Drain oil from sardines, then carefully open them and remove the backbones. Place the fish on a dish. Sprinkle with a dessert-spoon of vinegar, and stand 10 minutes. Drain well. Mince shrimps, then pound with the chopped capers, butter and cayenne pepper to taste, until into a thick paste. Stuff sardines. Arrange on a dainty dish. Sprinkle each lightly with sieved egg yolk. Serve with thin brown bread and butter. Serves 6.

SCOTCH WOODCOCK

There are several versions of this old-fashioned Scottish savoury. Some suggest using chopped anchovies, others anchovy paste.

WITH ANCHOVIES: Cut 4 slices bread into triangles, then remove the crusts. Wash, scrape and chop seven anchovies. Beat 4 egg yolks with ½ pint of thin cream. Now toast the bread on both sides. Spread thinly with butter and sandwich the triangles with the chopped anchovies. Place on heated plates. Season the egg yolk mixture with salt and cayenne pepper and stir in the top of a double boiler over boiling water until thick. Pour over the toast. Sprinkle with minced parsley. If wanted as a savoury enough for 4. If wanted for a snack enough for 2.

WITH ANCHOVY PASTE: Pour 3 beaten egg yolks into the top of a double boiler. Gradually stir in ¼ pint cream, and cayenne pepper.

Cut 3 slices of bread into rounds as large as possible. Toast them, then butter and spread each with anchovy paste to taste. Stir the yolk mixture over boiling water till scrambled. Divide equally between the toasts. Serve at once. Serves 3.

BREAD, SCONES AND TEABREAD

Scotland has long been famous for her baking. Nowhere in the British Isles do you find better bread, and the variety of scones she offers defies description. Time was when the girdle took the place of the oven in Scotland, but not now. With the advent of solid fuel cookers and the development of electricity nearly every Scottish home has a modern oven.

After I had my first lessons in baking at the age of ten, I baked the puff pastry for our mince pies, choux pastry for our éclairs, shortbread and other teabread in our old coal range after testing the heat of its oven with my hand. When I was twelve I took on all the baking for our household of twelve. Twice a week I turned out a batch of bread and 'teabread' as we call all fancy buns and cakes. In my early 'teens I added currant and wholemeal breads to my repertoire.

MRS MACPHERSON'S BROWN BREAD
(*A Skye Recipe*)

8 oz. wholemeal
4 oz. self-raising flour
½ teaspoon salt
1 teaspoon bicarbonate of soda

1 teaspoon cream of tartar
golden syrup as required
milk as required

Mix the wholemeal, flour, salt, soda and cream of tartar with enough golden syrup to fold round a knife, and then with enough fresh milk to form a soft dough. Place in a greased tin with a lid. Mrs Macpherson suggested a round dried milk tin. Cover with lid. Bake in a moderate oven, 350° F., for 50 minites, then uncover and bake for 10 minutes.

CARAWAY LOAF

1 *tablespoon butter*	1 *teaspoon cream of tartar*
1 *lb. sifted flour*	1 *teaspoon salt*
1 *teaspoon caster sugar*	2 *teaspoons caraway seeds*
1 *teaspoon bicarbonate of soda*	*buttermilk as required*

Rub butter into flour. Mix the sugar with the soda, cream of tartar, salt and caraway seeds. Stir into flour mixture. Mix to a light dough with buttermilk. Place in a cake or loaf tin, greased and floured. Bake in a moderate oven, 350° F., till dry in the centre in about 1 hour.

PLAIN CURRANT BREAD

2 *lb. flour*	1 *pint tepid water*
1 *oz. bakers' yeast*	2 *teaspoons salt*
1 *teaspoon caster sugar*	¾ *lb. cleaned currants*

Sift flour into a heated basin. Make a bay in the centre. Cream the yeast with the sugar. Add ½ pint of the water. Pour into the bay. Stir in enough of the flour from the sides, to make a thick batter. Sprinkle the salt over the flour round the edge of bay. Cover and stand in a warm place for 15 minutes. Stir in the remainder of water, alternately with the remainder of flour till you have a soft, dry dough. Knead in the currants. At the end of 5 minutes, cover with a cloth. Stand in a warm place till well risen in about 30 minutes. Shape into 2 loaves. Place each in a greased loaf tin, filling it half full. Cover and stand in a warm place for about 20 minutes until the dough has risen to the rim of the tins. Brush tops lightly with milk. Bake in a hot oven, 450° F., for 15 minutes, then lower to 375° F. Bake for about ½ hour till loaves sounds hollow when tapped. Turn on to a wire tray to cool.

DUNDEE BREAD

1 oz. bakers' yeast
1 teaspoon caster sugar
1 tablespoon butter

1 tablespoon lard
4 lb. flour
1 tablespoon salt

Mix the yeast and sugar to a cream. Cut up butter into a quart measure. Fill up measure with cold water. Turn into a large jug. Add 1 pint of scalded milk. Cool till between 90° and 100° F., and then pour over the yeast. Turn into a bread mixer, slightly heated in the oven. Add flour. Cover mixer with lid, then stir for 3 minutes. Cover and place in a lukewarm oven till dough doubles its size. Remove from oven. Stir for a second, then pull out dough on to a slightly heated floured pastry board. Divide in four equal portions. Knead each well. Place each in a greased loaf tin. Stand in a warm place, covered with a large cloth and protected from all draughts until the loaves have doubled their size, in about 20 minutes. Bake in a hot oven, 450° F., for 15 minutes, then lower to moderate and bake till ready.

SPICED FRUIT BREAD: Follow the above recipe, but use 2 oz. yeast, and increase butter to ¾ lb. Beat in 3 eggs, 1 lb. cleaned currants, 1 lb. cleaned sultanas, ¼ lb. roughly chopped raisins, ¼ lb. minced candied peel, ¾ teaspoon ground cinnamon, 1 teaspoon ground ginger, 1 teaspoon ground mace and 1½ teaspoons ground all-spice.

OAT BREAD

1 cup scalded milk
1 cup water
½ cup golden syrup
1 teaspoon salt

1 oz. bakers' yeast
1½ lb. flour
2 cups rolled oats

Cool milk to 80° F. and heat water to the same temperature. Pour both into a large slightly heated basin and add syrup and salt. Crumble in the yeast. Stir occasionally till the yeast is dissolved. Sift flour. Add 1 lb. Beat with a wooden spoon until smooth, then cover. Stand in a warm place to rise till double its size in about 2½ hours. Stir in rolled oats and remainder of flour. Knead till dough is elastic and smooth, then place in a greased basin. Turn dough in basin till slightly greased all over. Cover and leave in a warm place to rise for about 1¾ hours till double its size. With your fingers draw the corners down into the centre. Punch well down. Cover again and leave in a warm place for 1 hour. Turn on to a floured board. Cut in two equal portions. Knead into loaves. Cover. Stand for 10 minutes, then shape neatly and place each in a well-greased loaf tin. Brush the tops with melted butter. Cover. Leave in a warm place for 40 minutes. Bake in a moderately hot oven, 375° F. to 400° F., for 20 minutes then lower to moderate, 350° F., and continue to bake for about 40 minutes until nicely browned.

WHOLEMEAL BREAD

2 *lb. stone ground wholemeal*	½ *teaspoon sugar*
1 *lb. flour*	*about ¼ pint tepid water*
3 *oz, butter*	½ *pint tepid milk*
1 *oz. bakers' yeast*	1½ *teaspoons salt*

Place the wholemeal in a warm basin. Sift in flour. Mix well. Rub in butter. Mix the yeast and the sugar till liquid. Stir in tepid water and milk. Make a hollow in the centre of dry ingredients. Pour in the liquid. Sprinkle the salt over the surrounding flour. Mix to a smooth dough with a wooden spoon. Cover with a cloth. Leave in a warm place to rise, but not too near the fire, till doubled its size, in about an hour. Knead till smooth and free from stickiness. Divide in equal portions. Shape each into a neat loaf, then place in greased loaf tins. (They should half fill the tins.) Cover and leave in a warm place to rise for about 30 minutes when the dough should have reached near the top of the tins. Bake in a fairly hot oven, 425° F., for about 15 minutes, then lower temperature to moderate, 350° F., and bake from 25 to 35 minutes till the loaf sounds hollow when tapped below.

AULD YULE LOAF
(*Forres Recipe*)

6 *oz. butter*
6 *oz. lard*
1½ *lb. sifted flour*
1 *lb. moist brown sugar*
1½ *lb. currants*
½ *lb. sultanas*
2 *oz. chopped candied peel*

4 *oz. chopped almonds*
½ *teaspoon salt*
½ *teaspoon grated nutmeg*
4 *beaten eggs*
2 *oz. bakers' yeast*
¼ *pint warm milk*

Rub the butter and lard in turn into the flour. Stir in sugar, currants, sultanas, peel, almonds, salt and nutmeg. Make a well in the centre. Add eggs. Dissolve yeast in the milk. Pour over the eggs. Beat in flour from edge with a wooden spoon then beat with hand till into a dough. Cover. Stand in a warm place to rise for 1 hour. Turn into a large greased cake tin about 10 inches in diameter. Bake in a slow oven, 300° F., for about 3 hours.

Note: I am told that in bygone days a teaspoon of bicarbonate of soda was dissolved in a tablespoon of the warm milk and added to flour mixture with the yeast. I cannot understand why. It could be substituted for the yeast, I should say.

NEWBARNS FRUIT LOAF

½ *lb. cooking fat*
½ *lb. caster sugar*
1 *lb. flour*
2 *teaspoons baking powder*
2 *beaten eggs*

½ *lb. cleaned currants*
½ *lb. cleaned sultanas*
2 *oz. blanched almonds*
2 *tablespoons milk*

Use either butter or margarine, or half and half. Beat with sugar till creamy. Sift flour and baking powder. Add flour and eggs alternately to the fat and sugar. Lightly stir in fruit. Chop almonds and add with the milk. Mix lightly till blended. Pour into a large, greased loaf tin. Bake in a moderate oven, 350° F., for 2½–3 hours, till dry when tested in the centre with a heated skewer.

SELKIRK BANNOCK

In the summer of 1867 when Queen Victoria was in residence at Floors Castle, she paid a visit to Melrose Abbey and then went on to Abbotsford where a rich repast was awaiting her. To the surprise of everyone all she wanted was a cup of tea and a piece of Selkirk Bannock.

2 lb. bakers' dough	½ lb. cleaned sultanas
¼ lb. lard	½ lb. cleaned currants
½ lb. butter	¼ lb. minced, candied orange
½ lb. caster sugar	peel

Place dough in a basin. Rub in the fats, then knead in the sugar and fruit. Knead till thoroughly blended. Shape into a round. Place in a greased cake tin. Cover and place in a warm place until well risen in about 30 minutes. Bake in a moderate oven, 350° F., till lightly browned in about 1¼ hours, time depending on size of tin.

A SIMPLE TEA LOAF

½ lb. flour	6 oz. butter or margarine
½ teaspoon bicarbonate of soda	milk as required
1 teaspoon cream of tartar	¼ lb. cleaned currants
½ teaspoon salt	¼ lb. cleaned sultanas
1½ oz. caster sugar	2 oz. minced candied peel

Sift dry ingredients into a basin. Rub in fat. Stir in milk as required to make a moist dough, then fruit and peel. Turn into a greased loaf tin. Bake in a moderate oven, 350° F., for fully one hour, brushing top if liked with milk or equal quantity of beaten egg and milk when loaf is almost ready. Keep for 24 hours before cutting.

TO VARY: Substitute 1 oz. of chopped crystallized ginger for half the peel, and sift ½ teaspoon of mixed spice with the dry ingredients. If liked, substitute 2 oz. chopped walnuts for 1 oz. each of the currants and sultanas.

GLAZED DINNER ROLLS

2 *lb. flour*
1¾ *teaspoons salt*
1 *teaspoon caster sugar*

1 *oz. bakers' yeast*
about 1½ *gills tepid milk*
about 1½ *gills tepid water*

Sift flour and salt into a basin. Beat sugar and yeast to a cream. Mix the milk with the water. Stir half the mixture into the sugar and yeast. Make a hollow in the centre of flour. Stir in the yeast mixture, then enough of the flour round the edge to make a stiff batter. Sprinkle a little of the flour over the batter. Cover with a clean cloth. Stand in a warm place till the mixture in the centre is into a sponge in about 10 minutes, then stir in all the remaining flour from the sides, and add the remainder of milk and water as required to make a stiff dough. Knead well, then make a cross-cut with a knife over the centre. Cover and stand in a warm place to rise for about 1 hour. Divide into 2½ dozen equal portions. Knead each up into a small roll. Place a little apart in a slightly floured baking sheet. Stand in a warm place to rise for about 15 minutes. Bake in a hot oven, 450° F., for about 15 minutes. When almost ready, brush with beaten egg or milk.

MORNING ROLLS

There are many kinds of Morning Rolls in Scotland, bearing different names, according to where they are made, such as Baps, Butteries and 'Softies'. They vary not only from town to town, but shop to shop, depending on the baker, the fat, the flour and the oven.

SOFTIES

I am sorry I haven't been able to trace the method of making Softies, but here are the ingredients for anyone who cares to experiment.

1 *lb. strong flour*
½ *pint water, 100° F.*
fully ½ *oz. bakers' yeast*

fully ¼ *oz. salt*
1¼ *oz. fat*
1 *oz. caster sugar*

ABERDEEN MORNING ROLLS

1ST MIXTURE

1 *lb.* 2½ *oz. strong flour*   *fully* ¾ *oz. yeast*
1¼ *oz. fat*   *barely* ½ *pint water*
¼ *oz. salt*

2ND MIXTURE

5¼ *oz. fat and margarine*   2 *oz. flour*
barley ½ *oz. salt*

Make the dough with the first mixture, the water heated to 85° F., and the other ingredients added at normal temperature which will give you a finished dough approximately 72° F.

METHOD FOR FIRST DOUGH: Sift the flour into a basin. Make a well in the centre. Place salt and fat in the well. Dissolve yeast in the water at temperature given, and place in centre of well. Gradually work in all the flour from the sides. When thoroughly mixed, keep it cosy with dry cloths. When risen, in about ½ hour, knock the air out of the dough, and wrap the basin up well again. Repeat this in another ½ hour.

METHOD FOR SECOND DOUGH: Mix the ingredients in the second list thoroughly, but only till blended. If you overdo this mixture, they will 'oil'. When the first dough has lain for 1½ hours, spread it out as flat as possible and spread the second mixture over it, either with your knife or hands. Fold dough in two and roll out as for flaky pastry. Divide into pieces of equal size to form ovals or rounds according to taste, about 3 inches long and 2 inches wide if oval, and 3 inches across if round. If desired floury, dust with flour after brushing them with milk and water, but if preferred glazed, simply brush with milk and water. Repeat this treatment after standing a little apart on a greased, floured tin or baking sheet in a warm place for 15 minutes, then press a finger into the centre of each to prevent blisters. Bake in a hot oven, 450° F., for about 15 minutes. Serve warm or cold but they must be eaten fresh.

BAPS

1 *lb. plain flour* 1 *teaspoon sugar*
¾ *teaspoon salt* ¼ *pint milk*
2 *oz. lard* ¼ *pint water*
1 *oz. yeast*

Heat mixing bowl. Sift in flour and salt. Rub in fat. Place yeast in small basin. Add sugar. Rub with the bowl of a wooden spoon till liquid. Heat milk and water till tepid, 98° F. Add to yeast, then strain into the flour. Mix to a soft dough. Cover and stand in a warm place for about an hour until bulk is doubled. Knead lightly, then divide into small, squarish pieces. Dust with flour. Place on a greased tin dredged with flour. Cover and stand in a warm place until double their size, in about ¼ hour. Bake in a hot oven, 425° F., for about ¼ hour. Serve hot.

ABERDEEN BUTTERIES

1 *lb. flour* ¾ *pint tepid water*
1 *oz. bakers' yeast* 6 *oz. lard*
1 *level tablespoon salt* 6 *oz. butter or margarine*
1 *level tablespoon caster sugar*

See that all utensils are warm, as they should be when working with yeast. Sieve flour. Mix yeast, salt and sugar and add to the flour along with the tepid water. Mix together and set in a warm place to rise until twice its bulk, keeping it covered with a warm damp towel while it proves. Beat fats till blended, then divide fats into three equal parts. Roll out dough on a floured board into a strip. Dot the first part of the fat over it in small pats. Fold in three and roll out as for flaky pastry. Repeat twice until fat is used up. Divide into 'Buttery' shapes. Put a little apart on a greased and floured tray and prove in a warm place for another thirty minutes, then bake in a fairly hot oven for 20–25 minutes.

OATMEAL CAKES

Oatcakes are a delicate relish
When eaten warm with ale.
BURNS

May the mouse ne'er leave our meal-pock, wi' the tear in its e'e.

Visitors to Scotland are usually bewildered by the many forms our teabread takes, and confused when they find that on the Braes of Angus a thick oatcake is labelled a bannock, whereas in Selkirk a bannock is a fruit scone. Both are 'fired' on a girdle.

To make perfect girdle cakes, you need not only a girdle which in early days took the place of the modern oven, but a spathe, a heart-shaped, long-handled iron implement used for lifting cakes from board to girdle, and a rolling pin for all rolled out cakes and a banana-rack, or toaster for toasting oatmeal bannocks and oatcakes. *Always heat girdle before starting to prepare batter or dough.*

DROP BANNOCKS

1 *egg*	¼ *teaspoon salt*
1 *pint milk*	*oatmeal as required*
¼ *teaspoon bicarbonate of soda*	

Beat egg. Stir in milk. Stir in soda, salt and enough oatmeal to make a dropable batter. Pour into a jug. Rub the girdle over with a piece of suet. Pour the batter into small rounds as for drop scones. Fire over moderate heat till bubbles form on top, then turn and fire on the other side.

BRANDON BANNOCKS

To make these in the old-fashioned way, you need a brander such as our grandmothers used for grilling steaks over charcoal or live coal.

1 *large breakfast cup oatmeal*	2 *tablespoons dripping*
a small pinch of bicarbonate of soda	*tepid water as required*

Place the oatmeal in a basin. Stir in soda, dripping and enough water to make a dough. Strew the pastry board with medium oatmeal. Place the dough on the board. Sprinkle with oatmeal. Knuckle it out into a round cake from $\frac{1}{4}$ to $\frac{1}{2}$ inch thick, then cut in quarters. Lift one quarter up at a time, and shake lightly, then place on brander. Toast over a clear fire, then turn and toast on the other side. Place in a toaster to finish off. In bygone days, the toaster used for this operation was hooked to the bars of the grate.

GARRION BARLEY BANNOCKS

1 *lb. barley meal*
$\frac{1}{4}$ *lb. flour*
$\frac{1}{2}$ *teaspoon salt*

1 *pint buttermilk*
2 *small teaspoons bicarbonate of soda*

Mix the barley meal with the flour and the salt. Pour the buttermilk into a jug. Add the soda. As the mixture fizzes up, pour it into the meal and flour. Work into a soft dough, then dredge with flour and roll lightly to about $\frac{1}{2}$ inch thickness. Cut into large rounds. Fire on a hot girdle, turning scones when brown below so that they brown on other side.

BANNOCKS

Up to the last century, from time immemorial, a special kind of bannock was 'fired' for every Highland quarter day. On the first of February, the 'Bonnach Bride' helped us to celebrate the dawn of spring. On May Day, the 'Bonnach Bealltain' was produced to greet the summer. On the first of August, the 'Bonnach Lunasstain' heralded the autumn, while the last quarter day, the first of November, demanded a 'Bonnach Samhthain' to announce the arrival of winter.

There were rites attached to the service of many bannocks, most of which were made of oatmeal, in those times. We read in *The Scots Kitchen* about the sweet 'Cryin' Bannock' that was served to the 'kimmers' in attendance when a child was born, of the 'Teethin' Bannock' made with oatmeal and butter or cream, sometimes with a ring in it, for a child cutting teeth, and of the

'Bonnach Salainn' (Salt Bannock) served in the Highlands on Hallowe'en because it was claimed that those who partook of it would dream of the future so long as they neither spoke nor drank water after eating it.

With the passage of the years many of the old customs my maternal great grandmother used to crack about have died out and the popularity of cakes made of oatmeal has unfortunately slightly waned. It is a pity as they are an excellent accompaniment to broth, cheese and herrings in any shape or form, and if there is anything more delicious for breakfast than a well-made oatcake, spread with good butter and marmalade or heather honey, I have yet to meet it.

OATCAKES

When thin oatcakes are required, roll dough to one-eighth of an inch in thickness then cut into quarters. If thick are preferred, pat or roll into large rounds about 6 inches across, then cut into 4 quarters, then halve them if liked. If thick 'bannocks' are wanted, roll only to $\frac{1}{4}$ inch thickness.

$\frac{1}{2}$ lb. oatmeal	small $\frac{1}{4}$ teaspoon bicarbonate
$\frac{1}{2}$ teaspoon salt	of soda
$\frac{1}{2}$ to 1 tablespoon melted fat	about $\frac{1}{2}$ teacup hot water

Heat girdle slowly. Mix the oatmeal with the salt, and bicarbonate of soda. Make a bay in the centre. Pour in the melted fat, using bacon or ham fat or dripping, then stir in enough hot water to make a very stiff dough. Turn onto a board rubbed with plenty of medium oatmeal. Knead thoroughly. Divide in 2 equal portions. Knead into 2 smooth balls, then shape into 2 rounds. Press out a little, then roll out to $\frac{1}{4}$ inch in thickness. Cut out neatly with a plate, and rub with oatmeal. Now you have 2 bannocks ready to be fired. If thinner cakes are preferred, roll each to an eighth of an inch in thickness, then cut into 4 farls or 8 triangles. With a spathe or spatula slip on to girdle, smooth side uppermost. Bake over moderate heat until the edges of the cake or cakes begin to curl. Remove carefully to board. Rub smooth side with oatmeal, and either toast in front of a clear fire, in a moderate oven or

240

under the grill till crisp and faintly brown. When cold, store in the girnel or meal chest, and take out as required.

HINTS ON MAKING OATCAKES. 1. To make good oatcakes, you must work quickly, and rub frequently with oatmeal when kneading to prevent dough sticking. 2. To keep edges even pinch them with thumbs and forefingers as they show signs of breaking when rolling out cakes. 3. If you haven't a girdle use a strong frying pan. 4. Reheat if not freshly fired shortly before serving. 5. Serve with butter and honey or marmalade for breakfast, with broth or cheese for dinner, and with boiled, fried or grilled herring for lunch, high tea or supper.

MIDLOTHIAN OATCAKES

8 oz. oatmeal
4 oz. flour
½ teaspoon salt

1 teaspoon caster sugar
1 teaspoon baking powder
3 oz. butter

Place oatmeal in a basin. Sift in flour, salt, sugar and baking powder. Rub in butter or use half butter and half lard. Mix to a stiff dough with cold water. Turn dough onto a board sprinkled with oatmeal. Knead lightly. Roll to ¼ inch thickness. Cut into rounds to taste. Bake in a moderate oven, 350° F., for about 25 minutes.

BALLATER SCONES

1 lb. flour
2 teaspoons cream of tartar
3 oz. butter

1 small teaspoon bicarbonate
    of soda
½ pint tepid milk

Sift flour and cream of tartar into a basin. Rub in butter. Dissolve soda in the milk. Stir into dry ingredients. Knead to a stiff paste. Roll out on a lightly floured board into a round ½–¾ inch thick. Cut into rounds, 2 or 2½ inches across. Bake a little apart on a lightly greased baking sheet in a hot oven, 450° F., for 10 to 15 minutes. When done, brush tops lightly with milk. Serve split and buttered hot. *Yield:* About 2 dozen.

BARLEY MEAL SCONES

¼ pint milk
¼ pint water
7 oz. barley meal

1 teaspoon butter or dripping
¼ teaspoon salt

Pour the milk and water into a small saucepan. Add barley meal, fat and salt. Bring to a boil, stirring constantly, then remove pan from stove, and stir in enough additional barley meal to make a soft dough. Turn out onto a floured board. Knead rapidly till smooth and firm. Cut into thin round scones about the size of a bread and butter plate. Quarter. Bake on a hot girdle on one side, till turning brown, then turn and bake on the other. Serve hot, with salt butter. *Yield:* About 1 dozen.

BERE MEAL SCONES

1 lb. flour
1 lb. bere meal
2 teaspoons bicarbonate of soda
1 teaspoon cream of tartar

1 teaspoon salt
½ oz. butter
milk as required

Sift the flour with the meal, soda, cream of tartar and salt into a basin. Rub in butter. Mix to a dough with milk or buttermilk. In the Highlands buttermilk is used. Roll out on a floured board. Cut into rounds with a large pan lid, then in quarters. Fire on a floured heated girdle till brown below, then turn and brown on the other side. In the north these are sometimes baked on a brander on a hearth with a peat fire.

BROWN SCONES

½ lb. flour
¾ cup wholemeal
¾ cup flaked oats
½ teaspoon bicarbonate of soda
½ teaspoon cream of tartar

½ teaspoon salt
1 dessertspoon cornflour
2 tablespoons caster sugar
2 tablespoons butter or lard
about ½ pint sour or buttermilk

Mix the flour with the wholemeal, flaked oats, soda, cream of tartar, salt, cornflour and sugar. Rub in fat. Mix to a stiff dough with the milk. Roll on a lightly floured board into a round about 1½ inch in thickness. Cut in four triangles. Bake on a floured baking sheet at 425° F. for about 25 minutes.

BROWN FARMHOUSE SCONES

2 oz. flour
½ teaspoon salt
1½ oz. caster sugar
2 oz. butter or margarine

6 oz. wholemeal flour
3 teaspoons baking powder
½ gill milk

Sift flour, salt and sugar into a basin. Rub in fat. Stir in wholemeal flour and baking powder. Mix well, then add milk, using more if required to make a soft dough. Knead lightly into a flat round on a lightly floured board. Place on a greased baking sheet. Mark into 6 triangles with the back of a floured knife. Bake in a hot oven, 450° F. for about ¼ hour. When nearly cooked, break the triangles apart. Split and butter hot.

BUTTERSCOTCH SCONES

7 oz. flour
1 oz. cornflour
1 teaspoon baking powder

pinch of salt
1 oz. butter
milk to mix

FILLING: *butter and brown sugar*

Sift the flour with the cornflour, baking powder and salt into a basin. Rub in the butter. Mix to an elastic dough with milk. Turn onto a floured board and knead lightly. Roll out into an oblong shape ¼ inch thick. Spread with butter and sprinkle liberally with soft brown sugar. Roll up like a Swiss roll. Cut into slices and bake in a hot oven, 475° F., for 8–10 minutes.

CINNAMON FARLS

½ lb. self-raising flour
½ teaspoon ground cinnamon
¼ teaspoon salt
1½ oz. bacon fat

1 teaspoon sugar
½ gill milk
½ gill water

Sift flour, cinnamon and salt into a basin. Rub in fat. Add sugar. Mix to a soft dough with the milk and water. Shape lightly into a round on a lightly floured board. Roll to ½ inch thickness. Cut into triangles with a floured knife. Bake a little apart on a greased baking sheet in a fairly hot oven, 425° F., for about 9 minutes, until dry and lightly coloured. *Yield:* 9 Farls.

HOT COBBS

1 tablespoon butter
1 dessertspoon lard
1 lb. flour
1 teaspoon bicarbonate of soda
1 dessertspoon caster sugar

2 small teaspoons cream of
  tartar
pinch of salt
about 2 cups milk

Rub the fats into the flour. Stir in soda, sugar, cream of tartar, salt and milk to make a soft dough. Turn onto a floured board. Knead as little as possible. Roll out and cut into rounds about 2 inches across. Place a little apart on a greased baking sheet. Brush tops with beaten egg. Bake in a hot oven, 450° F., until risen and golden in 8–10 minutes. Split and butter hot.

CREAM SCONES

½ lb. flour
1 small teaspoon cream of
  tartar
½ teaspoon bicarbonate of soda

2 teaspoons caster sugar
½ teaspoon salt
2 oz. butter
about ¼ pint thin cream

Sift the dry ingredients into a basin. Rub in the butter. Stir in the cream and a little milk if necessary so as to form a soft dough. Turn on to a lightly floured board. Roll out to about ¼ inch in thickness. Cut into small or large rounds. Place a little apart on a lightly greased baking sheet. Bake in a hot oven, 450° F., for about 10 minutes. Split, butter and serve hot piled on a hot dish or in a muffineer, lined with a doily.

CRUMPETS

¼ lb. flour
¼ teaspoon salt
½ oz. butter
about 1¼ gills milk

½ oz. bakers' yeast
1 teaspoon caster sugar
1 beaten egg

Sift flour and salt into a basin. Melt butter. Add milk. Stand until tepid. Cream the yeast with the sugar. Add milk to egg. Stir into yeast mixture. Make a well in centre of flour. Strain yeast into well. Mix flour to a batter with the yeast mixture. Beat until smooth. Cover. Stand in a warm place to rise for about 45 minutes. Grease a heated girdle. Drop batter in rounds a little apart from a tablespoon or jug. Bake till brown below, then turn and bake on other side. Butter and roll up. Serve hot on a hot plate covered with a paper doily or in a muffin dish with boiling water below.

Note: If a thinner crumpet is wanted, increase milk to ½ pint.

DROPT SCONES

½ lb. sifted flour
½ teaspoon salt
1 oz. caster sugar
½ teaspoon bicarbonate of soda

½ teaspoon cream of tartar
1 beaten egg
about 1½ gills buttermilk

Heat girdle. Mix the dry ingredients thoroughly in a basin. Make a bay in the centre. Add egg and half the milk. Stir till thick, then thin with remainder of milk to the consistency of thick cream. Pour into a jug. Rub girdle with a piece of suet held in a cloth or tissue paper. Pour batter out into rounds about 3 inches across, placing them a little apart. Fire till light brown below, and bubbles form on top, then turn and fry on other side. Place in a folded towel as cooked until all are ready. Serve buttered hot, or cold with butter and honey or strawberry jam. Children like them buttered hot, then topped with fine brown sugar.

MEMUS MUFFINS

1 *lb. flour*
2 *teaspoons cream of tartar*
1 *oz. bicarbonate of soda*
3 *oz. caster sugar*

2 *oz. butter*
1 *beaten egg white*
sweet or buttermilk as required

Sift flour with cream of tartar, soda and ½ teaspoon salt. Stir in sugar. Rub in butter. Mix the egg white with a ¼ pint milk. Stir into flour with enough additional milk to make a soft dough. Turn onto a floured board. Roll out lightly to 1 inch thickness. Cut into rounds with floured biscuit cutter, about 3 inches across. Place a little apart on a lightly greased baking sheet. Bake in a very hot oven, 450° F., for about 12 minutes.

PAPA'S FAVOURITE SCONES

1 *lb. barley meal*
½ *lb. medium oatmeal*
½ *lb. flour*
1 *teaspoon bicarbonate of soda*

½ *teaspoon cream of tartar*
½ *teaspoon salt*
buttermilk as required

Mix the dry ingredients with a wooden spoon in a basin. Stir in enough buttermilk to make a soft dough. Roll on a lightly floured board. Cut into large rounds and fire on a heated floured girdle, till brown on one side, then turn and brown on the other.

STRONE GIRDLE SCONES

¾ *pint buttermilk*
½ *cup cream*
1 *teaspoon bicarbonate of soda*
½ *teaspoon baking powder*

1½ *tablespoons caster sugar*
½ *saltspoon salt*
sifted flour as required

Grease girdle before placing on stove. Pour the buttermilk into a large basin. Stir in the cream, soda, baking powder, sugar, salt and as much flour as required to make a battery dough that can be 'lifted nicely' with a tablespoon. Fire 1½ inches apart on floured girdle until small bubbles appear on top. Turn carefully and brown on the other side. *Yield:* 6 or 7 large scones.

Note: The scones were usually about the size of a small meat plate, but can be made any size to taste. Serve with butter and heather honey or strawberry jam. When you become expert at making these scones, do not spoon them onto girdle. Dredge board with flour. Spoon the batter, made like a thick pancake batter, onto flour till the scone is as large as you want it, then pat the flour round the edge and gradually get your hands under it and lift it quickly onto hot girdle. Repeat till all are fired on both sides.

THRUMS POTATO CAKES

2 oz. butter	½ teaspoon baking powder
½ lb. cold boiled potatoes	¼ teaspoon salt
4 oz. flour	

Beat butter into potatoes. Sift flour with baking powder and salt. Stir into potato mixture. Turn onto a lightly floured pastry board. Roll out thinly. Cut into rounds about the size of a saucer. Prick well with a fork. Fire for 3 minutes on each side on a hot girdle or strong frying pan. Serve hot or cold.

TREACLE GIRDLE SCONES

½ lb. flour	½ teaspoon ground cinnamon
¾ teaspoon bicarbonate of soda	½ teaspoon ground ginger
1 teaspoon cream of tartar	½ oz. butter
½ teaspoon salt	1 tablespoon black treacle
2 teaspoons caster sugar	buttermilk as required

Sift the flour with the soda, cream of tartar, salt, sugar and spices.

Melt butter slowly with the treacle until both run freely. Stir into the flour with enough buttermilk to make a soft dough, firm enough to knead. Turn onto a lightly floured board. Divide in two. Gently knead each into a round about ½ inch thick. With a floured knife, divide each in quarters. Fire on a hot floured girdle over moderate heat till dry and lightly browned below in 5 or 6 minutes, then turn and cook on the other side. Serve with butter.

YETHOLM GIRDLE CAKES

1 *lb. flour*
½ *lb. butter*

½ *teaspoon salt*
cream or milk as required

Sift flour into a basin. Rub in butter. Stir in salt. Mix to a rather firm paste with thin cream or milk. Roll out to about ¾ inch thickness. Cut into rounds. Bake on a heated girdle over moderate heat until brown below, then turn and brown on other side. Split and butter hot.

SCOTCH COOKIES

1 *lb. flour*
1 *teaspoon salt*
2 *oz. butter or lard*
1½ *gills warm milk*
1 *beaten egg*

¾ *oz. bakers' yeast*
2 *oz. caster sugar*
1½ *oz. cleaned currants or*
  sultanas

Sift flour and salt into a basin. Dissolve the butter or lard in the milk, then stir in the beaten egg. Beat yeast to a cream in a small heated basin with a teaspoon of the sugar, then stir in the milk gradually. Make a hollow in centre of flour. Stir in creamed yeast, then draw in enough flour from the sides to make a stiff batter. Sprinkle a little flour over the top, then cover with a clean cloth. Stand in a warm place for about an hour until well risen, then knead in remaining sugar and fruit. Turn onto a lightly floured board. Divide in ten equal portions. Mould, and roll each into a round. Place a little apart on a greased baking sheet. Place in a warm spot for about 15 minutes until risen, then bake in a fairly hot oven, 425° F., for about 20 minutes. When ready, glaze with a piece of butter held in a piece of muslin. *Yield:* 10 cookies.

TO VARY: Omit the fruit. When cold, split and fill with raspberry jam and whipped cream.

ATHOLE CAKES

3 *oz. butter*	$\frac{1}{2}$ *teaspoon baking powder*
2$\frac{1}{2}$ *oz. caster sugar*	1 *oz. finely-minced candied*
2 *eggs*	*lemon peel*
5 *oz. cornflour*	

Cream butter. Gradually beat in sugar. Beat till fluffy, then beat in 1 egg at a time. When blended, stir in the cornflour, baking powder and peel, and a little milk if necessary to make a batter. Three-quarter fill greased gem tins, dusted with rice flour. Bake in a moderate oven, 350° F., for 15–20 minutes. When cold, coat tops with white glacé icing, flavoured rum. Decorate with chocolate shot or pink coconut or sugar.

BALMORAL BONNETS

$\frac{1}{2}$ *pint water*	1 *walnut of butter*
1 *cinnamon stick*	2 *beaten egg yolks*
peel of 1 *lemon*	*pinch of salt*
3 *tablespoons flour*	

Pour water into a saucepan. Add cinnamon stick and lemon peel. Simmer for 10 minutes, then strain. Leave until nearly cold, then stir enough into the flour to make a smooth cream. Add remainder of water. When blended, turn into a saucepan. Cook for 2 or 3 minutes, stirring constantly, then add the butter. Stir till blended, then remove from heat and leave until cold. Beat in egg yolks and salt. When thoroughly blended, drop into hot deep fat from a dessertspoon. Fry till golden brown, turning in the fat as necessary, then drain on absorbent paper. Serve on a hot plate, covered with a paper doily. Dredge with sifted icing sugar. Garnish with lemon.

BACHELORS' BUTTONS

¼ lb. butter   2 oz. caster sugar
10 oz. sifted flour   2 eggs

Beat butter till creamy. Stir in half the flour, then the sugar. Beat eggs. Stir into mixture, then stir in remainder of flour and vanilla essence to taste. Divide into small pieces, thumb size, and flatten each into a round the size of a shilling piece. Dredge with caster sugar. Bake in a moderately hot oven, 375° F., for about 12 minutes until light brown.

COBURG CAKES
(Drynoch Recipe)

¼ lb. butter   ½ lb. self-raising flour
¼ lb. brown sugar   ½ teaspoon ground ginger
¼ lb. golden syrup   ½ teaspoon ground allspice
2 beaten eggs

Place butter, sugar and syrup in a saucepan. Heat almost to boiling point, stirring occasionally, then remove from stove. Gradually beat in eggs. When blended, sift flour with spices and stir rapidly into egg mixture. Beat till smooth. Three-quarter fill 24 greased patty tins. Bake in a moderate oven, 350° F., for about 20 minutes. Remove from oven. Stand for 2 or 3 minutes, then turn onto a wire rack to cool.

Note: If using plain flour, sift ½ teaspoon bicarbonate of soda with the flour and spices.

TO VARY: Add ½ teaspoon of ground cinnamon, and place a split blanched almond in the bottom of each tin before adding batter.

COFFEE BUNS

½ lb. flour
1 teaspoon baking powder
2 oz. butter
2 oz. caster sugar

1 beaten egg
1 dessertspoon coffee essence
about ½ gill milk

Sift flour and baking powder. Rub in butter. Stir in sugar. Mix the egg with the essence, and add with as much of the milk as is necessary to make a stiff dough. Divide into about a dozen small equal portions. Roll each lightly into a ball. Place a little apart on a floured baking sheet. Brush with equal quantity of beaten egg and black coffee. Dredge with caster sugar. Bake in a hot oven, 425° F., for about 20 minutes.

CLUNIE ROCK BUNS

2 oz. butter
8 oz. flour
3 oz. caster sugar
2 tablespoons grated chocolate
2 oz. chopped nuts

2 oz. stoned raisins
¼ teaspoon mixed spice
1 teaspoon baking powder
1 beaten egg
milk as required

Rub butter into the flour. Stir in sugar, chocolate, nuts, raisins, mixed spice and baking powder. Add egg and enough milk to make a stiff dough. Shape into balls with floured hands. Place a little apart on a floured tin. Bake in a moderate oven, 350° F., for about 20 minutes till golden brown. Dredge with caster sugar. *Yield:* About 18.

CUPID CAKES

1 oz. glacé cherries
1 oz. citron peel
3 oz. butter or margarine
3 oz. caster sugar

2 beaten eggs
¼ lb. flour
¼ teaspoon baking powder
½ teaspoon vanilla essence

Chop cherries and citron peel. Beat fat until softened. Gradually beat in sugar. Beat until creamy. Beat eggs. Sift flour with baking powder. Add flour and eggs alternately to the fat and sugar, beating between addition. Stir in cherries, citron peel and vanilla essence. Mix lightly. Three-quarter fill greased patty tins. Bake in a moderately hot oven, 375° F., for about 20 minutes. Cool on a wire rack. Spread with rum glacé icing. Decorate with silver balls, or with a cherry cut like a flower on top of each, and angelica leaves and stalks. *Yield:* About 12 cakes.

FAIRY CAKES

¼ *lb. butter*	*pinch of salt*
¼ *lb. caster sugar*	*2 oz. quartered glacé cherries*
2 eggs	*2 oz. cleaned currants*
½ *lb. self-raising flour*	*milk as required*

Cream butter. Beat in sugar. When fluffy, beat in 1 egg at a time. Sift flour with salt. Stir 2 or 3 tablespoons into the cherries and currants, then add to batter with enough milk to make a dropable batter. Stir in fruit. Three-quarter fill greased patty tins. Bake in a moderately hot oven, 375° F., till golden in 15–20 minutes. Dredge with vanilla sugar. *Yield:* 20–24 cakes.

FLY CAKES

½ *lb. flour*	*3 drops lemon essence*
1 oz. caster sugar	¼ *lb. cleaned currants*
¼ *lb. butter*	

Mix the flour with the sugar. Rub in butter. Stir in enough ice-cold water, mixed with the lemon essence, to make a soft but dry dough. Roll out thrice on a lightly-floured pastry board, rolling the last time into a rectangle. Spread half the dough thickly with the currants. Cut off the other half and lay on top. Press lightly together. Cut into fingers, about 2 × 1 inches, or 2 inch squares. Bake in a hot oven, 450° F., till golden brown.

HOLYROOD ROUT CAKES (1851)

Beat ½ lb. of butter to a cream. Add to the beaten yolks of twelve eggs. Stir in ½ lb. of fine sifted sugar, the freshly grated rind of a lemon, and 12 oz. of sifted flour. Add a few drops of orange flower water, or a few pounded blanched almonds. When blended, pour mixture into a greased, paper-lined mould, or baking tin. Let the batter be scarcely 1 inch thick. Bake it and when cool cover it with icing. When icing is set, cut with a sharp knife and ruler into squares, diamonds, lozenges, etc.

JAM THUMBS

½ lb. flour
3 teaspoons baking powder
¼ teaspoon salt
1 tablespoon caster sugar

3 tablespoons butter
about ¾ cup milk
1 banana
strawberry jam as required

Stir flour with baking powder and salt. Stir in sugar. Cream butter and stir into flour mixture, then add enough of the milk to make a soft dough. Roll out on a lightly floured board into a found about ¼ inch thick. Cut into rounds about 2½ inches across, and cut out the centres of half the rounds with a doughnut cutter or a liqueur glass. Brush edges of solid rounds with lightly beaten egg white and place a ring on top of each. Peel, chop and mash banana with about 2 tablespoons strawberry jam, and spoon this into the centre of each. Bake in a hot oven, 450° F., for about 20 minutes. *Yield:* 1 dozen.

MELTING MOMENTS

6 oz. butter
4–6 oz. caster sugar
2 beaten eggs

8 oz. cornflour
2 teaspoons baking powder
grated rind ½ lemon

Beat butter till creamy. Add sugar. Beat till fluffy. Add egg alternately with the cornflour and baking powder sifted together. If necessary, which may be if the eggs are small, stir in a little milk so as to have a fairly soft mixture. Stir in lemon rind or ½ teaspoon flavouring essence to taste. Half fill greased patty tins or use paper baking cases. Bake in a fairly hot oven, 425° F., for 15–20 minutes. *Yield:* About 24.

TO VARY: Substitute 2 oz. flour for 2 oz. of the cornflour. Sift with cornflour mixture. Use vanilla essence, and add about a tablespoon of milk to the batter.

ORANGE GINGER BUNS

¾ *lb. flour*	½ *teaspoon cream of tartar*
6 *oz. caster sugar*	1 *teaspoon ground ginger*
3 *oz. butter*	*grated rind 2 oranges*
½ *teaspoon bicarbonate of soda*	2 *eggs*

Sift flour and sugar into a basin. Rub in butter. Stir in soda, cream of tartar, ground ginger and orange rind. When blended, beat and stir in eggs with enough milk to make a rather stiff dough. With a dessert or tablespoon place rough heaps of the mixture a little apart on a greased baking sheet. Bake in a moderate oven, 350° F., until golden brown in about 30 minutes. Dust with orange icing sugar.

TO VARY: Omit ginger and substitute 2 oz. chopped candied orange peel for the orange rind.

QUEENIE'S NUT SLICES

PASTRY

½ *lb. butter*	½ *lb. flour*
½ *cup moist brown sugar*	½ *teaspoon salt*

TOPPING

1 *level tablespoon flour*	1½ *cups moist brown sugar*
1 *teaspoon baking powder*	2 *eggs*
1 *cup desiccated coconut*	1 *teaspoon vanilla essence*
1 *cup chopped walnuts*	

Beat the butter till creamy, then stir in the sugar. Sift the flour with the salt and add to butter and sugar. Knead to a dough. Roll out thinly into a rectangle, on a baking sheet covered with a greased paper. Bake in a moderate oven, 350° F., for 15–20 minutes. Mix all the ingredients for the topping in the order given, while the pastry is cooking. Spread quickly and thinly over the pastry. Bake in a moderate oven for about 35 minutes.

PARLEYS
(PARLIES)

½ lb. butter or margarine
1 small cup treacle
1 lb. flour

1–1½ oz. ground ginger
½ lb. moist brown sugar

Melt the fat and the treacle until boiling. Sift the flour with the ground ginger. Stir in sugar, then add the fat and treacle. As soon as the mixture has cooled sufficiently, knead it until smooth. Roll out into a rectangle on a sheet of greased paper to fit a baking sheet. Mark in 4 or 4½ inch squares with a knife. Grease baking sheet lightly and carefully draw paper on to the baking sheet. Bake in a slow oven, 300° F., until risen and lightly browned in about 40 minutes. Break into squares.

TO VARY: In some parts of Scotland a beaten egg is added after the fat and treacle.

RASPBERRY OR STRAWBERRY BUNS

6 oz. ground rice
6 oz. flour
¼ lb. butter
¼ lb. caster sugar
1 teaspoon baking powder

1 egg yolk
a little milk
raspberry or strawberry jam
1 egg white

Mix the ground rice with the flour. Rub in butter. Stir in sugar, and baking powder. Mix to a stiff paste with egg yolk and a little milk. Divide into small equal-sized balls. Hollow each in the centre and insert a teaspoonful of raspberry or strawberry jam. Brush the edge of hollows with beaten egg white, then pinch them together. Dip the balls in beaten egg white. Flatten slightly with a knife. Bake a little apart, in a fairly hot oven, 425° F., for about 20 minutes. Dredge with caster sugar when half cooked. *Yield:* 15 buns.

RASPBERRY FINGERS

¼ *lb. flour*
3 *oz. butter*
1 *oz. ground almonds*
1 *oz. caster sugar*
1 *egg yolk*
2 *drops almond essence*
raspberry jam

Sieve flour. Rub in butter. Stir in almonds, sugar, egg yolk and almond essence. When into a stiff paste, chill. Roll out into thin equal-sized sheets on a baking sheet covered with lightly greased paper. Bake in a moderate oven, 350° F., till pale yellow in about 15 minutes. Remove carefully to wire racks. Pair with raspberry jam. Cut into fingers. If liked, coat top and sides of fingers with glacé icing flavoured with raspberry essence. Decorate with chopped blanched pistachio nuts.

GLENOGIL SAND CAKES

¼ *lb. butter*
3 *oz. caster sugar*
5 *oz. cornflour*
2 *beaten eggs*
½ *teaspoon baking powder*
few drops vanilla essence

Cream butter. Beat in sugar. When blended, sift in cornflour, then gradually stir in the eggs, baking powder and vanilla essence in order given. Half fill greased patty tins. Bake in a moderately hot oven, 375° F., for about 20 minutes. Turn out, then dredge with caster sugar. *Yield:* 14 or 15 cakes.

WEST LOTHIAN NUTS

$\frac{1}{4}$ lb. butter
$\frac{1}{4}$ lb. caster sugar
1 small egg

$\frac{1}{4}$ lb. cornflour
$\frac{1}{4}$ lb. flour
$\frac{1}{2}$ teaspoon baking powder

Cream butter. Gradually beat in sugar. When fluffy, stir in egg and cornflour sifted with the flour and baking powder. Shape into small equal-sized balls. Flatten them a little. Bake a little apart on a greased baking sheet in a moderately hot oven, 400° F., until a pale gold in about 15 minutes. Cool on a wire rack, then pair with apricot jam or lemon curd. Dust tops with caster sugar.

BALMORAL FRUIT CAKE

$\frac{3}{4}$ lb. unsalted butter
$\frac{3}{4}$ lb. caster sugar
6 eggs, separated
$\frac{3}{4}$ lb. sifted flour
6 oz. chopped candied orange
  peel

4 oz. candied citron peel
$\frac{1}{2}$ nutmeg, grated
1 teaspoon ground caraway
  seeds
3 oz. blanched Jordan almonds
$\frac{1}{2}$ wineglass brandy

Beat the butter with your hand to cream, then beat in the sugar. Add 1 egg yolk, sprinkle with a little of the flour, and beat till blended. Continue in this way until all the yolks are added, then place the orange peel in a basin. Cut the citron peel into thin narrow strips and add. Stir in a little of the remaining flour, the grated nutmeg, caraway seeds and the almonds, split in two. Gradually stir in the fruit mixture, then the flour. Beat egg whites to a stiff froth. Fold into mixture, then stir in the brandy, and a teaspoon of rose water if liked. Place in a greased cake tin, smoothly lined with 3 layers of greased paper, 8 × 3 or 3$\frac{1}{2}$ inches. Smooth the top with a palette knife. Sprinkle lightly with caraway comfits. Bake in a fairly slow oven, 325° F., for about 3$\frac{1}{2}$ hours, until dry in the centre when tested with a warm skewer.

BLACK BUN

PASTRY

¾ lb. flour
pinch of salt
4 oz. butter

½ teaspoon baking powder
beaten egg as required

FILLING:

1 lb. flour
½ lb. caster sugar
2 lb. Muscatel raisins
2 lb. cleaned currants
6 oz. almonds
2 oz. mixed candied peel
½ teaspoon black pepper
½ oz. Jamaica pepper

½ oz. ground ginger
½ oz. ground cinnamon
1 rounded teaspoon cream of
  tartar
¾ teaspoon bicarbonate of soda
½ pint milk
1 tablespoon brandy or sherry
beaten egg as required

TO MAKE PASTRY: Sift the flour with the salt. Rub in the butter. Stir in baking powder and enough beaten egg to give you a dough like shortcrust. Roll out pastry and line a large cake tin.

TO MAKE FILLING: Sift the flour. Stir in sugar. Prepare fruit. Stone and chop raisins. Mix with half the flour, then stir in currants, chopped blanched almonds, chopped peel and the peppers mixed with the spices. Sift remainder of flour with the cream of tartar and soda. Stir into fruit mixture, then stir in milk and brandy or sherry. Pack into lined tin. Level filling, then roll remainder of pastry into a round to make a pastry lid. Brush top of pastry edge with cold water. Lay lid on top. Make 4 holes right down to the bottom with a skewer. Prick all over top with a fork. Brush with beaten egg. Bake in a moderate oven, 350° F. (Regulo 3), for about 3 hours, until dry when tested with a skewer. Keep for at least 10 days before cutting.

BRAEMAR FRUIT CAKE

1 *lb. cleaned currants*
¼ *lb. stoned raisins*
¼ *lb. mixed candied peel*
2 *oz. blanched almonds*
½ *lb. butter*
½ *lb. moist brown sugar*
4 *eggs*
½ *lb. flour*

¼ *teaspoon salt*
½ *teaspoon baking powder*
1 *teaspoon mixed spice*
grated rind 1 *lemon*
1 *teaspoon rose water*
½ *gill brandy*
2 *teaspoons browning*

Line a greased 8-inch cake tin smoothly with 3 layers of greased paper. Place currants in a basin. Chop and add raisins. Mince the peel with the almonds and add to the fruit. Beat butter till softened, then gradually beat in sugar. Beat till fluffy. Drop 1 egg into the mixture. Sprinkle with a little of the flour and beat till blended. Continue beating in eggs in this way until all are added. Sift remaining flour with the salt, baking powder and spice. Gradually beat into the fat mixture, then stir in the lemon rind, rose water, brandy and browning, in this order. When blended, place in prepared tin. Bake in a slow oven, 300° F., for about 3¾ hours, until dry in the centre when tested with a warm skewer.

CELESTIAL CAKE

10 *oz. flour*
5 *oz. butter*
5 *oz. caster sugar*
ginger as required

3 *oz. chopped green citron peel*
3 *eggs*
milk as required
1 *large teaspoon baking powder*

Sift flour. Cream butter. Beat in sugar. When frothy, stir in half the flour. Mix the remainder with 3–6 oz. chopped, crystallized or preserved ginger, and citron peel. Beat the 3 eggs one at a time, into the butter mixture, then stir in the fruit mixture and milk as required to make a dropable batter. When blended, stir in baking powder. Bake in a greased cake tin 8 × 3 inches, smoothly lined with greased paper, in a fairly slow oven, 325° F., for about 1¾ hours until dry when tested in the centre with a heated skewer. Remove from tin. Peel off paper and cool on a wire rack. Cover with boiled almond paste, then with fondant icing, to taste and decorate.

BOILED ALMOND PASTE: Dissolve ½ lb. caster sugar in ½ gill water, then boil to 250° F. Remove pan from stove. Add 5½ oz. ground almonds. Stir till blended, then stir in 1 egg yolk. Pour over cake and spread smoothly with a palette knife. Leave until set.

FONDANT ICING: Place 1½ lb. loaf sugar in a saucepan. Add ½ pint cold water. Stir over low heat till sugar is dissolved. Add 1 dessertspoon glucose. Stir till dissolved, then stop stirring and place a sugar-boiling thermometer in pan. Bring to boil, then skim. Boil rapidly until the thermometer registers 238° F. Remove pan to side of stove and take out thermometer and place it in boiling water. Leave the syrup to settle for 2 or 3 minutes, then pour it into a large basin rinsed with cold water. When cool enough to 'work', start stirring sides to centre, then beat until stiff and thick. Knead with your hands till smooth. If to be kept, store in a jar. Cover with waxed paper. If to be used shortly, cover basin with a towel and stand for 1 hour, then place in the top of a double boiler with cold water in pan below. Heat very slowly till fairly warm, but it must not be hot. If too thick for pouring, thin with water. As this icing sets rapidly, it must be used at once, coloured to taste if liked.

GLENOGIL CHRISTENING CAKE

¾ lb. butter	3 oz. candied orange peel
¾ lb. caster sugar	2 oz. candied citron peel
1 lb. sifted flour	¼ lb. cherries or raisins
1½ teaspoons ground ginger	¾ lb. cleaned currants
1 teaspoon baking powder	¾ lb. cleaned sultanas
8 separated eggs	¼ lb. almonds
3 oz. candied lemon peel	1 teaspoon browning

Line a greased cake tin, 9 inches across, with 3 layers of greased paper. Cream butter. Beat in sugar. Beat till fluffy. Sift flour with ginger and baking powder. Beat egg yolks for 5 minutes. Add a little egg to fat and sugar. Dredge with a little of the flour. Beat till blended. Continue mixing in this way until all the egg is incorporated, then stir in half the flour. Add remaining to chopped peels, halved cherries or raisins, currants and sultanas. Stir into batter. Add split blanched almonds, a teaspoon of browning and the egg whites beaten till stiff. Fold them in as lightly as possible. Bake in a moderate oven, 350° F., until dry in the centre when tested with a heated skewer, in about 4 hours. Cool on a wire rack, then cover with almond paste and frost.

ALMOND PASTE: Mix 1 lb. ground almonds with the whipt whites of 4 eggs. Stir in 1 lb. sifted icing sugar. Beat well. Spread on cake coated with beaten egg white. Place in a cool oven to dry. Stand for 12 hours, then cover with

SUGAR ICING: Beat 4 egg whites to a stiff froth. Sift in 1 lb. icing sugar mixed with 1 oz. fine starch. Spread evenly with a palette knife. Leave in a cool place to harden.

CHRISTMAS CAKE

1½ lb. flour
4 level teaspoons baking powder
1 teaspoon salt
¾ lb. butter
1 small nutmeg, grated
¾ lb. moist brown sugar
¼ lb. ground almonds
1 lb. raisins or sultanas
2 lb. cleaned currants
1 lb. shredded candied peel
6 eggs and ¼ lb. brown sugar
½ pint milk

Line a greased cake tin, 10 inches across, with 4 folds of greased paper. Wrap a fold of brown paper round the outside of tin, and tie in place. Imbed the tin in salt packed in a baking tin. Sift flour with baking powder and salt. Rub in butter. Stir in nutmeg, sugar and almonds. Put half the raisins or sultanas through a mincer. Stir into remainder. (If preferred, use only ¾ lb. raisins or sultanas, and a ¼ lb. halved glacé cherries.) Add currants and peel. Stir fruit mixture into the flour mixture. Beat eggs with the brown sugar for 10 minutes. Stir in half the milk. Add to dry ingredients,

then stir in remainder of milk. Mix well. Half fill tin. Hollow out
centre. Bake in a moderate oven, 350° F., till dry in the centre
when tested with a heated skewer, in about 3½ hours.

DUNDEE CHRISTMAS CAKE

¾ lb. butter
¾ lb. brown sugar
1 lb. flour
¼ teaspoon bicarbonate of soda
½ teaspoon salt
¾ lb. cleaned sultanas
½ lb. chopped mixed peel
6 oz. halved glacé cherries

grated rinds of 2 lemons
grated rinds of 2 oranges
3 oz. Jordan almonds
8 eggs
1 teaspoon vanilla essence
1 dessertspoon sherry
¼ teaspoon browning or ½ gill
    caramel

Beat butter till softened. Gradually beat in sugar. Beat till fluffy.
Sift flour with soda and salt. Prepare the fruit, peel and lemon and
orange rinds. Blanch and chop almonds. Beat 1 egg. Drop it into
the butter and sugar. Sprinkle with a teaspoon of the flour and
beat till blended. Add all the eggs in this way, then stir in half
the remainder of flour. Stir the remainder of flour into fruit mixture and almonds and rinds. Stir the vanilla essence, sherry and
browning or caramel into the butter mixture, then fold in the
fruit and nuts. (If no orange rinds are available, substitute 1 tablespoon orange marmalade.) The batter should be dropable. If not,
add buttermilk or sour milk as required. Pack lightly into a
greased cake tin 9 inches across, lined smoothly with 3 folds of
greased paper. Hollow out the centre slightly. Place tin inside a
baking tin thickly lined with kitchen salt. Tie a thick fold of brown
paper round the outside of tin. Bake in a slow oven, 300° F., for
about 6 hours, until dry in the centre when tested with a warm
skewer.

CREAM FINGERS

2 *unbeaten eggs*
$\frac{1}{2}$ *lb. caster sugar*
$1\frac{1}{4}$ *gills thin cream*
8 *oz. flour*
$2\frac{1}{4}$ *teaspoons baking powder*

$\frac{1}{4}$ *teaspoon salt*
$\frac{1}{4}$ *teaspoon ground cinnamon*
$\frac{1}{8}$ *teaspoon ground mace*
$\frac{1}{8}$ *teaspoon ground ginger*

Beat the eggs, sugar and cream vigorously together till blended. Lightly stir in the flour, sifted with the baking powder, salt and spices. Spread in a shallow greased baking tin. Bake in a moderate oven, 350° F., for about $\frac{1}{2}$ hour. Cut into fingers. Dust with sugar.

CURLY MURLY

2 *oz. yeast*
1 *cup tepid milk*
1 *lb. 2 oz. flour*
$\frac{1}{4}$ *lb. caster sugar*
$\frac{1}{2}$ *lb. butter*

2 *or 3 eggs*
$\frac{3}{4}$ *teaspoon salt*
$1\frac{1}{2}$ *teaspoons grated lemon rind*
1 *oz. chopped citron peel*
1 *cup chopped hazelnuts*

Dissolve the yeast in the milk. Sift the flour. Stir $\frac{1}{4}$ lb. flour into the milk. Cover. Stand in a warm place for about 30 minutes until well risen. Sift sugar. Beat butter till softened. Gradually beat in sugar. When creamy, beat in one egg at a time. Add salt and lemon rind and beat well, then gradually stir in the remaining flour. Beat for 5 minutes. Add the citron peel and the nuts. Cover with a cloth. Stand in a warm place until double its bulk in about 2 hours, then divide dough in two equal portions, and roll each portion out into three long strips. Plait each set and shape into a wreath, wetting the ends and moulding them neatly together, so that you have two wreaths, about 9 inches in diameter. Place them on a greased baking sheet. Cover and leave in a warm place to rise for 30 minutes. Brush the tops with melted butter. Bake in a moderate oven, 350° F., until golden brown in about 30 minutes. Cool on a wire rack. Cover with vanilla or lemon icing made by mixing 1 cup sifted icing sugar with about 2 tablespoons boiling water, and $\frac{1}{2}$ teaspoon vanilla essence, or $\frac{3}{4}$ teaspoon lemon juice.

TO VARY: Omit the citron peel and nuts from the batter, and sprinkle ½ cup shredded blanched almonds mixed with 2 oz. caster sugar, equally over the wreaths. When hazelnuts are in season, sprinkle one or two shredded hazelnuts over the rolls as they are iced. Sometimes the Curly Murlies used to be filled with an almond paste before plaiting. To make the paste, beat 1½ oz. butter to a cream with ½ cup caster sugar, then stir in ½ cup ground almonds, a pinch of grated lemon rind and 1 lightly beaten egg. Roll the strips very thinly. Spread the filling down the middle. Wet the edges. Fold in two, then plait as described.

SCOTTISH DIET CAKE (1851)

Place 1 lb. of sifted fine sugar in a basin. Add 1 lb. of eggs (an egg in its shell weighs approximately 2 oz.) very well whisked. Beat together for 20 minutes. Flavour to taste with grated lemon rind and ground cinnamon. Add ¾ lb. of sifted flour. Stir till smoothly blended. Turn into a greased baking tin, smoothly lined with greased paper. Strew with sifted fine sugar. Bake in a moderately hot oven, 400° F., until light, pale golden and spongy. If preferred, omit the sugar at the end and ice when cold.

DUNDEE CAKE

6 oz. butter	pinch of salt
5 oz. caster sugar	3 oz. cleaned sultanas
4 eggs	4 oz. cleaned currants
8 oz. flour	2 oz. chopped stoned raisins
1 teaspoon baking powder	4 oz. chopped mixed peel
½ teaspoon mixed spice	4 oz. Jordan almonds

Beat butter to a cream. Gradually beat in sugar. When fluffy beat eggs and sift flour with baking powder, spice and salt. Add a little egg to fat and sugar. Dredge with a little flour. Continue in this way until all the egg is added, then stir in flour, fruit, peel and almonds. If eggs are small you may need 5 or substitute a little milk. The mixture should be rather stiff. Place in a greased cake tin, 8 inches across, smoothly lined with greased paper. Smooth top with a palette knife. Bake in a moderately hot oven, 400° F., for about 1¼ hours till dry in centre when tested with a warm skewer, but after baking for 15 minutes, place 1 oz. split blanched almonds over the top.

TO VARY: Substitute rice flour for half the flour and add the grated rind of a lemon with the fruit.

DUNDEE DOUGH CAKE

½ quartern bread dough
¼ lb. cleaned currants or
    sultanas
1–2 oz. chopped candied peel
¼ lb. caster sugar
2 eggs
2 oz. butter
½ teaspoon mixed spice

Place the dough in a slightly heated basin. Add fruit, peel, sugar and eggs. Cut the butter in small pieces, and add with the spice and a ¼ teaspoon of salt. Beat well till thoroughly blended. Turn into a greased, floured cake tin. Prick well. Cover and stand in a warm place to rise for about 1 hour, or until the dough reaches three-quarters of the way up the sides of tin. Bake in a moderately hot oven, 375° F., for about 35 minutes. When lightly browned, before removing from oven, brush top with a tablespoon of caster sugar dissolved in a tablespoon of water. Cool on a wire rack. Serve sliced and buttered.

DUMBARTON CAKE

4 eggs
½ pint new milk
rose or orange flower water
½ lb. butter
½ lb. caster sugar
½ gill brandy
¼ oz. ground cinnamon
¼ oz. grated nutmeg
pinch of bicarbonate of soda
1 tablespoon hot water
sifted flour as required

Beat eggs till yolks and whites are smoothly blended. Gradually stir in the milk and rose or orange flower water to taste. Cream

265

butter. Gradually beat in sugar. Beat till fluffy. Mix the brandy and spices. Dissolve in the water as much bicarbonate of soda as will lie flat on a shilling. Stir ½ cup of flour into the fat mixture, then a little of the egg mixture, beating well after each addition. After all the liquid has been absorbed, stir enough flour, as is required to make a dropable batter, in with the soda-water and brandy. Bake in a 9 inch cake tin, smoothly lined with greased paper, in a slow oven, 325° F., for about 2¾ hours until dry in centre when tested.

EASTER CAKE

½ lb. butter
½ lb. caster sugar
12 oz. sifted flour
¼ oz. mixed spice
¼ teaspoon salt
1 teaspoon baking powder
6 eggs

8 oz. cleaned sultanas
2 oz. halved glacé cherries
2 oz. chopped citron peel
1 oz. chopped preserved ginger
4 oz. cleaned currants
¼ cup milk
almond paste

Cream butter. Beat in sugar. When fluffy, sift 10 oz. of the flour with spice, salt and baking powder. Drop an egg into the butter and sugar. Sprinkle with a little of the remaining flour. Beat till blended. Continue adding eggs in this way until all the egg and the 2 oz. of flour are added. Mix the remainder of the flour with the sultanas. Stir in cherries, peel, ginger and currants. Lightly stir the milk into the egg mixture, then stir in fruit mixture. Place half the batter in a greased 9 inch cake tin, smoothly lined with greased paper. Spread a third of the almond paste over the batter. Add remainder of cake batter. Press it lightly over the almond paste. Bake in a moderately hot oven, 375° F., until dry in centre when tested with a heated skewer, in 3 to 3½ hours. Cool slightly. Mould remainder of almond paste into a thick ring to fit round top edge of cake. Brush edge of cake lightly with heated apricot jam. Lay the ring on top. Ornament it with the prongs of a fork or notch with forefingers. Make side of ring smooth with a palette knife. Cover cake in centre with a thick round of paper. Brush top of ring lightly with beaten egg. Return cake to oven. Leave until ring is delicately browned. Cool cake. Remove paper. Fill hollow in centre with pale green water icing. When almost set, decorate with tiny Easter eggs and one or 2 chickens.

ALMOND PASTE FOR EASTER CAKE: Mix 10 oz. ground almonds with 10 oz. caster sugar and the juice of 1 lemon. Moisten with beaten egg white. Flavour to taste with orange flower water and vanilla essence.

EDINBURGH SANDWICH

½ lb. flour
pinch of salt
1 teaspoon bicarbonate of soda
2 tablespoons cocoa
2 oz. caster sugar

2 oz. lard
2 tablespoons syrup
1 cup milk
1 tablespoon vinegar

Sift flour, salt, soda and cocoa, with the sugar. Heat lard and syrup gently until melted. Stir into dry ingredients, then gradually stir in the milk. Beat well, then stir in vinegar. Divide between two greased sandwich tins, 9 inches across. Bake in a moderately hot oven, 400° F., for about 20 minutes. Cool on a wire rack, then pair with Cocoa Creme. Cover with Chocolate Frosting.

COCOA CREME: Beat 2 oz. butter till softened. Mix 1 cup sifted icing sugar with 1 dessertspoon cocoa. Gradually beat this into the butter. When creamy, stir in 1 tablespoon hot water, and ½ teaspoon vanilla essence.

CHOCOLATE FROSTING

1½ oz. chocolate
¼ pint scalded cream
1 egg yolk
½ teaspoon melted butter

a few grains of salt
sifted icing sugar as required
½ teaspoon vanilla essence

Melt the chocolate in a basin over hot water. Gradually stir in the cream, then the egg yolk, butter and salt. When blended, stir in enough icing sugar to make a spreadable frosting, then the vanilla essence.

YARROW FRUIT CAKE

½ lb. butter	2 lb. cleaned currants
½ lb. lard	1 lb. cleaned sultanas
1¼ lb. caster sugar	½ lb. chopped candied peel
8 eggs	2 oz. blanched almonds
1½ lb. flour	1 grated nutmeg
½ lb. ground rice	¼ teaspoon essence of lemon

Cream butter. Beat in lard. When blended, gradually beat in the sugar. Beat till fluffy. Beat eggs. Sift the flour with the ground rice. Add a little egg to the fat and sugar. Sprinkle with a little of the flour mixture. When all the eggs are added, stir in half the remaining flour and ground rice. Stir the remainder into the currants, then add the sultanas, and peel. Chop almonds and add. Stir lightly into fat mixture with the nutmeg and essence. Stir till thoroughly blended. Turn into a large greased cake tin, smoothly lined with 2 layers of greased paper. Bake in a moderate oven, 350° F. for 30 minutes, then lower to 300° F. and finish baking. Do not remove from oven until when tested with a skewer it comes out clean.

GRIZEL'S LAYER CAKE

¼ lb. butter	2 tablespoons milk
½ lb. caster sugar	1½ teaspoons baking powder
½ lb. flour	grated rind ½ lemon
3 eggs	½ teaspoon vanilla essence

Cream butter. Add sugar. Beat till creamy. Sift flour. Beat eggs. Lightly stir the flour and egg alternately into the fat mixture, then stir in the milk and baking powder. (If eggs are small you will need 4.) Stir in lemon rind and vanilla essence. Grease two 9-inch sandwich tins. Dust with flour then shake well. Divide batter equally between the tins, bringing it slightly higher round the edge than in the centre. Bake in a moderate oven, 350° F., for about ½ hour till risen, firm and golden. When cold pair layers with custard cream. Coat with chocolate icing (*see below*).

CUSTARD CREAM: Cream 1 dessertspoon cornflour with 1 tablespoon water. Add an egg. Beat well. Stir in ¼ pint milk at boiling point. Pour into an enamel saucepan. Stir till boiling. Simmer for a minute or two, then remove from stove. Add a pat of butter and vanilla to taste. Stir frequently till cold, then use.

CHOCOLATE ICING: Pour ½ gill water into a saucepan. Add 3 oz. grated chocolate. Stir till boiling. Boil for a few seconds, stirring constantly, then remove from stove and stir in ½ lb. sifted icing sugar very quickly and ½ teaspoon vanilla essence. Pour over cake. Decorate with halved walnuts.

HALLOWE'EN GINGERBREAD

1¼ lb. sifted flour	1 oz. crystallized ginger
1¼ oz. ground ginger	¼ lb. butter
¼ teaspoon salt	1 lb. treacle
1 tablespoon caster sugar	2 beaten eggs
3 oz. glacé cherries	1 teaspoon bicarbonate of soda
4 oz. almonds	½ pint warm milk
4 oz. citron peel	

Sift the flour with the ginger and salt. Stir in sugar. Quarter cherries. Blanch and chop the almonds and chop the citron peel and ginger. Stir into dry ingredients. Melt butter slowly with the treacle. Stir gradually into the eggs, then stir into the dry ingredients. Dissolve the soda in the milk, and stir in quickly. When thoroughly blended, pour into a 10 inch square well-greased shallow baking tin, smoothly lined with greased paper. Bake in a moderate oven, 350° F., for about 1 hour.

JAM SHORTCAKE

1 *egg*	*weight of* 1 *egg in sifted flour*
weight of 1 *egg in butter*	1 *teaspoon baking powder*
weight of 1 *egg in caster sugar*	*milk as required*

Beat egg. Cream butter and sugar. Stir a tablespoon of milk into egg. Mix the flour with the baking powder and the weight of the shell egg in ground rice (failing ground rice use rice flour). Stir into the butter and sugar alternately with the egg and milk. Divide dough in equal portions. Knead till smooth. Press into 2 lightly greased 9-inch sandwich tins, or shape into flat rounds 10 inches wide and bake on greased enamel or fireproof plates in a hot oven, 425° F., until pale brown. Cool on a wire rack. Spread one layer thickly with jam or lemon curd. Place other layer on top. Dredge with caster sugar. Cut in 8 triangles for serving.

SPONGE GINGERBREAD
(*Kirriemuir recipe*)

½ *lb. sifted flour*	2 *beaten eggs*
¼ *lb. caster sugar*	1 *tablespoon golden syrup*
1 *teaspoon ground cinnamon*	1 *tablespoon treacle*
1 *teaspoon ground ginger*	½ *teaspoon bicarbonate of soda*
½ *teaspoon mixed spice*	*about* ½ *cup buttermilk*

Sift the flour with the sugar and spices. Stir in eggs, syrup, treacle and the soda dissolved in the milk. Beat well. Bake in a well-greased, shallow baking tin 9 inches × 12 inches, in a fairly hot oven, 425° F., for about 11 minutes. Cut into squares or oblongs when cold.

HOGMANAY BUN

FILLING

4 *lb. raisins*	½ *oz. ground ginger*
2½ *lb. cleaned currants*	½ *oz. ground cloves*
½ *lb. Jordan almonds*	½ *oz. Jamaica pepper*
¼ *lb. candied lemon peel*	

PASTRY

1½ *lb. butter*
½ *teaspoon salt*

4 *lb. flour*
¼ *pint fresh yeast*

Stone the raisins. Add currants. Blanch and add almonds. Chop peel. (If preferred, substitute orange peel, or use 2 oz. of orange and 2 oz. of lemon.) Add to the fruit mixture then stir in the spices. Mix well. Beat butter until creamy. Sift salt with flour. Rub in butter, then add enough warm water with the yeast to make a smooth paste. Cut off about one third. Add the remainder to the fruit mixture and knead it into a flat round like a cheese, about 5 inches high. Roll out remainder of pastry thinly. Cut two rounds, one for the top and one for the bottom, then gather up remainder and knead and roll it into a strip, to encircle cake. Place the cake on one round. Brush edge with cold water. Wrap the strip carefully round the cake so that the bottom edge lies on the top edge of the bottom round. Brush ends of strip with cold water and mould smoothly together. Brush top edge of strip with cold water. Lay on top. Press the edges lightly together with a rolling pin. Run a small thin skewer from top to bottom about 2 inches apart. Prick all over the top with a fork. If liked, decorate the top edge with the prongs of a fork. Cover a baking sheet with floured paper. Draw floured paper closely round the outside of bun. Bind it in place with a piece of tape. Bake in a moderate oven, 350° F., for about 2½ hours.

LAWN TENNIS CAKE

5 *oz. flour*
2 *oz. cornflour*
¼ *teaspoon salt*
2 *teaspoons baking powder*
¼ *lb. butter or margarine*

5 *oz. caster sugar*
3 *oz. glacé cherries*
¼ *lb. cleaned sultanas*
2 *oz. chopped candied peel*
4 *separated eggs*

Grease a cake tin 7 × 3½ inches. Sift flour with cornflour, salt and baking powder. Beat fat till softened, then gradually beat in sugar. Beat till fluffy. Halve cherries and mix with sultanas and peel. Add egg yolks to fat and sugar, one at a time, and dredge with a little of the flour. Beat between each addition. Stir in remainder of

271

flour and the fruit. Beat egg whites to a stiff froth, then fold lightly into batter. Pack the mixture into tin. Place in a moderately hot oven, 375° F. Bake for 1–1½ hours till dry in centre when tested with a skewer. Turn onto a rack, base downwards. Leave for 12 hours. Cut crosswise in two. Fill with a layer of almond paste. Coat all over with orange glacé icing. Pipe it crisscross with green glacé icing, bringing the 'lines' down over the side of cake.

SODA CAKE

1 *lb. flour*	2 *separated eggs*
1 *teaspoon ground cinnamon*	1 *teaspoon bicarbonate of soda*
½ *teaspoon ground ginger*	½ *cup warm milk*
6 *oz. butter*	6 *oz. cleaned currants*
4 *oz. caster sugar*	

Sift the flour with the spices. Cream butter. Beat in sugar. When creamy, beat in egg yolks. Dissolve soda in the milk. Gradually work in the dry ingredients, then the milk. Stir in the currants. Fold in stiffly whipped egg whites. Bake in a moderate oven for about 2 hours till dry in centre when tested.

TO MAKE A RICHER SODA CAKE: Decrease butter to 6 oz. Double amount of sugar. Decrease currants to 4 oz. but add in addition 4 oz. each of cleaned sultanas, chopped raisins and chopped candied peel, and stir the grated rind of a lemon into the batter before adding egg whites.

MARTINMAS CAKE

½ *lb. sifted flour*	3 *oz. chopped crystallized*
1 *heaped teaspoon baking*	*ginger*
powder	¼ *lb. butter*
¼ *teaspoon salt*	1 *cup light brown sugar*
1¼ *teaspoons ground cinnamon*	2 *egg yolks*
¼ *teaspoon ground ginger*	2–3 *cup milk*

Sift flour thrice with baking powder, salt and spices. Stir 1 cup of the mixture into the ginger so as to separate the pieces. Cream butter. Gradually beat in sugar. Beat yolks till light. Stir into sugar mixture, then add to flour mixture alternately with milk. Stir in ginger. Turn into a floured greased baking tin about 8 inches square. Cover with Brown Meringue Frosting. Sprinkle to taste with split blanched almonds. Bake in a fairly slow oven, 325° F., for about 50 minutes.

BROWN MERINGUE FROSTING: Beat 2 egg whites with a few grains of salt till stiff but not dry. Gradually beat in 1 cup light brown sugar, and use as described.

MONDAMIN CAKE

4 oz. butter
5 oz. caster sugar
6 oz. cornflour

1 teaspoon baking powder
3 eggs

Prepare a Mondamin tin (7 × 3 inches with a central pipe) by greasing and dusting with 1 teaspoon cornflour mixed with 1 teaspoon caster sugar.

Beat butter till soft. Add sugar and beat till white and creamy. Beat in the eggs, one at a time, with 1 tablespoon of the cornflour and baking powder sifted together. Beat thoroughly between each addition. Mix in the rest of the cornflour, flavouring as liked. Spoon lightly into the prepared tin. Bake at 375° F. for 35–40 minutes, then cool slightly in the tin before turning out onto a wire rack.

NO-EGG CAKE

1 lb. sifted flour
¼ lb. butter
½ lb. caster sugar
½ lb. cleaned sultanas
½ lb. stoned raisins

2 oz. chopped, candied orange
  peel
1 teaspoon bicarbonate of soda
1 large tumbler milk

Sift flour again. Melt butter slowly until creamy. Stir in the sugar,

273

then beat in a little of the flour. Stir remainder of flour into the fruit and peel and add to batter. Meanwhile, dissolve the soda in the milk and beat into flour mixture. Beat very well. Spread in a shallow buttered baking tin about 10 × 6 inches. Bake in a moderate oven, 350° F., for 45 to 60 minutes, until golden brown.

NORANSIDE CAKE

1 *lb. butter*	1 *lb. cleaned currants*
2 *cups brown sugar*	1 *lb. raisins*
4 *well-beaten eggs*	6 *oz. finely-chopped candied*
½ *cup treacle*	*peel*
2 *teaspoons ground cinnamon*	2 *oz. almonds*
1 *teaspoon ground mace*	1¼ *lb. flour*
1 *teaspoon ground cloves*	2 *teaspoons baking powder*

Melt butter a little, then beat it well. Beat in the sugar, then the eggs, one at a time. Continue beating while adding the treacle and spices, then stir in the currants, raisins (stoned), peel, and the almonds, blanched and chopped. When blended, sift the flour with the baking powder and a pinch of salt, and lightly stir into the batter. Pack into a large, greased cake tin, 9 to 10 inches across, smoothly lined with 2 layers of greased paper. Bake in a moderate oven, 350° F., for about 3¼ hours, depending on size of tin. When cold, beat an egg white with the juice of ½ lemon and stir in enough sifted sugar to make a soft paste. Spread over the top of the cake.

A FINE SEED CAKE (1851)

Take 12 oz. flour and eight well beaten eggs. Place in a basin with 12 oz. of fine sugar. Beat thoroughly until blended and light. Throw in ¼ lb. of chopped candied citron, lemon and orange peel mixed and 2 oz. of chopped blanched almonds. Beat 6 oz. of butter to a cream. Gradually beat in the flour and egg mixture. Add ground cinnamon and ground cloves to taste, as well as caraway seeds. Place in a greased cake tin smoothly lined with greased paper. Cover lightly with sugared caraway seeds and bake till dry in the centre when tested.

OLD-FASHIONED SEED CAKE

1½ lb. butter
1½ lb. caster sugar
12 separated eggs
1½ lb. sifted flour
½ lb. chopped candied citron
  peel
¾ lb. chopped candied orange
  peel

6 oz. chopped Jordan almonds
1 grated nutmeg
1 teaspoon ground caraway
  seeds
½ gill brandy

Beat butter till creamy. Gradually beat in sugar. When fluffy, add a little egg yolk at a time, then dredge with a little of the flour. Beat until blended after each addition. Continue in this way until all the yolks are absorbed, then give a sharp beat. Lightly sift the half of remaining flour into a basin. Stir in peels and almonds. Sift remaining flour with the nutmeg and caraway seeds and stir into fat mixture. Do not beat. Stir in peels and almonds mixed with the flour, then the brandy. Beat egg whites to a stiff froth. Fold into mixture. Pour into a large greased cake tin 10½ or 11 inches across, smoothly lined with greased greaseproof paper. Place in the centre of a moderate oven, 350° F., and strew with caraway comfits. Bake until dry in the centre when tested with a heated skewer in about 4 hours.

MRS STEWART'S JAM SANDWICH

½ lb. sifted flour
½ lb. salt butter
4 separated eggs

½ lb. caster sugar
1 teaspoon baking powder
flavouring to taste

Cream flour with the butter. Cream egg yolks with the sugar. Beat egg whites to a stiff froth. Beat the yolks and sugar gradually into the flour and butter. Stir in baking powder, then fold in egg whites with flavouring to taste. Pour into two greased sandwich tins 9 inches across. Bake in a moderately hot oven, 400° F. for about 20 minutes. Turn onto a sheet of paper dredged with caster sugar. When cold, put together with raspberry jam.

MISS BRECHIN'S SPONGE CAKE

6 eggs
weight of 3 eggs in caster
 sugar

weight of 3 eggs in flour
1 teaspoon lemon juice
½ teaspoon vanilla essence

Grease a cake tin, 8 inches across and 3½ inches deep. Dust inside with equal quantity of rice flour and caster sugar. Beat eggs and sugar for 20 minutes till creamy and foamy. Sift the flour. Fold lightly into egg mixture, then lightly stir in lemon juice and vanilla essence. Turn mixture lightly into tin. Bake in a slow oven, 300° F., for about 1 hour until cake shows signs of shrinking from the sides. Invert on a wire rack to cool. At the end of an hour, ease out with a palette knife and place, face downwards, on rack. Dredge top and sides with sifted vanilla icing sugar.

MARYE CAMERON-SMITH'S SPONGE SANDWICH

3 eggs
3½ oz. caster sugar

4 oz. self-raising flour

Separate the eggs. Whisk the whites until very stiff. Add yolks and sugar. Whisk until sugar dissolves. Fold in sieved flour. Bake in a greased glass flan dish, 8½ inches in diameter in a moderate oven, 350° F., for 30 minutes. Cool on a wire rack. Split in two crosswise. Sandwich the layers with jam.

SPONGE ROLL

pinch of baking powder
3 oz. sieved flour
4 oz. caster sugar

3 eggs
¼ teaspoon vanilla essence

Sieve the baking powder with the flour. Beat the sugar and egg till light and full of air bubbles (if using an ordinary egg beater, the beating should take from 15–20 minutes). Lightly stir in the flour and baking powder, then the essence. Pour gently into a greased, shallow oblong baking tin 9 × 12 inches, smoothly lined with greased paper. Spread evenly all over and into the corners, and draw the batter slightly towards the edges. Bake in a hot oven, 425° F., for 10 to 12 minutes. Turn quickly onto a paper sprinkled with caster sugar. Spread quickly with heated jam, and roll up. Cool on a wire rack, join downwards.

TO VARY: Follow above method, but allow only 2 oz. flour and 3 oz. caster sugar, and use a smaller baking tin.

CHOCOLATE ROLL: Grease a shallow baking tin, 9 × 12 inches and line smoothly with greased paper. Whip 3 eggs, 4 oz. caster sugar and ½ oz. grated chocolate in a basin over hot water till beginning to thicken, then beat until almost cold. (If using unsweetened chocolate, allow only 2 oz. sugar.) Lightly shake out the whisk, then gently fold in 3 oz. flour sifted with a pinch of baking powder and stir in 1 teaspoon vanilla essence. Pour into tin and bake and roll up. See Sponge Roll. Coat with Chocolate Icing.

CHOCOLATE ICING FOR ROLL: Sift 4 tablespoons icing sugar with 1 dessertspoon chocolate powder. Mix to a coating consistency with boiling water, then add vanilla essence to taste.

SULTANA SLAB CAKE

6 oz. butter
6 oz. caster sugar
grated rind of an orange
2 eggs
8 oz. cleaned sultanas
2 oz. chopped glacé cherries
2 oz. chopped candied orange peel
12 oz. flour
3 teaspoons baking powder
¼ teaspoon salt
about ¾ cup milk

Grease a shallow cake tin, about 11 inches by 7, and line smoothly with greased paper. Cream fat, sugar and orange rind. Beat in eggs. Stir in fruit. Sift flour with baking powder and salt. Stir into fat mixture alternately with the milk. Turn into tin. Bake in a moderate oven, 375° F., for about 1 hour.

TARTAN SLAB CAKE

6 *oz. butter*
6 *oz. caster sugar*
2 *well-beaten eggs*
about ½ cup milk
10 *oz. flour*
¼ *teaspoon salt*

1 *teaspoon baking powder*
lemon flavouring and colouring
1 *tablespoon grated chocolate*
few drops rum, vanilla essence
and rose water
green and pink colouring

Beat butter till creamy. Gradually beat in sugar. Beat till fluffy. Gradually beat in the egg and milk (8 tablespoons) alternately with the flour sifted with the salt and baking powder. Grease 2 Russian cake tins. Line each side of each tin separately with greased paper. Place a quarter of the mixture, flavoured and coloured lemon, into one side of one tin, smoothing it level with a palette knife and working it well into the corners. Stir 1 tablespoon grated chocolate, melted in a basin sunk in boiling water, into the second portion with 4 drops vanilla essence. Colour third portion a warm green. Flavour it with a saltspoon of rum. Add 1 saltspoon rose water and cochineal colouring to taste to last portion. Now fill remaining half of first tin with one of the portions, fixing it like the first, then place the remaining two portions in remaining tin. Bake in a moderate oven, 350° F., for about 15 minutes till risen firm, and slightly browned. Place on a wire rack. When cold, cut each portion in halves lengthwise, using the loose division as a ruler. Trim neatly. Place the sections together in this order; after spreading them thinly with apricot jam or lemon curd so that they adhere. Lemon over pink, chocolate over green, pink over lemon, and green over chocolate. This gives you a rectangular cake. Cover with almond paste.

ALMOND PASTE FOR TARTAN CAKE: Mix ¾ lb. sifted icing sugar with ¼ lb. ground almonds. Stir in a pinch of salt and enough beaten egg white to make a stiff paste. Knead paste until smooth. Place on a board covered with greaseproof paper. Roll into an oblong long and wide enough to cover the whole of the cake except the ends. I should say about 4 inches × 6. Brush paste over with slightly beaten egg white. Carefully but firmly press the paste on to the sides of the cake with the help of the greaseproof paper, and mould edges neatly together over the top. Now turn cake upside down. Decorate down the centre with a trail of crystallized violets with angelica leaves.

WALNUT LAYER CAKE

$\frac{1}{4}$ *lb. butter*

9 *oz. caster sugar*

4 *eggs*

10 *oz. flour*

pinch of salt

$\frac{1}{2}$ *teaspoon baking powder*

$\frac{1}{2}$ *gill milk*

2 *oz. chopped walnuts*

1 *teaspoon vanilla essence*

Cream butter. Beat in sugar. Beat till fluffy, then beat in eggs one at a time. Sift flour with salt and baking powder, and add half the mixture alternately with half the milk. Stir till blended. Add remainder of flour and milk, walnuts and vanilla essence. Divide equally between 3 layer cake tins, 8 inches across, well greased and floured. Bake in a moderately hot oven, 400° F., for about 20 minutes. When cold, put together with apricot filling. Dredge top with sifted icing sugar.

APRICOT FILLING: Mix 3 tablespoons apricot jam with 3 tablespoons ground almonds, 1 tablespoon chopped walnuts and 1 teaspoon vanilla essence.

WEDDING CAKE

Unless you are able to have two ovens in use simultaneously, you will have to halve the following mixture, and bake it in a large cake tin about 12 inches in diameter, then make the same quantity on another day and divide it in two portions, two-thirds and one-third. Bake the larger portion in a tin $9\frac{1}{2}$ to 10 inches across, in the morning. It will take about $5\frac{1}{2}$ hours at 300° F. In the afternoon, stir $\frac{1}{2}$ teaspoon baking powder into remaining mixture, and bake in a 7-inch tin at 300° F. from $3\frac{1}{2}$ to $3\frac{3}{4}$ hours. If you wish to have only a two-tiered cake, use three-quarters of the ingredients I am given, and divide in two-thirds and one-third. Bake the larger portion in an $11\frac{1}{2}$ to 12-inch tin, and the smaller in an $8\frac{1}{2}$ or 9-inch tin. The larger will take about $6\frac{1}{2}$ hours, and the smaller about 5 hours. Prepare tins as described below, and test in the same way before removing from oven.

2 *lb. minced candied orange peel*	*¾ teaspoon mixed spice*
1 *lb. minced candied lemon peel*	*¾ teaspoon ground cinnamon*
1 *lb. minced candied citron peel*	*½ teaspoon ground mace*
5 *lb. cleaned currants*	*½ oz. allspice*
3 *lb. cleaned sultanas*	*½ teaspoon salt*
¼ lb. halved glacé cherries	2 *lb. ground almonds*
2½ *lb. butter*	*¼ teaspoon lemon essence*
2½ *lb. caster sugar*	1½ *teaspoons rose essence*
3 *lb. eggs, in shells*	2 *teaspoons vanilla essence*
2 *lb.* 14 *oz. flour*	*juice of* 1 *lemon*
	1 *glass brandy (½ gill)*

Grease three cake tins, 12 inches, 9½ to 10 inches and 7 inches. Line each with five folds of greased paper. Tie a thick band of brown paper around the outside. Mix the minced peels with the prepared fruit. Beat butter till softened, then gradually beat in sugar. Beat till fluffy, using your hand instead of a spoon. Beat eggs till light and frothy. Sift flour with spices and salt. Add flour mixture and egg alternately with the fat and sugar mixture, till all the egg is used up, then stir in remainder of flour alternately with the peel and fruit mixed with the ground almonds, beating with your hand all the time. Lastly, stir in essences, lemon juice, and brandy. If preferred, use half brandy and half sherry. Pack mixture lightly into prepared tins, filling them half full. Hollow out centres lightly with the back of your hand. Place each cake tin on a bed of kitchen salt in a baking tin, pushing the salt close to the sides, if baking in an oven with bottom heat. Bake largest cake at 300° F. for about 6½ hours, second size for about 5½ hours, and the smallest for 3½–3¾ hours. Test each cake when nearly ready with a heated skewer. When ready the skewer comes out dry. If any batter is attached, continue to bake and test again. When ready, remove from oven, stand cakes for ½ hour in tins to allow them to shrink slightly, then turn out carefully onto a wire tray, placing them on their bases. Remove all paper at once. Cool overnight away from draughts. Tie cakes in three layers of greaseproof paper and store in tightly-closed tins, until ready to cover with almond paste and decorate.

ALMOND PASTE FOR
THREE-TIERED CAKE

2½ lb. ground almonds
1 lb. sifted icing sugar
1 lb. sifted caster sugar
5 teaspoons lemon juice
2½ teaspoons rose water

10 drops almond essence
1 teaspoon vanilla essence
3 egg yolks
6 eggs

Mix the almonds with the sugars. Stir in flavourings. Beat egg yolks and eggs, and gradually stir into the mixture, until you have a rollable paste. You may need a little extra egg yolk or egg, depending on the size of yolks used. Knead paste until smooth. Divide in three portions, suitable for each cake. Brush tops of cakes with melted apricot jam, then knead and roll each portion of paste into a round to fit the top of the cake concerned. Roll lightly with a rolling pin to get a smooth surface, and see that the sides are on a sharp level with the edge of the cakes. Cover loosely with butter muslin or greaseproof paper and stand in a warm room for 2 or 3 days until dry. Cover almond paste and sides of cake with a coat of water icing, and leave until set.

Note: If you wish to cover the sides of the cake with almond paste, as well as the tops, you will need 9–10 lb. of almond paste.

ROYAL ICING FOR A
THREE-TIERED CAKE

4½ lb. sifted icing sugar
4½ teaspoons lemon juice
9 egg whites

4 teaspoons pure glycerine
a few drops of blue colouring

Place icing sugar in a basin. Add lemon juice. Beat egg whites slightly and stir into sugar. Beat until smooth in about 10 minutes. While beating, gradually incorporate the glycerine and the blue colouring. Do not beat after icing forms peaks. Keep a damp cloth over the icing bowl while applying or piping on cake, as it dries out quickly. Place a smooth coating over the water icing, with a palette knife, then thicken icing a little with sifted icing sugar, and decorate cake according to taste. The last wedding cake I made I decorated with white roses, sprigs of white heather and lovers' knots by piping, then after standing for a fortnight, I placed silver pillars on the large bottom tier, and lifted the medium-sized cake on top. I put 1 or 2 pillars on the second cake, and crowned it with the smallest cake. I then filled a squat silver vase with white blossoms and trailing smilax, then I piped icing round the edge of the silver boards on which each cake stood, and added a wreath of white artificial orange blossom and silver leaves round the base, and decorated the other cakes with real white heather, and waxen orange blossoms, etc.

BISCUITS

I do not need to sing the praise of Scottish biscuits. Their high quality is responsible for their excellent reputation. Unfortunately I cannot trace the recipes for many of the large biscuits I used to enjoy. 'Couttie's Handmade' I loved with our homemade damson jam; I always took some home with me from Dundee. 'Hecklies' accompanied me from Forfar, and Cinnamon and Rice Biscuits from Thrums. Many a time I've dashed into Peter's in Thrums on my way home to buy a dozen of the paste biscuits for which they were also famous. My mother, when she was too busy to make pastry, heated them and served them with stewed apple or rhubarb. Nowadays many of the varieties of biscuits that used to be made by bakers seem to have gone, with the conversation sweeties that lads and lassies used to exchange when they were too shy to tell their love. When I was a schoolgirl we bought more biscuits from a baker than from a grocer.

ABERNETHY BISCUITS

½ lb. flour
½ teaspoon baking powder
3 oz. butter
3 oz. caster sugar

1 small teaspoon caraway seeds
1 beaten egg
about 1 tablespoon milk

Sift flour and baking powder into a basin. Rub in butter. Stir in sugar, seeds, egg and milk to make a stiff dough. Turn onto a floured board. Roll out thinly. Cut into rounds about 3 inches across. Prick the centres with a fork. Bake a little apart on a greased baking sheet, in a moderately hot oven, 375° F., for about 10 minutes. Cool on a wire rack.

ALMOND MACAROONS (1851)

Pound 1 lb. Jordan almonds, blanched and peeled, with the whites of four eggs until blended. Gradually beat in 2 lb. of fine sugar and pound to a paste. Shell and separate eight eggs. Gradually beat the egg whites into the almond mixture. When blended, squirt through an icing syringe on to a baking sheet covered with wafer paper, placing a little apart. Fire them very slowly till crisp.

RATAFIA MACAROONS: Follow the above recipe, but use $\frac{3}{4}$ lb. of Jordan almonds and $\frac{1}{2}$ lb. of bitter almonds. If a more solid macaroon is wanted, substitute a little rice flour for part of the almonds.

CINNAMON BISCUITS

$\frac{1}{4}$ lb. butter	$\frac{1}{2}$ heaped teaspoon cinnamon
$\frac{1}{2}$ lb. flour	$\frac{1}{2}$ teaspoon baking powder
3 oz. caster sugar	1 beaten egg

Rub the butter into the flour. Stir in sugar, cinnamon and baking powder, then enough egg to bind ingredients stiffly together. Roll out to $\frac{1}{8}$ inch thickness. Stamp into oval or round biscuits. Bake a little apart on a lightly greased baking sheet in a moderately hot oven, 375° F., until crisp in about 10 minutes. Cool on a wire rack, then pair with raspberry jam. Cover with cinnamon icing.

CINNAMON ICING: Dissolve $\frac{1}{2}$ lb. sugar in $\frac{1}{2}$ cup of water, then bring to boil. Boil for 5 minutes. Turn into a basin. Stir till mixture turns creamy. Stir in a large teaspoon of ground cinnamon and use.

COCONUT ROCKERIES

2 egg whites	2 oz. caster sugar
1 dessertspoon rice flour	2 oz. fine desiccated coconut

Beat egg whites to a stiff froth. Stir in rice flour, sugar and coconut. Mix lightly till blended. Place mixture in tiny heaps about

2 inches apart in a greased baking tin. Bake in a moderate oven, 350° F., until lightly browned all over in about 20 minutes.

MANSE BISCUITS

¼ lb. butter
½ lb. flour
¼ lb. caster sugar

grated rind ½ lemon
½ teaspoon baking powder
1 beaten egg

Rub butter into flour. Stir in sugar, lemon rind and baking powder. Moisten with egg. Roll to ¼ inch thickness. Cut in fancy shapes with biscuit cutters. Bake a little apart on a greased baking sheet in a moderate oven, for about 20 minutes until pale gold. Dredge with caster sugar.

MILK BISCUITS

¼ pint milk
1 oz. butter
½ lb. flour

1 teaspoon baking powder
½ teaspoon salt

Heat milk and butter slowly till butter melts. Sieve flour with baking powder and salt. Mix to a smooth but very stiff dough with the milk and butter. Knead well. Roll out on a floured board as thinly as possible. Prick all over. Cut into 2 inch rounds with a floured cutter. Bake a little apart on a lightly greased baking sheet in a moderately hot oven, 375° F., for 10 to 12 minutes, until a pale straw colour. Cool on a wire rack. Serve with cheese.

OATMEAL BISCUITS

5 oz. flour
½ teaspoon baking powder
½ teaspoon salt
¼ lb. butter

1 teaspoon caster sugar
7 oz. medium oatmeal
1 egg
2 tablespoons cold water

Sift flour, baking powder and salt. Rub in butter. Stir in sugar and oatmeal. Beat egg. Add cold water. Stir into flour mixture. Mix to a stiff dough. Roll out thinly on a floured pastry board. Cut into squares. Mark neatly with a knife. Bake a little apart on a greased baking sheet in a moderate oven, 350° F., for about 20 minutes. Serve with cheese.

SWEET OATMEAL BISCUITS

1½ tablespoons flour
½ teaspoon baking powder
¼ teaspoon salt
1 tablespoon butter
3 tablespoons golden syrup

2 tablespoons caster sugar
1 beaten egg
½ teaspoon lemon essence
1 teaspoon vanilla essence
1½ cups medium oatmeal

Sift flour with baking powder and salt. Melt butter in a saucepan. Stir into syrup. Add sugar, egg, essences, flour mixture and oatmeal. Beat till blended. Drop from a teaspoon in rounds 1½ inches apart onto a greased baking sheet. Bake in a moderately hot oven, 375° F., for 10–15 minutes.

PRESTONPANS BISCUITS

8 oz. flour
8 oz. cornflour
¼ teaspoon bicarbonate of soda
½ teaspoon cream of tartar

8 oz. caster sugar
8 oz. butter
2 beaten eggs

Sift all dry ingredients into a basin. Rub in butter. Mix to a dough with the eggs and a little milk if required. Roll out on a lightly floured board. Cut into rounds. Bake a little apart on a lightly greased baking sheet in a moderately hot oven, 375° F., for 10 to 12 minutes. Dredge with caster sugar.

RICE BISCUITS

¼ lb. flour
¼ teaspoon salt
½ teaspoon baking powder
¼ lb. ground rice
3 oz. caster sugar

¼ lb. butter
¼ teaspoon lemon or vanilla
  essence
¾ beaten egg

Sift flour, salt and baking powder. Stir in ground rice and sugar. Rub in butter. Stir lemon or vanilla essence into egg, then stir egg into dry ingredients. Knead slightly. Roll out on a lightly floured board. Cut into rounds or fancy shapes. Bake in a moderately hot oven, on a lightly greased baking sheet for 10–12 minutes at 400° F. Pair if liked with apricot or raspberry jam. Dredge with caster sugar.

ALMOND SHORTBREAD BISCUITS

½ lb. flour
¼ lb. rice flour
¼ lb. caster sugar
6 oz. butter

2 oz. chopped, blanched
  almonds
beaten egg as required

Mix the flour with the rice flour and sugar. Rub in butter. Stir in almonds, and enough beaten egg to make a rollable dough. Roll out thinly on a lightly-floured board. Cut into fancy shapes. Place a little apart on a greased baking sheet. Bake in a moderate oven, 350° F., for about 20 minutes, till pale gold. Dredge lightly with caster sugar. Cool on a wire rack.

SHORTBREAD FINGERS

¼ lb. flour
2 oz. rice flour

4 oz. butter
2 oz. caster sugar

Sift the flours into a basin. Beat butter till creamy, then beat in sugar. Beat till fluffy. Gradually beat in the flour, and continue beating until mixture is stiff, then knead it until smooth. Roll out dough on a lightly floured board to ⅓ of an inch in thickness. Prick all over with a fork. Cut into oblongs 3 inches by 1 inch. Place ¼ inch apart on a greased baking sheet covered with greased paper. Bake in a moderate oven, 350° F., for 15 minutes until crisp and straw-coloured. Dredge with caster sugar.

AYRSHIRE SHORTBREAD

¼ lb. flour
¼ lb. rice flour
¼ lb. butter

¼ lb. caster sugar
1 egg yolk
2 tablespoons cream

Sift flour and rice flour into a basin. Lightly rub in butter. Add sugar. Mix to a stiff paste with the egg yolk and the cream. Roll out thinly. Prick all over with a fork. Cut into small rounds. Bake on a baking sheet covered with greased paper in a moderate oven, 350° F., till pale gold in about 15 minutes. Dust with caster sugar. Cool on a wire rack.

PAISLEY SHORTBREAD

12 oz. flour
4 oz. cornflour
8 oz. butter

4 oz. caster sugar
yolk of egg

Sieve the flour and cornflour into a basin. Rub in the butter. Stir in sugar and egg yolk, then knead the mixture thoroughly with the hand into a firm smooth dough. Turn onto a lightly floured board. Shape into 2 or 3 round cakes. Notch the edges with the forefingers and thumbs and bake in a moderate oven, 350° F., for 30 to 40 minutes, time depending upon the thickness. Cool on a wire tray.

PETTICOAT TAILS

Some say that Petticoat Tails are a corruption of the French Petites Gatelles. Others claim that the name has its origin in the

288

shape of the cakes which resemble the bell-hoop petticoats of the court ladies of a bygone century.

1 *lb. flour*	6 *oz. caster sugar*
8 *oz. butter*	*water as required*

Sift flour into a basin. Rub in butter. Stir in sugar and enough water to make a smooth dough. Divide in two equal portions. Pat or roll each into two round cakes the size of a dinner plate. Remove the centre of each with a cutter about 4 inches across. Carefully divide the ring left into 8 equal portions. Slip rounds and 'tails' onto a lightly-greased baking sheet covered with greaseproof paper, placing them a little apart. Dust with caster sugar. Bake in a moderate oven, 350° F., for about 20 minutes. Cool on a wire rack, then place the round cakes in the centre with the 'tails' round. In some parts of Scotland, caraway seeds are added, allowing from $\frac{1}{4}$–$\frac{1}{2}$ oz., according to taste, and milk is substituted for the water.

PITCAITHLY BANNOCK

There are many versions of this bannock. This is the one I always made for my mother who belonged to Edinburgh where this variety of shortbread is a speciality.

8$\frac{1}{2}$ *oz. butter*	2 *oz. rice flour*
6 *oz. caster sugar*	2 *oz. minced blanched almonds*
13 *oz. sifted flour*	2 *oz. minced candied citron peel*

Beat butter till softened. Gradually beat in sugar (if not sweet-toothed, allow only 4 oz. sugar). Knead in first the flour then the rice flour, using your hand when the mixture becomes too stiff to mix with a spoon. Knead in almonds and peel (use orange peel if preferred to citron). When free from cracks, mould into an oblong, round or square on a baking sheet covered with greaseproof paper. Chill. Prick well over the centre with a fork. Notch the edges with thumbs and forefingers. Bake in a slow oven, 325° F., until biscuit-coloured in about 1 hour, the time depending on the thickness of cake which is a matter of taste. I like mine about

$\frac{3}{4}$–1 inch. Some prefer it to be $\frac{1}{2}$ inch thick. Slip onto a wire rack to cool.

WHOLEMEAL SHORTIES
(*Aberdeen Recipe*)

$\frac{1}{4}$ *lb. butter*   *pinch of salt*
$\frac{1}{2}$ *lb. wholemeal*   1 *egg yolk*
2 *oz. caster sugar*

Rub fat into wholemeal. Stir in sugar and salt. Knead in egg yolk till into a stiff paste. Roll to $\frac{1}{4}$ inch thickness. Stamp into $1\frac{1}{2}$ inch rounds. Place a little apart on a greased baking sheet. Bake in a moderate oven, 350° F., until lightly browned in about 15 minutes.

EDINA WINE BISCUITS

Rub 3 oz. of butter into 1 lb. of the finest flour. Add fine sugar and salt to taste. Mix to a dough with warm milk and a spoonful of yeast. Knead quickly, then leave the dough to repose for 1 hour. Roll out and stamp into rounds. Prick the biscuits with a dabber. Bake in a quick oven.

BEVERAGES

Gae bring to me a pint o' wine
And fetch it in a silver tassie
That I may drink, before I go,
A service to my bonnie lassie.

BURNS

If whisky is now the national beverage of Scotland, it was not always so. My father has often told me about the convivial habits of the Lowlanders when he was a boy, when drinking bouts were the fashion, and no man had proved himself a good fellow until he had drunk himself under the table. Apropos of this, Dean Ramsay quotes this anecdote: 'He had been involved in a regular drinking party. He was keeping as free from the usual excesses as he was able, and as he marked companions around him falling victims to the power of drink, he himself dropped off under the table among the slain, as a measure of precaution, and lying there, his attention was called to a small pair of hands working at his throat; on asking what it was, a voice replied: "Sir, I'm the lad that's to lowse the neck-cloths." '

I have also been told the story of how my great-grandfather on my mother's side once went to a horse fair in the wilds of Aberdeenshire. After a few drinks he bought nineteen Shetland ponies and then returned to the bottle! About nightfall a Shetland pony trotted back to the farm carrying great-grandfather on his back 'bung fou' and driving the other ponies in front. You see, he had nineteen children!

In the days when the Scottish Kings imported French wives to the Scottish Court, French wines were freely imbibed by the courtiers and the Scottish gentry, and no Scottish home of any standing was properly furnished if it had not a proper cellar.

It was not until about 1750 that Scottish women replaced wine with tea, and claret began to fight a losing battle with whisky. During the eighteenth century, Scottish women, particularly in the Lowlands, became famous for their home-made wines prepared from flowers and fruit. To quote Lady Nairne's *The Laird o' Cockpen*:

> *Mistress Jean, she was makin' the elder-flo'er wine:*
> *'And what brings the Laird at sic a like time?'*
> *She put off her apron and on her silk goon,*
> *Her mutch wi' red ribbons, and gaed awa' doon.*

One of the most unpleasant memories of my childhood was of standing in a row at the head of my seven brothers and sisters waiting for my share of what we called 'Papa's White Mixture'. This was some horrible concoction which he doled out to us in the spring, and tried to make more palatable by mixing it with equal quantity of cowslip wine, made from a recipe given him by his grandmother.

Somewhere on the Braes of Angus at the head of Glenquiech is buried a whisky still. It was bequeathed to my father by 'Rashiebog' when I was an infant. He had a map of the location. When, full of years and very tired, the Minister of Memus passed on, I found no trace of this heritage. It is possible that my father washed his hands of it. A strict teetotaller, though he enjoyed making wine and liqueurs, he may have resented the suggestion that he might take to making Mountain Dew. I wish he had treasured this inheritance. I would have liked to have had it as an heirloom of the days when Scotland willed she found a way.

Among the drinking habits that have changed in Scotland is the habit of calling for a toast each time glasses were filled. It is now in abeyance, although many of the old toasts still survive. One of the most popular from a lad to his lass was: 'May the hinges o' friendship ne'er rust, nor the wings o' love lose a feather.' The only other Scottish toast to a lass that I know was given in my presence by a Scottish judge to his lass at a shooting lodge near Hawick many years ago:

Here's tae the wings o' love
May they never lose a feather!
Till your little shoon an' ma big boots
Are ootside the door thegether.

ALE

As I said in *Beer and Vittels*, in olden days beer was the common beverage in Lowland Scotland. More than once did Sir Walter Scott immortalize it. In the north in medieval days it shared with claret the honour of being served at what was then known as 'Four-hours', until tea, which was introduced to the Scots about 1681 by Mary of Modena, it is said, took its place.

Stoups of ale and bread and cheese figured on many a Scottish table for many a long year. In the early eighteenth century you are told by travellers that beer always appeared at breakfast in the homes of Scottish chieftains, when it was served in large quaighs, or in silver flagons that had escaped the predatory hands of Cromwell and his followers, and it was popular alike in cottage and hall.

SKEACHAN
(*Yule Ale*)

4 *lb. molasses*   *a handful of hops*
7 *gallons soft water*   *fully* 1 *pint beer yeast*

Place the molasses and water in a large pan. Add the hops, tied in boiled muslin. Stir till boiling, then boil for 25 minutes. Pour into a tub kept for the purpose. Leave until cool, then add the yeast. Cover with a double piece of blanket. Pour it off from the lees and bottle.

ATHOLE BROSE

Aye since he wore the tartan trews
He dearly lo'ed the Athole Brose.

NEIL GOW

This is a very old Scottish beverage which used to be popular on Hogmanay. The original recipe is said to consist of whisky and oatmeal, but it has almost as many versions as Egg Nog.

ATHOLE BROSE I: Dissolve ½ lb. extracted honey in about ¼ pint of cold water. Stir with a silver spoon until thoroughly blended, then gradually stir in ¾ pint whisky. Stir rapidly till the brose froths. If not to be used at once, bottle and cork tightly.

ATHOLE BROSSE II: Mix 3 oz. medium oatmeal to a thick paste with cold water. Stand for 30 minutes. Strain thoroughly and use the liquor for making this brose. Mix it thoroughly with 4 dessertspoons heather honey, using a silver spoon. Pour into a quart bottle. Fill with whisky. Cork tightly. Shake well before serving.

BRUCE RUSSELL'S ATHOLL BROSE

3 *cups oatmeal*
½ *pint cold water*
¼ *pint Drambuie*

4 *dessertspoons liquid heather*
honey
¼ *pint cream*

Place the oatmeal in a basin. Stir in the water. When blended, set aside for about 1 hour, then strain, pressing well until about a ¼ pint of creamy liquid is obtained. Mix this with the honey, Drambuie and cream. Pour into a punch bowl. Serve in wine glasses at room temperature. If to be served as a toast, enough for 6–8 persons.

AULD MAN'S MILK

I feel sure that the egg nog so popular in the United States at Christmas parties, is a descendant of Auld Man's Milk.

6 *separated eggs*
½ *lb. sugar*
1 *quart new milk or thin cream*

about ½ pint brandy, rum or
whisky

Beat yolks and whites of eggs separately. Add sugar and milk or cream to the egg yolks. Stir till the sugar is dissolved, then add the brandy, rum or whisky by degrees. Beat egg whites to a froth. Pour the liquor into a china or glass punch bowl. Slip in the egg white. Mix very gently. Add grated nutmeg to taste. Serve in punch glasses.

BOSTON CREAM

As I have only met this beverage in Scotland I am giving the recipe here though its name does not suggest a Scottish origin.

2 *lemons*
3 *quarts boiling water*
2 *oz. tartaric acid*

1½ *lb. sugar*
3 *egg whites*

Wash and dry lemons. Peel thinly. Place the peel with the lemon juice in a basin. Add water, acid and sugar. Stir till sugar is dissolved. When quite cold, stir in the beaten egg whites. Bottle. When required, dilute to taste with chilled soda water.

BRAMBLE BRANDY

1 *quart brandy*
brambles as required

port wine as required
sugar and water as required

Fill wide-mouthed bottles a third full of brandy. Wash and well drain sound brambles. Fill the bottles up with the berries. Cork and tie down corks tightly. Store in a dark cellar for 3 months, then strain off the liquor. Place the fruit in a crock. Press it until all the liquor has been extracted. Strain off this liquor and add to the brandy with first extraction. Measure. Add port wine, water and crushed loaf sugar in the proportion of 1 pint port wine, 1 pint water and ½ lb. crushed loaf sugar to every quart of brandy mixture. Dissolve sugar in the water over low heat. Cool. Add port wine and bramble brandy. Strain through a jelly bag. Bottle, cork, label and seal. Ready for use in 2 months' time.

CARAWAY BRANDY

½ lb. loaf sugar
½ pint water
1 oz. caraway seeds

2 bitter almonds
1 quart brandy

Dissolve the sugar in the water in a saucepan, then bring to boil. Boil for a minute or two until into a thin syrup. Place caraway seeds in a fireproof jar. Add boiling syrup. Cover and stand for 10 minutes, then shell and add almonds. Pour in brandy. Cover and leave until quite cold, then bottle and cork tightly. Stand in a cool place for 10 days, then strain into smaller bottles and cork tightly.

GEAN GIN

2 lb. geans
1 quart gin

1 lb. light brown sugar

Rinse geans thoroughly and dry on a cloth. Prick each all over with a darning needle. Place in a large sweetie bottle or jar with the gin and sugar. Cork tightly. Shake every day for 2 months, then strain and bottle. Cork tightly. Keep for at least 6 months before serving

HET PINT

This is a beverage that was always served on the eve of a wedding and on New Year's morning in the Scottish Borders in days gone by. It was usually made from new ale seasoned with spice, laced with whisky, and thickened with beaten egg.

2 *quarts mild ale*	2 *eggs*
1 *nutmeg*	1 *egg yolk*
sugar to taste	½ *pint whisky*

Pour the ale into a sound enamel saucepan. Grate in the nutmeg. Bring to boiling point. Sweeten with sugar to taste. Beat the eggs with the egg yolk, then gradually stir in the hot ale. If you add too quickly, the beverage will curdle. Stir in whisky. Pour into saucepan. Stir till nearly boiling, then pour it from a height into a tankard heated with boiling water and pour backwards and forwards from tankard to pan till it froths. If liked, add to the ale with the nutmeg, 1 teaspoon ground ginger.

MEAL 'N ALE

In Victorian days, no harvest home was complete without this beverage. It was made in the morning and served at the end of the meal. Sometimes a ring was put inside, and the one who got it was the first to be married. So says the legend.

Pour 2 quarts of ale into a large basin. Heat 6 oz. treacle until it runs freely, then stir into ale. When blended, stir in ½ lb. medium oatmeal. Stir till smooth, then add Scotch whisky to taste.

BIRK WINE
(BIRCH WINE)

This wine used to be made about the end of March in Aberdeenshire, Glen Spey and wherever the birch tree flourished in Scotland. A hole was bored and a faucet inserted in the trunk and after all the juice required was run off, a pin was placed in the hole. If the tree was only tapped for two or three days it did not suffer.

1 *gallon birk juice*	½ *oz. crude tartar*
3 *lb. preserving sugar*	1 *oz. almonds*
1 *lb. raisins*	

Pour the juice, sugar and raisins into a preserving pan. Stir over low heat till sugar is dissolved, then boil for 25 minutes. Turn into a tub. Add the tartar. Allow it to ferment for 6 or 7 days. Strain into a cask. Tie almonds in a muslin bag. Add to juice. When the fermentation ceases, remove muslin bag. Bung up cask. Leave for 5 months, then fine and bottle the wine. Store bottles upright in a cool cellar. This is important. If laid down, the corks may fly off or the bottles burst.

MY FATHER'S COWSLIP WINE

Allow 3 lb. loaf sugar, the rind of a washed lemon and orange and the strained juice of a lemon to each gallon of water. Dissolve the sugar in the water, then bring to boil. Boil for 30 minutes, skimming frequently and carefully, then measure and pour over the fruit rinds and juice. Stand until the temperature of new milk, then add 1 gallon of cowslip blossoms for every gallon of water used in making this wine, and to every gallon allow 2 tablespoons yeast, spread on toast. This means gallon of liquid measured after boiling for 30 minutes, not only the water. Leave for 24 hours, then turn wine into a cask. Closely stop cask. Leave from 24 to 48 hours to ferment, and bottle 7 weeks later. If preferred, keep in cask.

ELDERFLOWER WINE

1 *pint elderflowers*   4 *lb. loaf sugar*
1 *lb. halved large raisins*   2 *tablespoons yeast*
2 *gallons water*

Only fully blown elderflowers should be used. Gather them on a dry day just before their petals begin to fall. Shake off the blossoms on to a sheet of paper. To do this first press the heads lightly to loosen the flowers without breaking off the buds, as they would make the wine slightly bitter. Measure the flowers loosely. Do not pack them down in the pint measure. Place the flowers, raisins and water and sugar in a barrel. Stir frequently till the sugar is dissolved, then add the yeast. Allow to ferment for 7 days, stirring every morning. Stop up barrel closely. Leave for 6 weeks, then strain and bottle.

MY FATHER'S GINGER WINE

March is the best time to make ginger wine. To make nine gallons, prepare a nine-gallon cask. Take 7 gallons water, 28 lb. loaf sugar, 10 lemons, 2 lb. muscatel raisins, 14 bitter oranges, 1 oz. isinglass, 2 oz. yeast, 5 oz. cream of tartar, $\frac{3}{4}$ lb. ginger.

Bring water to the boil in clean copper, add the sugar while stirring slowly, also the ginger bruised, and the rinds of oranges and lemons. Boil for 20 minutes after the sugar is melted. Cut and stone raisins, and put them in the cask. Cut in thin slices the oranges and lemons. Put them in a clean muslin bag. The cask should have a good-sized hole to admit the bag. When the liquor has cooled down to 80° F., put the mixture also into the cask. Now add the yeast and the cream of tartar. Brewers' yeast is best. Failing it, use German. The wine will ferment without yeast, but the fermentation is much slower. Stir well each day with a clean cane until active fermentation ceases, then dissolve the isinglass in a quart of the wine, slightly warmed, and add it to the cask. Stop the hole tightly, and it should stand from three to four months before it is bottled.

MY FATHER'S RHUBARB WINE

1 *pint water to* 1 *lb. fruit*   *sugar, lemon and whole ginger*

Trim off rhubarb foliage and ends of stalks. Wipe stalks with a damp cloth, then slice stalks. Place in a crock. Cover with cold water. Stand for 10 days, stirring daily. Measure and strain. Allow 1 lb. sugar to each pint of juice, and lemons and whole ginger in the proportion of 1 lemon and 2 oz. whole ginger, well bruised, to 8 pints of wine. Stir daily till the sugar is dissolved, then bottle or place in a large cask. If bottled, do not fill too full and cork only loosely till the wine has stopped fermenting. Cork tightly after fermentation has ceased.

Note: Use only earthenware or wooden vessels for wine making, not enamel or zinc.

GAY GORDON PUNCH

1 *quart whisky*
1 *pint brandy*
1 *quart claret*
1 *quart fresh lemon juice*

2 *sliced peeled bananas*
2 *sliced oranges*
3 *pints dry champagne*

Mix the whisky, brandy and claret in a punch bowl. Stir in strained lemon juice. Place a large block of ice in bowl. Sweeten punch with sugar to taste, stirring frequently till sugar is dissolved. Add banana, orange slices and champagne. *Yield:* About 5 quarts.

STIRRUP CUPS

In the eighteenth century ale was the most popular stirrup cup in Scotland. Apropos this, 'A brewster's wife, having one day brewed a "peck o' maut", placed it at the door to cool. A neighbour's cow passing by drank the browst. The ale wife was so annoyed that she took the case to court when it was decided that as by immemorial custom nothing was ever charged for a standing drink or stirrup cup. The defendant ought to be assoilzied. The cow having swallowed the browst standing at the door.'

Nowadays, whisky has taken the place of ale as a stirrup cup, usually diluted with cold water in Scotland, but sometimes with soda water. In cold weather, the whisky is often made into Toddy.

TODDY: Heat tumblers with boiling water, pouring it in very slowly until they are half full. Swill the water round until the whole surface is thoroughly heated. Pour out water, then add loaf sugar to taste and fill almost half full with boiling water. When sugar is melted, fill tumblers about three-quarters full with whisky, then add boiling water to taste. Stir with a silver spoon.

STOORUM

Place a heaped teaspoon of oatmeal in a tumbler. Add 2 table-spoons cold water and stir well, then pour in boiling water till tumbler is half full. Fill up with boiling milk. Season with salt to taste and strain into another tumbler. For 1 person.

CANDIES

Scotland has always been famous for her confectionery, particularly for rock, taiblet (tablet) and toffee. In my young days nearly every town had a shop celebrated for its special brand of confectionery. I never left Thrums without buying some of its delicious rock, nor Brechin without bringing home a large box of what we called toffees but which were really clove, peppermint and other kinds of cushions. When I cycled into Forfar I seldom came away without two or three boxes of 'Peter Reid' rock, flavoured with clove, lemon, cinnamon and peppermint as I remember. When I went to Edinburgh I always sent home some Edinburgh rock and almond cake, a glorified almond brittle sold in bars. There are many other forms of confectionery famous in Scotland such as Helensburgh toffee, and all the range of taiblets. As Wee Macgregor said, 'Taiblets are awfu' guid'.

I would like to be able to pass on the recipes for all these sweets, but this is not possible. Here you will mostly find recipes for sweets that were made in Scottish homes when the century was young.

TEMPERATURES FOR CANDIES

To be able to make candy without failures, you need a sugar boiling thermometer, but before using it for testing, place it in a saucepan of cold water and bring to boiling point, then transfer to the syrup. If you put it into the syrup without heating, it may crack. The moment the candy is ready, transfer thermometer to a jug of very hot water and let it cool slowly before drying and storing.

Types of Candy	Description	Temperature
Fudges	Very soft ball	234°–238° F.
Fondants	Soft ball	238°–240° F.
Caramels	Firm ball	242°–250° F.
Toffees	Hard ball	258°–270° F.
Butterscotch	Brittle under water	275°–300° F.
Brittles	Hard crack	295°–310° F.
Lollipops	Very brittle	310° F.

Note: To test without a thermometer, tip a few drops into a cup of ice-cold water and test with thumb and middle finger. Remove pan to one side of stove while testing.

ABERDEEN FUDGE

½ lb. caster sugar
½ cup rich milk

2 oz. butter
1 tablespoon golden syrup

Place all the ingredients in a saucepan. Stir over low heat till sugar is dissolved then to boiling point. Boil to soft ball stage when tested in cold water. Remove from stove. Cool slightly. Beat until creamy. Pour quickly into a buttered tin. Cut into squares when slightly cooled.

COFFEE FUDGE

½ lb. caster sugar
1 tablespoon butter
¼ pint rich milk

¾ cup golden syrup
1 to 2 tablespoons coffee
  essence

Place all the ingredients in a saucepan. Stir over low heat till sugar is dissolved, then till boiling. Boil for 15 minutes, stirring constantly. Pour into a buttered tin. Mark into squares before it firms, then cut out when cold.

ALMOND TOFFEE

2 oz. almonds
½ teaspoon cream of tartar
1 lb. caster sugar

1 dessertspoon unsalted butter
½ cup milk

Blanch and chop almonds. Dissolve cream of tartar in a table-spoon of milk. Place the sugar in a saucepan. Add butter and milk. Stir over low heat till the sugar is dissolved, then till boiling. Boil rapidly for 8 minutes without stirring, then add almonds. Boil for a minute and a half, then add cream of tartar. Stir until blended, then pour into a buttered dish. When nearly cold, cut with a sharp knife into strips.

BARLEY SUGAR

2 lb. loaf sugar
1 pint water
¾ teaspoon lemon juice

pinch of cream of tartar
saffron yellow to colour

Dissolve sugar in the water in a saucepan. Stir till boiling. Boil, without stirring, to between 236° and 240° F., soft ball stage. Add lemon juice, cream of tartar, and a drop or two of essence of lemon if liked. Boil to a very brittle stage, 310° F., without stirring. Add a drop or two of saffron yellow colouring to taste. Pour on-to a well oiled or buttered slab or platter. Leave till cool. Cut into narrow strips with oiled scissors. Twist each into a spiral 6 inches long and 1 inch wide, with hands dipped in cold water. Leave till quite cold. Store in an air-tight tin or box.

BLACK BOB

1 pint black currant purée   ¼ lb. sugar

Place the purée, made from black currants heated and mashed in a wet preserving pan, then rubbed through a hair sieve, into a clean pan, with ¼ lb. sugar. Stir over low heat till sugar is dis-solved, then till boiling. Boil for 45 minutes, stirring almost constantly. Pour into saucers. Place them before a fire to dry, and turn the cakes every day for 4 days. Place between folds of paper and hang up to dry. Cut into lozenges and store in jars with tight stoppers. Excellent for colds or sore throats.

BULL'S EYES

2 *lb. loaf sugar*
1 *cup cold water*
¼ *teaspoon cream of tartar*

yellow colouring to taste
¼ *teaspoon tartaric acid*
¼ *teaspoon lemon essence*

Stir the sugar, water and cream of tartar in a saucepan over low heat till sugar is dissolved, then stir till boiling. Boil without stirring till brittle. Pour a small portion onto a buttered or oiled slab. With gloved hands pull it out till it is creamy white. Stir a few drops of yellow colouring, tartaric acid and lemon essence into remaining portion. When blended, lay strips of the pulled portion an inch apart on the coloured portion. Fold the whole in two, stripes outwards, and draw the two ends together. With oiled scissors, cut in convenient strips, then into bull's eyes.

CARAMEL WALNUTS

3 *oz. sifted icing sugar*
3 *oz. ground almonds*
3 *oz. caster sugar*

beaten egg
shelled walnuts as required
caramel syrup

Mix the icing sugar with the almonds, caster sugar and enough beaten egg to make a very stiff dough. Flavour if liked with a drop or two of almond essence. Divide into equal-sized small portions about the size of a hazel nut, then roll each into a ball. Sandwich each ball between two halved walnuts. Lay aside for 24 hours. Coat balls with the caramel syrup, then let them dry on an oiled platter. Serve each in a little paper case. If to be kept for any length of time, store in a tightly closed tin box.

CARAMEL SYRUP: Pour ¼ pint of cold water into a small saucepan. Add 1 lb. caster sugar. Stir over low heat till the sugar is dissolved, then till boiling. Add a drop or two of caramel colouring if liked.

COCONUT ICE

1 *lb. loaf sugar*   5 *oz. desiccated coconut*
¼ *pint milk*   *cochineal to colour*

Place sugar in a saucepan. Add milk. Stir over low heat till dissolved, then till boiling. Boil to 240°–245° F., firm ball stage. Remove pan from stove. Stir in coconut. Quickly pour half the mixture into a small oiled shallow, oblong tin. Colour the remainder a delicate pink, and pour quickly and evenly over the first layer. When half set, mark into bars about 5 × 1½ inches long, with the back of a knife, and carefully break or cut up when cold.

MY FATHER'S VARIATIONS: Substitute coconut milk or water for the fresh milk, and freshly grated coconut for the desiccated. Boil steadily after sugar is dissolved for 10 minutes. Add coconut, increasing it to 6 oz. Boil for 10 minutes, then pour into a shallow dish. Sometimes he had to stir it a little after removing from stove before turning it out, and when using the desiccated coconut he always soaked it in milk for 30 minutes and drained it well. He substituted this milk for the fresh. Occasionally he made this tablet with half loaf and half brown sugar.

COCONUT TABLET

2 *lb. caster or loaf sugar*   1 *oz. butter*
¼ *pint milk*   1 *saltspoon cream of tartar*
¼ *pint water*   ¼ *lb. desiccated coconut*

Place, sugar, milk, water and butter in a saucepan. Stir over low heat till dissolved, then till boiling. Add cream of tartar. Boil to a firm ball, 245° F., stirring occasionally. Stir in coconut, and boil again to 245° F., stirring occasionally. Cool slightly. Beat with a wooden spoon till creamy. Pour into a buttered tin, 8 × 10 × 2 inches. When cool, cut into bars and wrap each in waxed paper. When coconuts are available, substitute coconut milk for part of the fresh milk and freshly grated coconut for the desiccated.

DUNDEE TOFFEE

½ lb. butter
½ lb. Demerara sugar
¾ lb. golden syrup

1 teaspoon lemon juice
1 teaspoon water

Melt butter. Add sugar, syrup, lemon juice and water. After sugar is dissolved, stir till boiling. Boil steadily, stirring constantly, till a few drops tossed into cold water snap when tested. Pour into buttered tins. Break with a hammer when cold.

EDINBURGH ROCK

1 lb. granulated sugar
¼ pint cold water

¼ teaspoon cream of tartar
colouring and essence to taste

Place sugar and water in a saucepan. Stir over low heat till sugar is dissolved, then till boiling. Add cream of tartar. Remove spoon and cover pan. Boil rapidly for 2 or 3 seconds, then remove lid, when all signs of sugar granules will have vanished. Gently insert heated thermometer. Boil to hard-ball stage, 262° F. in cold weather and 264° F. in hot. While syrup is boiling, brush a slab thoroughly with melted butter and brush a palette knife as well. When syrup reaches required temperature, remove pan from stove at once and pour syrup carefully over slab. Sprinkle a few drops of flavouring over the top and colouring as well. Remember that when the candy is pulled the colour will fade. Use lemon, ginger, vanilla or any other essence such as orange, raspberry or strawberry to taste. Gently fold the cooled edges over on to the centre with the greased palette knife. Repeat process as the remaining edges set. Continue to fold in this way until the mass is firm enough to take in your hand. Either grease your fingers, or dust them with sifted icing sugar, then pull the candy out into a roll over the slab. Pull roll out. Put the end in your right hand over the end in your left. Take the folded ends in your right hand, then pull strip evenly and gently but quickly. Again, put the end in your right hand over the end in your left, taking care not to twist roll and keeping the strip the same thickness all along. Continue doing this until the candy is firm enough to hold its shape when cut up. It should be nicely ribbed. Dust the board quickly with sifted icing sugar. Place strip on board. Pull out to thickness required. Cut into equal-sized lengths, 5 or 6 inches long, with scissors. Leave on a board in a warm room until the rock becomes powdery in 12 to 24 hours.

'GLESSIE'

1 *teaspoon cream of tartar*   ½ *oz. butter*
2 *tablespoons cold water*   1½ *lb. golden syrup*
½ *lb. moist brown sugar*

Place the cream of tartar, water, sugar and butter in an enamelled saucepan. Stir over low heat till sugar is dissolved then until boiling. Boil for 5 minutes. Add syrup. Stir till boiling, then boil rapidly without stirring for 30 minutes, until when tested in cold water a few drops soon become crisp. Pour out in thin sheets into buttered tins. When cold, break it with a hammer. If preferred it can be pulled out as soon as it is cool enough to handle and cut into sticks, either 6 or 8 inches long.

GUNDY

3 *cups golden syrup*   ¾ *teaspoon bicarbonate of soda*
1 *cup black treacle*   1 *teaspoon lemon juice*

Pour the syrup and treacle into a very large saucepan. Stir constantly until boiling and until the thermometer registers 290° F., when toffee should be brittle when tested. Stir in the bicarbonate of soda and lemon juice. Pour at once onto a buttered slab. When partly cooled, 'pull' until it turns light yellow. Draw out into a slab, six to eight inches long. Cut into sticks with oiled scissors.

HELENSBURGH TOFFEE

¼ *lb. unsalted butter*   1 *tin sweetened condensed milk*
2 *lb. caster sugar*   1 *teaspoon vanilla essence*
1 *cup water*

Melt butter. Add sugar, water and milk. Stir till boiling, then simmer steadily for about 25 minutes, stirring constantly, and then add vanilla essence. Pour into greased oblong or square tins. Mark into squares, before it becomes firm, then cut out.

HOREHOUND CANDY

$\frac{1}{4}$ lb. butter
a few drops water
2 lb. sugar

$\frac{1}{4}$ lb. honey
essence of horehound to taste

Place butter in a saucepan with the water, then stir in sugar and honey and essence of horehound. Stir over low heat till sugar is dissolved, then till boiling. Continue to boil, stirring constantly, until a little dropped into cold water snaps—290° F. Pour into a greased tin. Mark into small bars or squares when slightly cool, then divide when cold. Wrap in waxed paper.

PEPPERMINT DROPS

1 lb. caster sugar
$\frac{1}{2}$ cup cold water

$\frac{1}{4}$ teaspoon cream of tartar
10 drops oil of peppermint

Stir sugar, water and cream of tartar in a saucepan over low heat till sugar is dissolved. When boiling, cook quickly without stirring until soft ball stage is reached. Remove pan from heat. Stand for 2 minutes. Add oil of peppermint. Beat until creamy and slightly cooled, then drop from a teaspoon in rounds a little apart onto a baking sheet covered with waxed paper.

PETA'S PEPPERMINT CREAMS: Rub 1 lb. icing sugar and a pinch of cream of tartar through a hair sieve. Beat the white of a medium-sized egg slightly. Add 1 large tablespoon of cream and a few drops of essence of peppermint. Stir this mixture into the sugar. When blended, cover and leave for 1 hour in a cool place. Knead until smooth. Roll out on a board sprinkled with sieved icing sugar. Cut into small rounds. Place on a tin covered with greaseproof paper. Leave to dry for 24 hours. *Yield:* 20 creams.

RUSSIAN TOFFEE

1 *lb. loaf sugar*
½ *lb. butter*
1 *lb. red currant jelly*

½ *pint cream*
a few drops vanilla essence

Place all the ingredients in a saucepan. Stir over very slow heat till the sugar is dissolved then until the toffee leaves the sides of the pan clean. Pour into an oblong or square oiled tin. When set, mark into squares. Cut up when cold. Wrap each in wax paper. *Warning:* Do not allow mixture to boil.

DR KERR'S RUSSIAN TOFFEE

1 *lb. caster sugar*
2 *oz. butter*
1 *tin sweetened condensed milk*

1 *tablespoon golden syrup*
1 *tablespoon raspberry or red currant jelly*
a few drops of rum

Place all the ingredients in a rinsed saucepan, except the milk. Stir over slow heat till the sugar is dissolved, and the mixture is nearly boiling, then add the milk, stirring constantly. Boil for 15–20 minutes, till toffee is chewy when tested in cold water. Flavour with rum. Turn into an oblong or square oiled tin, and mark into squares when set. When almost cold, turn out onto a board and cut into squares.

STUFFED DATES

Slit and stone dates. Stuff with marzipan, or with marzipan wrapped round a piece of walnut. Close as tightly as possible and roll in caster sugar. Serve in little paper cases.

MARZIPAN: Mix 8 oz. ground almonds with 4 oz. each of caster sugar and sifted icing sugar. Make a hollow in the centre. Drop in two egg whites. Mix well, then gradually drop in a tablespoon of brandy, or flavour with a few drops of vanilla essence and a drop or two of almond essence.

TAIBLET OR TABLET

There are many versions of Scotch Taiblet. Here is a basic recipe with some variations.

2 lb. caster sugar   flavouring to taste
3 cups thin cream or top milk

Dissolve the sugar in the cream or top milk over slow heat, stirring constantly, then stir till boiling. Boil rapidly for about 10 minutes to soft ball stage, then remove from stove. Stir in flavouring to taste. Lower the pan into a bowl of cold water. Stir rapidly with a wooden spoon until the syrup shows signs of thickening round the edge. Keep stirring till the mixture turns slightly granular, then pour at once on to a buttered slab, or into a buttered tin. Cut into small rounds about 1½ inches across, or into bars 5 inches long and 1½ inches wide. When quite cold, wrap each bar in waxed paper.

CINNAMON OR CLOVE: Add a drop or two of oil of cinnamon or clove to taste.

FIG: Add 4–6 oz. minced, dried, washed figs, but stir a pinch of cream of tartar into the syrup just before it reaches soft ball stage.

LEMON OR VANILLA: Add ¾ teaspoon lemon or vanilla essence.

WALNUT: Reduce sugar to 1 lb. and increase cream or top milk to ½ pint. Add 1 tablespoon golden syrup. Stir until boiling after sugar is dissolved, then add 6 oz. chopped walnuts and boil rapidly for 10 minutes. Remove pan from stove. Add 1 teaspoon vanilla essence, and leave till slightly cool, then beat well till mixture shows signs of stiffening. Pour out and cut into bars as in basic recipe.

TREACLE ALMOND TOFFEE

1 *lb. black treacle*   ½ *lb. caster sugar*
¼ *lb. unsalted butter*   2 *oz. chopped blanched almonds*

Place the treacle, butter and sugar in a saucepan. Stir over low heat till sugar is dissolved, then till boiling. Boil for 20 minutes, stirring constantly. Remove from stove. Add almonds. Pour into a buttered tin. Leave till set. Break with a hammer.

PRESERVES

When I was very young my father made all our jams, jellies and marmalade, and never had a failure. When I was in my 'teens he was so busy in the summer extracting honey from the combs that he gradually transferred the summer preserving to me. You see, he had been brought up in a very strict household where everything was made at home, even candles.

ALMACK

4 *dozen halved stoned plums* 2 *dozen cored peeled pears*
2 *dozen cored peeled apples* 3 *lb. loaf sugar*

Place alternate layers of plums, quartered apples and sliced pears in an earthenware jar. Cover with a lid. Tie down closely with brown paper. Bake in a moderate oven till the fruit is quite soft. Place the sugar in a preserving pan. Sieve the fruit over it. Stir till blended and the sugar is melted then till boiling. Boil for about 1 hour, stirring frequently, then pour into a rather deep dish. Cover closely. When required, serve, cut in slices, like guava cheese.

APRICOT JAM

2 *lb. dried apricots* 4 *lb. loaf sugar*
2 *quarts cold water* 2 *oz. almonds*

Halve apricots. Wash in a colander under the cold water tap. Drain. Cover with the water. Soak for 24 hours. Turn apricots

313

and water into a preserving pan. Heat sugar slightly in the oven and add. Stir over slow heat till dissolved, then bring to boil. Boil steadily for about 45 minutes to setting point, 220°–222° F. Meanwhile, blanch and halve almonds, and add when jam has been cooking for 30 minutes. Pot and seal.

MY FATHER'S BLACKCURRANT JAM

If you prefer a rather stiff blackcurrant jam, use this recipe, but the currants must be large and juicy, and if any hard or unripened fruit is included, the jam will be spoilt.

6 *lb. blackcurrants*   6 *lb. loaf sugar*
1 *pint cold water*

Place the blackcurrants and water in a preserving pan. Simmer gently for 30 minutes. Meanwhile, heat sugar slightly in the oven. When fruit is tender, remove pan from stove. Add sugar. Stir until dissolved, then replace pan on stove. Bring to simmering point. Simmer gently for 15 minutes. Remove pan from stove. Stir jam for a moment or two, then pot and seal.

BLAEBERRY JAM

7 *lb. blaeberries*   5 *lb. loaf sugar*
1 *lb. sliced rhubarb*

Carefully pick over blaeberries, removing any bits of leaf or stem. Place rhubarb in a rinsed preserving pan. Heat the sugar and place over rhubarb. Stir over low heat till sugar is dissolved, then till boiling. Boil rapidly for 10 minutes. Add berries. Simmer gently until tender, skimming as required, then continue to simmer to setting point. Pot and seal. If preferred, cook the rhubarb in enough water to cover bottom of pan for 12 minutes, then strain, and use juice in place of the rhubarb.

GOOSEBERRY AND RASPBERRY JAM

3 *lb. green gooseberries*   *sugar as required*
cold water as required   6 *lb. raspberries*

Pick over, top and tail and wash the gooseberries. Place in a preserving pan. Cover with cold water. Bring slowly to boil. Simmer gently for about 1 hour until the berries are into a mush, then pour into a jelly bag. Leave without squeezing or mashing until all the juice is extracted, then measure. Pour into preserving pan, adding sugar, 1 lb. to each pint of juice, and 4½ lb. extra to sweeten the raspberries. Stir gently over low heat until the sugar is dissolved, then bring to boil. Add the raspberries. Bring to boil, and boil for about 15 minutes, until the jam sets when tested.

GOOSEBERRY AND STRAWBERRY JAM

Top and tail and rinse 10 lb. of freshly picked green gooseberries, all equally ripe. Hull and rinse 4 lb. fresh strawberries. Place the berries in a preserving pan. Heat slightly, then add 10 lb. preserving sugar. Stir gently over low heat till sugar is dissolved, then bring to boil. Boil quickly to setting point. Remove pan from stove. Stand for 5 minutes. Stir and pot and seal.

Note: If strawberries are not available, substitute 4 lb. strawberry jam.

WILD RASPBERRY JAM

6 *lb. raspberries*   4½ *lb. loaf sugar*

If you are not able to gather wild raspberries as I used to, use cultivated berries. Rinse very gently in a colander dipped in a basin of cold water. Drain thoroughly. Bring slowly to boil. Boil for 15 minutes. Remove pan from heat. Stir in sugar, and keep on stirring till all the sugar is dissolved, then return pan to stove. Bring to boil, stirring occasionally, then boil for 5 minutes. Remove pan from stove. Pot and seal.

MEMUS RHUBARB JAM

6 *lb. rhubarb*	1 *lemon*
3 *oz. preserved ginger*	6½ *lb. loaf sugar*

I usually make this jam in early June before the stalks turn stringy. Trim, wash and wipe sticks. Cut into ½ inch pieces. Chop the ginger. Wash and quarter the lemon, and discard the pips. Place the rhubarb, ginger, lemon and sugar in a large basin and cover closely. Stand for 3 days in a cool place, then turn into a preserving pan. Stir frequently till boiling. Boil for 35 minutes, then remove lemon. Pot and seal.

RHUBARB AND FIG JAM

6 *lb. rhubarb*	1 *lb. figs*
5 *lb. preserving sugar*	2 *oz. crystallized ginger*

Trim and wash rhubarb. Dry and cut into slices about ½ inch thick. Place in a basin. Cover with the sugar. Soak for 24 hours. Place in a preserving pan. Wash figs in warm water. Remove stalks. Cut up figs. Add to rhubarb with the ginger, finely chopped. Stir over low heat till sugar is dissolved, then till boiling. Boil steadily for about 30 minutes till a little sets when tested. Remove from stove. Stand for 5 minutes. Stir, pot and seal.

MY FATHER'S STRAWBERRY JAM

6 *lb. strawberries*	4½ *lb. loaf sugar*

Pick the berries on a dry day, choosing fruit of an equal size. Rinse in a colander in a basin of cold water, then drain thoroughly. Place in a preserving pan. Heat slowly till boiling. Boil for 20 minutes. Remove pan from stove. Add sugar. Stir till dissolved, then return pan to stove. Stir occasionally till boiling, then boil for 10 minutes. Pot and seal.

APPLE AND SLOE JELLY

4 *lb. crab apples or cooking*   2 *lb. sloes*
   apples   *sugar as required*

Wash and cut up the apples roughly. Remove stalks from sloes and rinse sloes. Place apples and sloes in a preserving pan. Cover with cold water. Bring to boil. Boil steadily until into a pulp. Strain through a jelly bag into a basin, but do not squeeze the bag or mash the pulp. Measure juice. Pour juice into preserving pan. Heat sugar slightly, allowing 1 lb. sugar to each pint of juice. Add to juice. Stir over low heat till sugar is dissolved, then till boiling. Skim carefully. Boil for 15 minutes. Pot and seal.

AVERN JELLY

If you're in Scotland in August you may be able to make jelly from 'Averns' which is the name the folks on the Braes of Angus give to wild strawberries to be found on the foothills of the Grampians. I remember walking about 13 miles up to the head of Glen Clova and climbing the steep tussocky hill to the shores of Loch Brandy, where they grew, singing *Excelsior* as I peched over the desolate haunt of the blackcock one hot afternoon in the long ago. From the basket of berries I made delicious jelly.

5 *pints of berries*   1 *quart cold water*
juice of 2 lemons   *sugar as required*

Place the berries in preserving pan. Add lemon juice and water. Bring slowly to boil. Simmer gently till all the juice is extracted. Strain and measure juice. Add sugar in the proportion of 1 lb. sugar to each pint of juice. Boil to between 220° and 222° F. till a little sets when tested on a cold saucer, then skim, pot and seal.

BRAMBLE JELLY

4 *lb. blackberries*   ½ *oz. tartaric acid*
½ *pint water*   *loaf sugar as required*

Rinse berries. Place in preserving pan. Add water and acid. Simmer slowly till fruit is quite tender, mashing occasionally. Strain through a jelly bag. Measure juice, then weigh out 1 lb. sugar to each pint of juice. Rinse pan. Add juice and sugar. Stir over low heat till sugar is dissolved, then till boiling. Boil rapidly without stirring for 8 minutes, then test. Continue to boil to setting point. Pot and seal.

KILLIECRANKIE JELLY

Remove stalks from ripe barberries. Place berries in a colander, and rinse in a basin of water, then drain. Place in a preserving pan with equal quantity of juice, strained from apples, cooked to a pulp in cold water to cover. Boil, stirring constantly, until the berries are into a pulp, then strain through a jelly bag and measure juice. Allow preserving sugar in the proportion of 1 pound to a pint of juice. Stir over low heat till sugar is dissolved, then till boiling. Boil for about 15 minutes to setting point. Pot and seal.

MEDLAR JELLY (1816)

Wipe ripe medlars and place in a preserving pan with water to cover them. Simmer slowly till into a pulp, then strain through a jelly bag and measure the juice. Allowing ¾ lb. sugar, caster for preference, to every pint of juice, turn into a preserving pan. Stir over low heat till the sugar is dissolved, then bring quickly to a boil. Boil until the syrup is quite clear and turns a pinkish shade, when it is ready to put in pots and seal.

MORNA'S ORANGE JELLY

4 *lb. bitter oranges*	*cold water as required*
3 *lb. sweet oranges*	*preserving sugar as required*
2 *lb. cooking apples*	

Wash fruit but do not pare it. Cut in quarters. Place in a preserving pan. Just cover with cold water. Bring to boil. Boil gently for 1½ hours. Strain through a jelly bag. Measure juice, and weigh out preserving sugar, allowing sugar in the proportion of 1 lb. sugar to 1 pint juice. Stir over low heat till sugar is dissolved, then till boiling. Boil rapidly until a drop jellies when tested on a cold plate. Pot and seal.

CARRIE'S RED CURRANT JELLY

The following two recipes have been passed on to me by my sister who was famous for her preserves.

12 *lb. freshly picked red*   *water as required*
  currants   *sugar as required*

Stem the currants. Place in a large preserving pan. Cover with water. Boil till soft. Turn into a jelly bag and let the juice drip without squeezing into a basin below, then measure juice. Allow 1 lb. sugar to each pint of juice. Place sugar and juice in rinsed preserving pan. Bring quickly to boil and allow it to come only once to the top of pan, then remove immediately and pot and seal. This jelly retains the colour and the flavour of the fruit.

RED CURRANT AND RASPBERRY JELLY

3 *lb. red currants*   *sugar as required*
1 *lb. raspberries*

Weigh a large basin. Squeeze fruit through a thin linen jelly bag into basin. Weigh again. Allow loaf sugar in the proportion of 1¼ lb. to each lb. of juice. Stir sugar and juice till sugar is dissolved. Pot and seal at once.

RODDEN JELLY

This jelly should be made in September when the berries are red and juicy.

2 *quarts rowan berries*   *loaf sugar as required*
3 *quarts cold water*

Rinse and drain berries. Place in a preserving pan. Add water. Bring to boil. Simmer until half the water is boiled away. Pour into a jelly bag and let the juice drip into a basin below. Measure. Weigh out sugar, allowing 1 lb. to each pint of juice. Rinse preserving pan. Add sugar and juice. Stir slowly till boiling, then remove any scum. Boil for about ½ hour, to setting point, 220°–222° F. Pot up in small jars. Leave for two or three days uncovered, then cover and seal. Serve with fried, grilled or roast venison.

ROSE HIP JELLY

Wash hips, then remove seeds, using a large needle. Place in an enamel-lined saucepan with cold water to cover. Simmer till soft. Strain through a jelly bag, and measure juice. Rinse pan. Add juice. Boil rapidly for 10 minutes, then add sugar, allowing ¾ lb. to each pint of juice. Stir over low heat till dissolved, then till boiling. Boil to setting point. Pot and seal.

TANNADICE FRUIT JELLY

1 *lb. black currants*
1 *lb. red currants*
1 *lb. gooseberries*
cold water as required

1 *lb. raspberries*
½ *pint rhubarb juice*
sugar as required

Stalk and top black currants. Strip the red from their stalks. Top and tail the gooseberries. Wash if necessary and drain thoroughly. Place the currants and gooseberries in a preserving pan with the raspberries. Add cold water to cover. Bring to simmering point. Simmer gently, stirring frequently, until fruit is into a pulp. Turn into a jelly bag. Allow to drip into a basin below without squeezing bag or mashing the fruit. Add rhubarb to the juice and weigh. Allow equal weight of sugar. Turn the sugar and juice into a preserving pan. Bring to boiling point. Boil for about 20 minutes to setting point. Pot and seal.

DUNDEE MARMALADE

2 lb. bitter oranges   2 quarts water
2 lemons   4 lb. heated preserving sugar

Wash oranges and lemons thoroughly. Place in a saucepan. Add water. Cover. Simmer for about 1½ hours until skins are so soft that you can easily pierce them. Remove oranges and lemons with a skimming spoon to plate. Leave until cool, then slice neatly. Pick out the pips and add them to the juice. Boil steadily for 10 minutes, then strain juice into preserving pan. Add the sliced pulp. Bring to boil. Add sugar. Stir over low heat until dissolved, then till boiling. Boil rapidly, without stirring, to setting point, 220° F., in about 20 minutes. *Yield:* About 3½ lb.

FOUR FRUIT MARMALADE

2 grapefruit   2 tangerines
4 lemons   6 pints water
2 bitter oranges   6 lb. preserving sugar

The total weight of fruit should be about 3 lb. Wash fruit. Peel off rind thinly. Cut into shreds. Strip off pith from fruit and put in muslin bag. Cut up flesh, removing coarse skin dividing sections of grapefruit and any coarse skin from other fruit. Put skin and pips into pith bag. Put fruit, peel and bag of pith and pips into large bowl and pour in the water. Leave for 12 hours. Turn contents of bowl into preserving pan. Simmer gently for about 2 hours, or till rind of bitter oranges is quite soft. When ready, lift up bag of pith, let liquid drip from it into pan, then discard pith and pips. Bring to boil. Stir in sugar. Remove pan from stove and continue stirring till sugar is dissolved, then boil rapidly till marmalade sets when tested. *Yield:* About 10 lbs.

GINGER MARMALADE

3 lb. tart apples   preserving sugar as required
1 quart water   1¾ lb. preserved ginger

Wash apples carefully. Cut them into thick slices without either peeling or coring. Put all the slices into a saucepan with the water. Simmer gently till fruit is well pulped, then strain through a jelly bag. Allow to drip for several hours. When all the juice is in the basin, measure it, and for every pint of juice allow 1 lb. of sugar. Turn juice and sugar into a preserving pan. Stir over low heat till sugar is dissolved. Add ginger cut into small pieces, then bring to boil. Boil quickly for 8 to 10 minutes or till preserve sets when tested on a cold plate. Pot and cover while hot. *Yield:* About 4½ lb.

HAMILTON MARMALADE (1838)

This marmalade should be made in March if possible. Wash two dozen oranges. Place in a preserving pan. Cover with cold water. Bring to boil. Boil slowly until so tender that they can be pierced with a skewer, then remove pan from stove. Lift the oranges out and let them cool until you are able to handle them, then peel off the outer skins. Scrape off the white pith and discard with the fibres and pips after slicing the fruit. Cut the outer skins into fine strips. Weigh strips and pulp. To every pound allow 2 lb. of sugar and 1 pint of water. Place rind, pulp, sugar and water in a preserving pan. Stir over moderate heat till sugar is dissolved, then bring to boil. Boil for about an hour, until setting point is reached, 220°–222° F. Pot up then cover and seal.

DAMSON CHEESE

Wash ripe damsons. Place in a basin. Stand basin in a pan of boiling water. Boil until the fruit is into a pulp. Rub the fruit and juice through a hair sieve, then measure the purée. Allow heated sugar in the proportion of 1 lb. to each pint of purée. Place purée and sugar in a preserving pan. Stir over low heat till the sugar is dissolved, then occasionally until boiling. Boil until the cheese sets rather stiffly in 30 to 40 minutes, stirring frequently, and almost constantly towards the end, as this preserve is liable to scorch. Pot in small moulds. Serve as a preserve at tea time, or with milk moulds.

MY LEMON CURD

¼ lb. caster sugar
¼ lb. loaf sugar
2 oz. unsalted butter

2 washed lemons
3 fresh eggs

Place the sugars in the top of a rinsed double boiler. Add the butter. Grate in the lemon rind. Extract and strain the lemon juice and pour into the top of boiler. Beat eggs. Stir into mixture. When blended, place over boiling water. Cook, stirring constantly, till the sugar is dissolved and the mixture thickens, but do not allow to boil. Pot and seal at once.

NIN'S LEMON CURD

¼ lb. unsalted butter
pinch of salt
2 well-beaten eggs
½ lb. caster sugar

grated rind of 2 lemons
strained juice of 2 lemons
1 level teaspoon cornflour

Place the butter, salt, eggs, sugar and lemon rind in the top of a double boiler. Gradually cream the lemon juice with the cornflour. Stir into egg mixture. Place in top of boiling water. Cook, stirring constantly, until thickened, but do not allow to boil. Pot and seal.

RHUBARB CHUTNEY
(Thurso Recipe)

1 lb. sliced rhubarb
1 peeled lemon
½ oz. chopped peeled garlic
½ oz. bruised root ginger
1 lb. moist brown sugar

½ pint vinegar
dash of cayenne pepper
1½ lb. washed sultanas
½ oz. salt

Place rhubarb, sliced lemon, garlic and all the other ingredients in an enamel-lined saucepan. Stir over low heat till sugar is dissolved, then until boiling. Boil till thick, stirring frequently, then pot and seal.

MINCEMEAT

2 *lb. shredded beef suet*
1½ *lb. loaf sugar*
1 *lb. brown sugar*
3 *lb. cleaned currants*
3 *lb. raisins*
2½ *lb. cooking apples*
¼ *oz. ground cinnamon*
¼ *oz. ground mace*
¼ *oz. grated nutmeg*
¼ *oz. ground cloves*
strained juice of 6 *lemons*

grated rind of 3 *lemons*
1 *oz. chopped candied citron peel*
3 *oz. chopped candied lemon peel*
3 *oz. chopped candied orange peel*
½ *pint white wine*
¾ *pint brandy*
a few grains of salt

Place the suet in a basin. Add the sugars, then the currants. Stone raisins, or use 2½ lb. of stoned raisins. Put half the raisins through a meat grinder and add with remainder to suet mixture. Peel, core and chop apples finely. Add to mixture with spices, lemon juice, lemon rind and candied peels. Sprinkle with the wine. Stir till blended. Stir once a day for 3 or 4 days until all the sugar is dissolved, keeping basin covered when not stirring. Stir in brandy, and salt. Cover and leave for about 1 hour, then stir, pot and seal. *Yield:* Between 13 and 14 lb.

APPLE PICKLE

20 *medium-sized apples*
½ *peeled onion*
½ *oz. mustard seed*
½ *dozen chilli peppers*

1 *lb. Demerara sugar*
½ *lb. cleaned sultanas*
2 *oz. salt*
1½ *pints vinegar*

Peel, core and cut up apples. Chop onion. Tie mustard seed and peppers in a muslin bag. Place the apple, onion, bag and remaining ingredients in an enamel-lined saucepan. Bring slowly to boil, stirring frequently until sugar is dissolved, then simmer gently until apple and onion are tender. Remove muslin bag. Pot and seal. Serve with cold duck, goose, or pork.

SALTED MARROW SEEDS

seeds from a medium-sized   *1 large tablespoon of butter*
  vegetable marrow   *salt to taste*

When halving a vegetable marrow for cooking, remove the seeds and spread them without washing in a baking tin. Sprinkle lightly with salt. Melt butter and stir into the seeds. There should be enough to cover them. If not, add some more. Bake in a very slow oven, 250° F., until brown and crisp.

TO CARAMELIZE MARROW SEEDS: Place the slightly browned seeds with sugar in a heavy frying pan, allowing 2 oz. caster sugar to 1 cup of the seeds. Heat slowly till sugar turns into a caramel, and all the seeds are coated. Remove from stove and separate seeds, then cool on waxed paper.

AYRSHIRE BACON

1 small side of pork   *1 oz. saltpetre*
6 oz. salt   *1 pint white vinegar*
8 oz. moist brown sugar

You must use home-fed pork for making this bacon. Bone it then mix the salt with the sugar and saltpetre, and rub it well into the pork, paying particular attention to the cut side from which the bones have been removed. Place in a dry pickling pan or crock, and sprinkle any of the pickle that remains over it. Leave for 3 days in a cool place, then sprinkle with the vinegar. Turn the pork in the pickle daily for a month, then remove from pickle and hang up to drain for 24 hours. Flatten it out on a board, then roll up tightly, the rind outwards, and fasten into a roll with strong string. Hang up in a current of air. Leave until quite dry, then boil and serve cold, or slice and fry or grill.

MUTTON HAM

Mutton hams are sometimes served at breakfast in the Highlands, after boiling as you would an ordinary ham. To make a mutton ham you need:

1 *shoulder of mutton*	$\frac{1}{2}$ *oz. saltpetre*
$\frac{1}{2}$ *lb. cooking salt*	2 *oz. black pepper*
2 *oz. bay salt*	4 *or* 5 *Juniper berries*
4 *oz. moist brown sugar*	

Place the mutton in a crock or pickling pan. Mix all the other ingredients together and pound well. Heat and rub half the mixture into the mutton. Leave for 2 days, then heat the remainder of the mixture and rub this in. Turn the mutton daily in the pickle for a fortnight, then smoke it or have it smoked, and it will keep well for 3 to 4 months. Soak in cold water to cover for 2 hours before boiling.

TO PICKLE HAMS

2 *medium-sized hams*	$\frac{1}{2}$ *lb. bay salt*
2 *lb. moist brown sugar*	$\frac{1}{4}$ *lb. Prunella*
3 *lb. cooking salt*	1 *pint old ale*

Place the hams in a large crock. Mix the sugar with the salt, bay salt, prunella and the ale. Rub this thoroughly all over the hams, and sprinkle with any remainder. Turn the hams and rub them every morning for two weeks, then hang them up to dry in an airy place and use without smoking.

LIQUID PICKLE FOR BEEF

1 *gallon water*	1 *oz. saltpetre*
$1\frac{1}{2}$ *lb. bay salt*	$\frac{1}{2}$ *oz. bruised peppercorns*
$\frac{3}{4}$ *lb. coarse brown sugar*	

Place all these ingredients in a large saucepan. Bring to boil. Skim carefully. Pour into an earthenware crock. Leave until quite cold before using.

HINTS ON PICKLING MEAT: There must be enough of the pickle to cover the meat entirely. See that the lid of the crock is kept on all the time. Allow a week in the pickle for a piece of beef weighing 6–8 lb. If the cut is larger, leave in pickle an extra day for each pound over 8 lb. Before cooking pickled beef, wash it well in cold water, and cook it in water that is fairly hot, but not quite boiling. Simmer it very gently the whole time.

FOR INVALIDS

As I feel no cookery book is complete without catering for the sick as well as for the hale, I am including a few recipes for the sick room that I follow myself.

BEEF TEA

8 *oz. lean, juicy beef*   salt, if allowed
½ *pint cold water*

Trim all the fat and skin from the beef. Wipe beef thoroughly with a damp cloth, then shred finely. Place in a strong straight-sided jar. Add water and a pinch of salt if allowed. Cover with a lid of greased paper, tying it on securely. Stand for 30 minutes, then uncover and stir well. Cover again. Place in a saucepan. Add enough cold water to come half-way up the side of jar. Bring slowly to boil. Simmer *very gently* for 2½–3 hours, then strain. If wanted at once, carefully remove any floating fat with blotting paper. If not, leave until cold, then heat up as required, removing fat if necessary. Serve with Fairy Toast.

Note: Only prepare as much beef tea as is required in one day. If raw beef tea is ordered by the Doctor, allow only 2 oz. to ¼ pint water, and strain into a covered cup after standing, without cooking. It is essential to make it fresh every time it has to be served.

ALBUMENIZED MILK

1 *egg white*   *½ cup fresh milk*

Place the egg white in a tumbler. Add milk. Cover tightly. Shake till blended, then pour into a fresh tumbler and serve.

MILK PUNCH

½ cup milk   1 *dessertspoon brandy or sherry*
¾ teaspoon caster sugar

Pour milk into a tumbler. Add sugar and brandy or sherry. Cover tightly and shake well. Pour into another glass.

PRUNE JUICE PUNCH

½ cup prune juice   *¾ teaspoon lemon juice*
¾ cup milk   *caster sugar to taste*

Pour juice into a tumbler. Gradually stir in the milk, then add lemon juice and sugar unless the juice is very sweet. If not, allow 1 teaspoon. Cover tightly. Shake well. Pour into a fresh tumbler.

GRUEL

Sometimes it is made with milk, sometimes with water, according to Doctor's orders.

WITH MILK: Mix a dessertspoon of fine oatmeal with 2 tablespoons of cold milk. Stir in ½ pint boiling milk, then pour into a lined saucepan. Simmer for 10 minutes, stirring constantly. Add salt and sugar according to taste. If brandy is ordered to be added, allow 1 tablespoon.

WITH WATER: Place 1 oz. of fine oatmeal in a basin. Add ½ pint cold water. Cover and stand for 1 hour. Strain. Pour liquid into a lined saucepan. Stir until boiling. Place pan over boiling water.

Simmer gently for 15 minutes, stirring occasionally. Add salt and sugar to taste.

BARLEY AND ORANGE GRUEL

1 *oz. well-washed pearl barley* 2 *or 3 strips orange rind*
1 *pint water* *honey or glycerine to sweeten*
½ *oz. cinnamon stick*

Place the barley in a lined saucepan. Add water, cinnamon stick and orange rind. Bring to boil. Boil until reduced to half its quantity, then strain. Return to pan. Sweeten to taste with honey or glycerine, and flavour to taste with lemon and orange juice or use only lemon. This is a good nightcap for people suffering from chills and coughs.

WHEY

1 *pint milk* 1 *teaspoon rennet*

Heat milk to the temperature of new milk. Stir in rennet. Stand till the milk curdles and the whey is clear. Leave until cool, then strain.

LEMON WHEY

1 *cup hot milk* 1½ *teaspoons caster sugar*
juice of 1 *small lemon*

Heat milk in a lined saucepan on top of hot water. Strain in lemon juice. Leave until the curd separates, then strain. Add sugar to the whey. Stir till dissolved. Serve hot or cold.

SHERRY WHEY

½ *cup milk*   ¼ *cup sherry*
1 *lump sugar*

Bring milk and sugar to a boil. Stir in sherry. Remove and leave
till curd forms. Strain whey into a glass.

A Hint on straining drinks: Use butter muslin, wrung out of hot
boiled water.

APPLE SAUCE

6 *cooking apples*   2 *teaspoons caster sugar*
1 *cup cold water*

Peel and quarter the apples. Remove cores. Place in an enamel
saucepan. Add water. Simmer for about 30 minutes until into a
sauce. Add sugar. Stir till dissolved. Strain. Serve for breakfast,
lunch or dinner with caster sugar.

APPLE SOUFFLÉ

2 *large apples*   1 *tablespoon caster sugar*
a few drops of lemon juice   1 *stiffly beaten egg white*

Bake apples in a greased covered dish containing 2 tablespoons of
water in a moderate oven, at 350° F. for about 30 minutes until
quite soft. Scrape out all the pulp into a basin. Beat until smooth.
Stir in lemon juice and sugar. Beat well. Fold in egg whites. Bake
in a small greased pie dish until fluffy and pale golden brown in
about 20 to 30 minutes.

BEEF CUSTARD

1 *beaten egg* $\frac{3}{4}$ *gill beef tea*
a few grains salt

Mix the egg with the salt and the beef tea. Pour into a greased custard cup. Cover with buttered paper. Steam gently for 20 minutes. Serve with dry, crisp toast.

CALVES' FOOT JELLY

$1\frac{1}{2}$ *pints stock*   *rind of* 2 *lemons*
5 *or* 6 *oz. loaf sugar*   3 *whole cloves*
2 *egg whites* $1\frac{1}{2}$ *inches cinnamon stick*
2 *egg shells* $\frac{1}{4}$ *pint sherry*
$\frac{3}{4}$ *gill lemon juice* $\frac{1}{2}$ *gill brandy*

Remove every particle of grease from the stock first with a spoon dipped in boiling water, then with a piece of muslin wrung out of hot water. Also wipe carefully round inside of basin containing stock with a piece of muslin dipped in boiling water. Rinse an enamel-lined deep saucepan with hot water. Add the stock, sugar, egg whites and shells, lemon juice, very thinly peeled lemon rinds, cloves and cinnamon stick, broken in small pieces. Whisk over moderate heat until almost boiling, then remove whisk. Bring to full boil. Draw pan to side of stove. Add sherry. Bring again to boil. Place a chair upside down on a table with seat resting on table, then tie a clean coarse linen cloth over the legs of the chair, and place a basin under the cloth. Now pour a little boiling water through cloth to ensure jelly running easily. Drain thoroughly. Pour water out of bowl, and replace bowl under bag. Pour a little jelly into bag. When it has dripped into the bowl, remove bowl. Replace it with a clean one, and pour the dripped jelly into the bag again and gradually pour in remainder of jelly. Stir brandy into the jelly in bowl. When all the remaining jelly has dripped through into the bowl, pot and seal. Store in a cold place.

TO PREPARE THE STOCK: Wash 2 calves' feet (if unable to buy a calves' foot and a jelly is wanted, substitute an ox foot). Divide each foot into 4 or 6 joints and carefully remove all fat and marrow. Wash again and scrape if necessary in hot water. Place in saucepan. Cover with cold water. Bring to boil, then drain and rinse well. Return to pan. Add 5 pints water. Simmer gently for 6 to 7 hours. Strain into a basin through a hair sieve. When cold, skim off fat with a spoon dipped in boiling water, then with butter muslin dipped frequently in boiling water. With the muslin, dipped in boiling water, wipe round inside of basin carefully. Now measure off 1½ pints. Skim again if necessary. If the stock is thin, dissolve, powdered gelatine in water, allowing ¼ oz. in winter and ½ oz. in summer to 2 tablespoons water. Stir stock only until melted before measuring for the jelly.

DARIOLES OF CHICKEN

¼ lb. raw chicken
1 beaten egg
salt to taste
pepper if allowed

1 tablespoon sieved breadcrumbs
1 stiffly beaten egg white
½ gill thick cream

Put chicken through a mincer. Stir in egg, salt and pepper if allowed and the crumbs. Fold in the egg white and cream, lightly whipped. Place in small buttered moulds. Cover with greased paper. Steam gently for 20 minutes. Turn each out onto a bed of spinach. Serve with fluffy mashed potatoes and egg or white sauce. For 2 invalids.

INVALID'S CHICKEN

1 freshly-boiled chicken
½ oz. butter
½ oz. flour
¼ pint chicken stock

1 tablespoon cream
salt and pepper to taste
½ teaspoon lemon juice
1 egg yolk

Remove the skin from the breast, then remove fillets as required. Place on a hot dish. Cover, and keep hot over boiling water. Melt butter. Stir in flour. When frothy, stir in the chicken stock. Stir until boiling, then simmer for 5 minutes, stirring constantly.

Gradually stir in the cream, salt to taste and pepper if allowed, then the lemon juice. When blended, dilute the yolk with 2 tablespoons of the chicken stock. Stir over slow heat until piping hot, but do not allow to boil or the sauce will curdle. Pour over the chicken breasts. Serve with mashed potato.

TO CODDLE AN EGG

Bring water to a boil in both top and bottom of a double boiler. Place egg in the upper part. Remove pan from stove. Leave egg in water over the bottom part from 4 to 8 minutes until coddled to taste. Do not return pan to stove. Serve in a cup or glass.

FISH CREAM

¼ *lb. haddock, sole or whiting*
½ *oz. butter*
½ *oz. white breadcrumbs*
½ *gill milk*
salt to taste

few drops lemon juice
½ *teaspoon minced parsley*
1 *tablespoon cream*
1 *stiffly beaten egg white*

Remove all skin and bones from fish before weighing, then wipe with a damp cloth and shred finely. Melt butter in a small saucepan. Add crumbs and milk. Stir over moderate heat until thick, then turn into a mortar. Add fish. Pound well until into a smooth paste, then rub through a fine wire sieve. Season lightly with salt, and pepper if allowed. Stir in lemon juice, parsley and cream. Fold in egg white. Pack lightly into a greased basin or mould, filling it three-quarter full. Tie on a round of greased paper. Steam gently till firm in about 25 minutes. Unmould. Coat with white or parsley sauce. Serve with fluffy mashed potato.

APPLE TART FOR AN INVALID

1 *large peeled apple*
2 *tablespoons cold water*
1 *teaspoon caster sugar*

1 *small sponge cake*
1 *beaten egg*

Core and slice the apple. Place in a saucepan with the water and sugar. Cover and simmer gently until tender. Remove from stove. Beat with a wooden spoon until into a pulp. Place in the bottom of a small greased fireproof dish. Slice sponge cake thinly. Lay over the apple. Beat up egg. Stir in a teaspoon of caster sugar and ¼ pint milk. Strain over sponge cake. Stand for 5 minutes. Bake in a rather slow oven, 325° F., for about 20 minutes until custard is set.

JUNKET

1 *pint tepid milk*
1 *teaspoon essence of rennet*

¾ *oz. caster sugar*

Pour the milk into a basin. Stir in the rennet and the sugar. (If using pasteurized milk, double quantity of rennet.) Pour into individual glasses. Grate a little nutmeg over the surface if allowed. Set at room temperature. *Yield:* 4 portions.

RICE CAKE

¼ *lb. rice flour*
¼ *lb. flour*
¼ *lb. butter*

¼ *lb. caster sugar*
1 *large teaspoon baking powder*
2 *beaten eggs*

Sieve rice flour with flour. Beat butter to a cream. Add sugar. Beat till fluffy. Stir in if allowed the grated rind of ½ or a whole lemon, then the flour, sifted with the baking powder, and the eggs by degrees. Turn into a small greased cake tin, smoothly lined with greased paper. Bake in a moderate oven, 350° F., for about 1½ hours till dry in centre when tested with a heated skewer. Dredge with vanilla sugar.

INVALID RUSKS

3 *oz. butter*
6 *oz. caster sugar*
6 *oz. lightly baked breadcrumbs*

3 *eggs*
1 *tablespoon thick cream*

Beat butter to a cream, then beat in the sugar. When blended, stir in breadcrumbs, then the eggs and cream. Mix well. Pour into a greased baking tin. Bake in a moderate oven, 350° F., until crisp in about ½ hour, then cut into fingers.

ICED SLAB CAKE

2 *oz. butter*
4 *oz. caster sugar*
1 *beaten egg*

8 *oz. flour*
1½ *teaspoons baking powder*
¼ *pint milk*

Cream butter. Beat in sugar, then egg sprinkled with a little of the flour. Sift remainder of flour with baking powder. Fold alternately into the fat mixture with the milk. Spread evenly in a shallow greased baking tin, 8 inches square. Bake in a moderate oven, 350° F., for about 30 minutes. Cool on a wire rack. Coat with chocolate icing. Cut in squares.

CHOCOLATE ICING: Melt 5 oz. chocolate in a wet basin over hot water. Stir in 5 oz. sifted icing sugar and about 2 tablespoons tepid water, just enough to give a coating consistency. Stir in ½ teaspoon vanilla essence.

TWO WAYS WITH SOLE

1. Grease a shallow fireproof dish with ¼ oz. butter. Place a small prepared Dover sole in dish. Season lightly with salt. Fleck with ¼ oz. butter. Cover with greased paper. Bake in a moderate oven, 350° F., for about 15 minutes till firm. Dish up. Coat with 2 tablespoons white sauce, flavoured with lemon juice or minced parsley if allowed. Serve with mashed potatoes and spinach.

2. Have a small Dover sole filleted. Sprinkle 2 fillets with salt to taste and a little lemon juice if allowed. Steam between 2 well-buttered plates over a pan of boiling water for about 20 minutes until firm. Serve with mashed potatoes and spinach.

TO PREPARE REMAINING FILLETS: Make into a cream of fish soup or a fish soufflé or custard.

ASPIC JELLY

1 *small peeled onion*
1 *small carrot*
1 *celery stick*
1½ *pints water*
¼ *pint sherry*
½ *gill malt vinegar*
½ *gill tarragon vinegar*

rind and juice of 1 *lemon*
½ *teaspoon salt*
8 *white peppercorns*
2 *egg shells*
2 *egg whites*
1½–2 *oz. powdered gelatine*

Place onion, carrot and celery in a saucepan. Cover with cold water. Bring to boil, then drain. Rinse a saucepan. Place all the ingredients including the scalded vegetables into pan. Stir until gelatine is dissolved. Whisk rapidly over a moderate heat until a good froth forms on top, then remove the whisk. Let the ingredients come to the boil rapidly, then draw pan to side of stove and leave for 10 minutes. Now strain through a jelly bag.

TO VARY: 1. Increase water to 2 pints, and omit sherry, celery and lemon rind and juice. Dissolve a cube of consommé in the water. Add to ingredients 1 sprig of parsley, 1 or 2 cloves, 1 blade of mace, 1 teaspoon chilli vinegar, and reduce the mixed vinegars to 2 teaspoons of each. Use 2 oz. gelatine. Follow above method.

TO VARY: 2. Follow recipe for aspic jelly, but add 1 pint of chicken or veal stock and reduce water to ¾ pint, and sherry to ½ gill.

TOMATO ASPIC

2 *lb. tomatoes*
2 *medium-sized onions*
1 *small lemon rind*
4 *whole cloves*
10 *black peppercorns*

2 *oz. powdered gelatine*
1 *lump of sugar*
¼ *pint vinegar*
2 *egg shells and egg whites*

Wash and slice tomatoes into a saucepan. (If fresh tomatoes are not available, substitute 1 quart tinned.) Peel and add onions with lemon rind, cloves and peppercorns. Bring to simmering point. Simmer for 20 minutes, then strain and measure. Add enough cold water to make a quart. Pour into a rinsed saucepan. Add gelatine and sugar. Stir till gelatine is melted, then add vinegar and egg shells and egg whites. Whisk until a froth forms on top after the liquid comes to a boil, then cover. Stand at side of stove for 20 minutes, then strain through a jelly bag.

TO MAKE BAKING POWDER

Rub 2 oz. each of bicarbonate of soda, rice flour and tartaric acid through a hair sieve four or five times. Store in tightly-corked bottles.

A FITLESS COCK

This traditional dish is rarely seen on Northern tables any more. Now the mixture is frequently used in Highland glens as a stuffing for a boiling fowl. History relates that a fitless cock was prepared and served on the Eve of Lent, called Fastern's E'en. In some parts of the country it was known as a Fitless Hen.

1 *cup shredded suet*
1 *cup medium oatmeal*
1 *medium-sized onion*

salt and pepper to taste
beaten egg as required

Mix the suet with the oatmeal. Mince and add onion. Stir in salt and pepper to taste, and egg to bind. Shape with floured hands into the form of a fowl. Wrap it in a pudding cloth wrung out of boiling water and sprinkled with flour. Tie cloth on gently with string. Drop carefully into a saucepan of rapidly boiling water to cover. Boil slowly, but steadily, for about 2 hours. Do not let the water uncover the 'bird'. Replenish when necessary. When ready, unwrap and turn on to a hot dish.

CONFECTIONERS' CUSTARD

½ oz. cornflour
½ pint milk
1 oz. caster sugar

2 egg yolks
1 egg white
vanilla essence to taste

Cream the cornflour with a little of the milk. Pour remainder into a small saucepan. Add sugar. Stir till dissolved over low heat, then bring to boiling point and remove from stove. Beat egg yolks and egg white. Stir into the cornflour. When milk is slightly cooled, stir it into the cornflour mixture, then pour back into pan and cook over hot water, stirring constantly until thick, but do not allow to boil. Strain into a basin. Stir in vanilla essence to taste. When cool, use for filling éclair cases or sponge sandwiches. To enrich custard, stir in ¼ oz. unsalted butter before straining.

CROWDIE

There are several kinds of Crowdie, which is known in the Highlands as 'Fuarag'. This is an Orcadian recipe.

Pour 3 pints of milk, direct from the cow, into a large milk pan. Stir in 1 teaspoonful of rennet. Leave until the curd forms, then cut it into dice. Heat a little over the stove to separate the whey from the curd, but take great care not to overheat or the curd will be tough. Remove pan from stove. When the whey rises to the top, turn gently into a colander. Drain without touching until free from whey. Transfer curd to a bowl. Add 1 tablespoon double cream and salt to taste. Stir until soft and creamy. Form into shapes. Serve with bread or toast and butter.

THE USE OF FLAVOURINGS

Almond, lemon and vanilla are the most popular flavourings for cakes and puddings. A combination of lemon rind and vanilla essence is also popular for sponge cakes and sandwiches made with butter.

MACE: Both the blade and the ground mace is freely used, the former for flavouring bread and white sauce, cream soups and soups and stocks, and the latter for rich fruit cakes.

FLOWERS: Elderflowers contribute a delicate muscat flavour to gooseberry jelly.

LEAVES: Rose-geranium leaves are not only used for flavouring apple jelly but sometimes they are placed on the bottom of greased and floured cake tins before adding the batter. They are not removed till the cake is cool. Lemon verbena leaves are sometimes used for flavouring cakes in this way as well.

BACON AND VEAL FORCEMEAT

This can be used as a stuffing for a chicken, duck, guinea fowl or rabbit, or it can be made into a pâté to serve as a first course.

1 *lb. fat bacon*	*pinch of grated lemon peel*
1 *lb. pie veal*	½ *teaspoon minced parsley*
salt and cayenne pepper to taste	½ *teaspoon crushed herbs*
1 *saltspoon grated nutmeg*	1 *or 2 eggs*

Remove rind from bacon. Cut bacon and veal into small pieces, then put through a mincer into a mortar. Beat with a pestle till blended, then gradually beat in the salt, cayenne pepper, nutmeg, lemon peel, parsley and herbs. Beat well till into a smooth paste. Beat egg or eggs. Strain, then gradually beat into the meat mixture. Use for stuffing, or turn into a pâté.

SAVOURY MEAT PÂTÉ: Fill a greased dish with alternate layers of forcemeat and chicken, duck, guinea fowl or rabbit, cut in small pieces. When dish is full, cover with greaseproof paper, then with pastry. Place in a baking tin containing a little hot water. Bake in a slow oven, 275° F., for about 8 hours. Remove pastry and paper. Drain off the stock from the paté. Add a quart of jellying stock obtained from the poultry or rabbit bones and a bacon bone and knuckle of veal. Bring to boil. Pour over paté immediately, inserting a knife here and there, so that the stock penetrates all the meat. Cool slightly. Cover with a thick layer of liquefied aspic jelly. When required, serve cut in slices with crisp toast and butter.

BROWN GLAZE I

1¼ oz. powdered gelatine
½ pint boiling water
salt to taste

2 teaspoons meat extract
gravy browning as required

Dissolve the gelatine in the water in a saucepan, but do not allow to boil. Stir constantly. Season with salt. Stir in meat extract and enough gravy browning to give a deep brown glaze. Boil 2 or 3 minutes to clarify it, then pour into a jar. Cover when cold as it must be kept airtight.

BUTTER FOR DECORATING GLAZED MEAT: Beat 1 dessertspoon or 1 tablespoon of butter as required until creamy, then thicken with a little flour.

BROWN GLAZE II

1 *quart beef consommé*

If the consommé is not clarified, clarify it at once, then boil it steadily until reduced to about 1 cupful, in an open saucepan. Pour into a jar and cover closely. It will keep for some time if stored in the coldest part of a larder or in the bottom of a refrigerator.

TO USE GLAZE: Heat in the top of a double boiler over hot water for garnishing cold meats. A little is useful for imparting richness and flavour to sauces when suggested in recipes.

HEALTH SALTS

2 oz. bicarbonate of soda 1½ oz. salt
1 oz. cream of tartar 2 oz. caster sugar

Mix all ingredients well, then rub through a sieve. Bottle and cork tightly.

MARAG

½ lb. medium oatmeal ½ teaspoon ground mace
3 oz. finely chopped suet ¼ teaspoon grated nutmeg
½ onion, finely grated 1 well-beaten egg
½ teaspoon salt a little stock
pepper to taste

This is the way oatmeal puddings are made in Iona. Toast the oatmeal in oven. Mix the other ingredients in order given with the egg and stock. Put into skins (from butcher) or place mixture in a greased bowl and boil 2 hours.

HOLYROOD PÂTÉ
(Adapted)

1 lb. pork fat 2 medium-sized onions
¼ lb. pork 2 celery sticks
1 lb. liver 6 peppercorns
1 bay leaf salt to taste
1 sprig thyme 1 dessertspoon made mustard
1 leaf sage

343

Cut the pork fat and pork into small squares and place in a sauce-pan. Wash and dry the liver, using calves' or chickens' or half and half, and cut in small squares. Place in saucepan. Stir over low heat until the fat starts to run, then add the herbs, peeled and chopped onions, and sliced, trimmed celery sticks. Stir over low heat until the mixture comes to a boil, then add peppercorns and salt to taste, and turn into a casserole. Cover, and cook in a slow oven, 275° F., for about 1 hour. Pass through a mincer, then press through a sieve with the back of a wooden spoon into a large basin. Stir in the mustard and a small wineglass of sherry by degrees. Whisk until like thick, whipped cream, then turn into a shallow dish. Spread with melted butter. Cover and chill over-night, or chill in the refrigerator for about 4½ hours.

MARINADE

1 *teaspoon minced onion*	*dash of pepper*
1 *teaspoon minced parsley*	2 *tablespoons salad oil*
2 *saltspoons salt*	3 *tablespoons malt vinegar*
dash of paprika	

Mix the onion with the parsley, salt, paprika and pepper. Stir in the salad oil, then vinegar. Use as required.

PORRIDGE

Porridge, referred to by Robert Burns as 'chief o' Scotia's food', is still a national breakfast dish. In Scotland porridge used to be eaten standing. This old custom I have been told has mystical significance, but many years ago when I was visiting Birnam I was told that the reason for standing or walking about when supping porridge was that 'A staunin' sack fills the fu'est'.

Porridge, which in Scotland is usually spoken of in the plural, is generally made of oatmeal. In Orkney and Shetland they are frequently made of bere-meal. To make them in the old-fashioned way, you should stir them with a porridge stick sometimes called a spurtle, sometimes a theevil. In bygone days, every girl had at least one theevil in her bottom drawer. I had three.

COARSE OATMEAL PORRIDGE

1 *quart boiling water*   4 *tablespoons coarse oatmeal*

Pour the water into a porridge pan. As soon as it comes to full boil, sprinkle in the oatmeal, stirring briskly all the time with a spurtle or theevil. If you haven't one, use a wooden spoon. You have to be very careful to stir rapidly, while sprinkling the oatmeal in slowly, to prevent lumps forming which ruins a dish of porridge. Stir till boiling and until the meal is slightly swollen in about 5 minutes, then cover with the lid and simmer for about 30 minutes, stirring frequently. If unable to attend to the stirring, cook them in the top of a double boiler over boiling water, when they do not need so much stirring. They are ready when they are of a good pouring consistency. When half cooked, add salt to taste—about ½ teaspoon. If you add the salt earlier, it tends to harden the oatmeal. Serves 4–5.

GARRION OATMEAL PORRIDGE

10 *oz. Garrion oatmeal*   1 *tablespoon salt*
3 *pints cold water*

Soak the oatmeal in a pint of the water for 5 minutes. Place remainder of water in a deep saucepan. When almost boiling, gradually stir in the oatmeal and keep stirring until the porridge is boiling. Boil for about 30 minutes, then stir in the salt and cook for a minute or two, still stirring. If there is no time to boil for 30 minutes in the morning, soak the meal overnight in half the water. Bring remainder to a boil and add the following morning. Cook as described, but only for 15 minutes, and keep the pan covered when not stirring. Serves 6–8.

BERE-MEAL PORRIDGE

1½ *pints cold water*   *about* 1 *teaspoon salt*
5 *oz. bere-meal*

Pour water into a saucepan. Stir in the bere-meal. When boiling, simmer over boiling water in the top of a double boiler with lid on pan and stirring occasionally for about 25 minutes, then add salt to taste. Serves 3.

TO SERVE PORRIDGE

There is an old Scots saying that goes 'When the porridge begin to say "Gargunnock" or "Perth", it's time they were dished'. Ladle porridge into porringers, soup cups or soup plates. Serve in the Scottish fashion with individual bowls of cream, milk or buttermilk. The correct way to sup them, is to take a spoonful of porridge and dunk them in the cream, milk or buttermilk before swallowing them. In these days, however, porridge is more often served with a jug of cream, milk or buttermilk which is poured directly over the porridge.

The Sassenachs who look on porridge with disfavour may not have tasted them at their best, made with freshly-ground oatmeal and served with thick cream. You can serve them with sugar or syrup, honey or treacle, or stewed prunes if you like, but some Scots prefer to drink beer or stout with them.

EGG PORRIDGE

1 *dessertspoon oatmeal*   2 *eggs*
1 *pint milk*

Sprinkle the oatmeal like rain over the milk. Stir to a simmering point, then simmer gently for 30 minutes, stirring frequently. Beat the eggs in a basin. Stir the oatmeal-milk rapidly into the egg, then sweeten with honey, sugar or syrup to taste, or flavour with salt as preferred. Serve in a tumber to drink. Serves 2.

SKIRLIE

¼ *lb. shredded suet*   *oatmeal as required*
3 *large chopped onions*   *salt to taste*

Melt the suet slowly in a frying pan. Add onion. Fry slowly until

346

evenly browned, stirring frequently with an iron spoon. Now add enough oatmeal to absorb the fat, and to give you a rather thick mixture. Cook for about 10 minutes, stirring constantly. Season with salt. Serve with potatoes.

FAIRY TOAST

The old-fashioned way of making it is to cut stale bread with crusts removed into wafer-thin slices, and bake them in a slow oven, 300° F., until evenly browned and crisp in about 15 minutes. Turn them several times to ensure even toasting and drying. Serve lightly piled in a bread basket.

The modern method is to toast slices of bread cut $\frac{1}{4}$ inch thick, with crusts or without them, till brown on both sides, then slit them through the centre and toast remaining sides.

OLD FESTIVAL FARE

Though with the march of time the custom of preparing and serving special fare on all feast days is not as religiously observed as it used to be, except perhaps in outlying districts, St Andrew's Day, Burns's Anniversary, Hallowe'en, Hogmanay and Yule (Christmas Day) still call for special efforts in the kitchen.

ST ANDREW'S DAY (30th November): Bawd Bree, Haggis, Howtowdie and Chappit Tatties, etc. (*see pages* 21, 183, 214, 164).

BURNS'S ANNIVERSARY (25th January): Cock-a-Leekie, Haggis, etc. (*see pages* 24, 183).

HALLOWE'EN (31st October): Chappit Tatties, Crowdie, Apples, etc. (*see pages* 164, 340).

HOGMANAY (31st December): Black Bun, Hogmanay Bun, Shortbread, Het Pint, Athole Brose, etc. (*see pages* 258, 270, 288, 294, 296).

YULE (Christmas): Roastit Bubbly-Jock, Mince Pies, Plum Pudding, etc. (*see pages* 217, 154, 126–7).

FARE ON FASTERN'S E'EN

In most homes pancakes are served on Fastern's E'en, as Shrove Tuesday is called in Scotland. In my grandfather's day housewives in rural Scotland tried to have a piece of boiled beef on this day, called in some parts of the country 'Brose Day', and in others 'Bannock Night'. Many farmers believed that if there was not meat for dinner on that day the stock would not thrive and some of them would be sure to die before next Fastern's E'en. Brose made of the beef bree was another famous dish at dinner. In it had been secreted a ring and a button. The ring signified 'marriage' and the button 'single blessedness'. The one who found the ring was not supposed to mention the find until the meal was finished. The ring, borrowed from a married woman present, had to be worn until next morning to give the finder a chance to dream of his or her future spouse.

Crowdie (*page* 340) was also a popular dish on Fastern's E'en with the unmarried folk. This dish was probably introduced in the Papal times to strengthen the Scots against the Lenten Fast. A ring was also slipped into it. It was said that whoever found it would be the first to marry in the next twelve months.

In some parts of Scotland young people used to visit their neighbours on Fastern's E'en to get their brose, each one carrying a spoon. At every house they gathered round a table, and then a large basin of hot savoury beef kale or mutton brose was placed on the centre. With a rush and a scramble, the feast began and didn't end until the basin was emptied.

Bannocks, fritters and pancakes were baked in the evening and everyone shared in the preparation in those days. The pancakes were made of beaten eggs, oatmeal and milk. Now flour takes the place of the oatmeal. When the last bannock, fritter and pancake had been cooked, the celebration ended with the baking and eating of the 'Sautie Bannock'. This was a thick oatmeal bannock, generously salted. The one who baked it was not allowed to speak. If she spoke, her place was taken by another. A ring had been placed in this cake. When thoroughly baked, it was divided into as many pieces as there were unmarried folks present. Each one had to take a piece, and the one who found the ring was sure to be the first married.

HALLOWE'EN

I can't very well leave the subject of Scottish parties without mentioning Hallowe'en. When I was in my 'teens, the games we played were more important than the fare. We used to sit cross-legged on the floor round black gypsy pots full of fluffy mashed potatoes and sup them with wooden spoons. There were charms embedded in the potatoes. If you came across a sixpence it guaranteed you wealth, if you found a ring you were the first to be married. The button ensured you single bliss, and so on. Then we used to 'dook' for apples in a tub of water and play forfeits, fortified by lemonade and cocoa and home-made biscuits and cakes. Sometimes we danced to the tinkle of a tinny piano. When I grew older the fare at Hallowe'en parties became more elaborate —sandwiches, lobster and oyster patties, jellies, creams and trifles and claret cup, and dancing, consequences and forfeits passed the evening away.

HOGMANAY

There are two ways of celebrating Hogmanay in Scotland. When I was young we used to dance up to midnight until the church bell pealed out across the snow (I cannot remember Christmas in Angus without snow), then the toast was drunk to the New Year and a thumping good supper was served, usually a choice of hot roast chicken with baked or boiled ham, and all the trimmings, and cold game or pork pie with jacket potatoes, followed by luscious creams, such as Stone Cream, a super trifle and hot mince pies and Athole Brose. Black Bun, Shortie and tea always followed later on because the dance lasted until cock crow. Nowadays it is more usual to invite a few friends in for the occasion and serve a buffet supper such as I have suggested.

At Hogmanay, various drinks used to be offered on the Braes of Angus such as port wine and whisky. In the Highlands Athole Brose sometimes took the place of both for the toast. Nowadays, it is more usual to start with sherry and drink a cider or wine cup throughout the meal, and offer champagne or port wine for the toast, but when there are men present there is always whisky in the offing.

ST ANDREW'S NIGHT DINNER I

at

THE OLD RED HOUSE

88 Bishopsgate in the City of London

30th November, 1950

In the Chair

ELIZABETH CRAIG

The Wines	*The Fare*
Madeira, Old Trinity House Bual	Bawd Bree
Old Highland Whisky	Haggis
	Chappit Tatties
1945 Chassagne Montrachet	Howtowdie
	Dunlop Cheese
Drambuie	Coffee

ST ANDREW'S NIGHT DINNER II

The Wines	The Fare
Chablis	Oysters
	Brown Bread and Butter
	Hotch Potch
Mountain Dew	Haggis
Burgundy	Roastit Grouse
	Bread Sauce Fried Crumbs
	Amber Puddin'
	Switched Cream
Port	Fruit and Nuts
Drambuie	Coffee

BURNS'S ANNIVERSARY

DINNER I		DINNER II	
The Wines	*The Fare*	*The Wines*	*The Fare*
	Cock-a-Leekie		Scotch Broth or Kail
Hock	Boiled Cod	Graves	Sole Wi' a Delicate Air
	Oyster Sauce		
Mountain Dew	Haggis	Mountain Dew	Haggis
	Chappit Tatties		Chappit Tatties
Claret	Roastit-Bubbly-jock	Claret	Boiled Mutton
			Caper Sauce
	Tipsy Laird	Sauterne	Venus Puddin'
	Bannock Dunlop Cheese Celery		Bannock Dunlop Cheese Celery
Port		Port	
	Dessairt		Dessairt
Toddy		Toddy	

HOGMANAY BUFFET PARTY

Shrimp Sandwiches

Turkey Sandwiches

Hot Mutton Pies
or
Forfar Bridies

Scotch Egg Salad

Black or Hogmanay

Bun

Shortbread

Fruit and Nuts

Stuffed Dates

Conversations

Athole Brose

GLOSSARY

Ashet	Meat platter
Bree	Broth or stock
Fired	Baked
Gean	Wild cherry
Gigot	Leg of Mutton
Girnel (*Girnal*)	Meal chest
Grosset (*Grosert*)	Gooseberry
Gudebread	Name for all bread and cakes prepared for feasts, particularly for the 'Daft Days', between Christmas and New Year's Day.
Hotch Potch	Vegetable broth
Howtowdie	A pullet
Kail	Member of the cabbage family which gives a continuous supply of greens during the winter when vegetables are scarce.
Kickshaws	Trifles or dainties
Lum	Chimney
Neeps	Turnips
Powsowdie	Sheep's head broth
Purry	Purée
Rizzared	Dried in the sun
Rowan (*Rodden*)	Berries of the mountain ash
Sippets	Small pieces of toast, usually cut in triangles
Stoved	Stewed
Switched	Whipped
Syes	Chives
Treacle	A dark brown syrup, not golden syrup.

INDEX

358

A SELECTED LIST OF TITLES
PUBLISHED BY CORGI BOOKS

WHILE EVERY EFFORT IS MADE TO KEEP PRICES LOW, IT IS SOMETIMES NECESSARY TO INCREASE PRICES AT SHORT NOTICE. CORGI BOOKS RESERVE THE RIGHT TO SHOW AND CHARGE NEW RETAIL PRICES ON COVERS WHICH MAY DIFFER FROM THOSE ADVERTISED IN THE TEXT OR ELSEWHERE

THE PRICES SHEWN BELOW WERE CORRECT AT THE TIME OF GOING TO PRESS (OCT. 79)

All these books are available at your bookshop or newsagent, or can be ordered direct from the publisher. Just tick the titles you want and fill in the form below.

CORGI BOOKS, Cash Sales Department, P.O. Box 11, Falmouth, Cornwall Please send cheque or postal order, no currency.

U.K. send 25p for first book plus 10p per copy for each additional book ordered to a maximum charge of £1.05p to cover the cost of postage and packing.

B.F.P.O. and Eire allow 25p for first book plus 10p per copy for the next 8 books, thereafter 5p per book.

Overseas Customers. Please allow 40p for the first book and 12p per copy for each additional book.

NAME (Block letters) ....

ADDRESS ....

(OCT. 79) ....